Assimilated Jews in the Warsaw Ghetto, 1940–1943

MODERN JEWISH HISTORY

Henry Feingold, *Series Editor*

Other titles in Modern Jewish History

American Jewish Political Culture and the Liberal Persuasion
Henry L. Feingold

The "Bergson Boys" and the Origins of Contemporary Zionist Militancy
Judith Tydor Baumel

Bundist Counterculture in Interwar Poland
Jack Jacobs

Contemporary Sephardic Identity in the Americas: An Interdisciplinary Approach
Margalit Bejarano and Edna Aizenberg, eds.

The Downfall of Abba Hillel Silver and the Foundation of Israel
Ofer Shiff

Judah L. Magnes: An American Jewish Nonconformist
Daniel P. Kotzin

Louis Marshall and the Rise of Jewish Ethnicity in America: A Biography
M. M. Silver

"Silent No More": Saving the Jews of Russia, the American Jewish Effort, 1967–1989
Henry L. Feingold

An Uneasy Relationship: American Jewish Leadership and Israel, 1948–1957
Zvi Ganin

We Are Many: Reflections on American Jewish History and Identity
Edward S. Shapiro

Will to Freedom: A Perilous Journey Through Fascism and Communism
Egon Balas

Assimilated Jews in the Warsaw Ghetto, 1940–1943

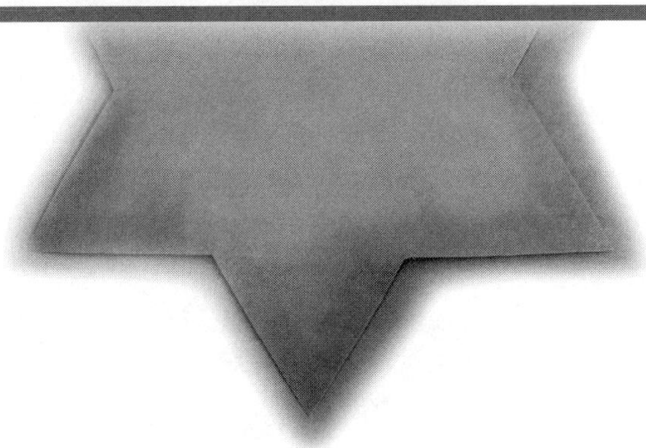

Katarzyna Person

Syracuse University Press

Syracuse, New York 13244-5290

First Edition 2014
14 15 16 17 18 19 6 5 4 3 2 1

Material is reprinted with permission from the following sources: Jewish Historical Institute Archive; Yad Vashem Archive; University of Southern California's Shoah Foundation's Visual History Archive; Archiwum Akt Nowych in Warsaw; Archiwum Historii Mówionej Muzeum Powstania Warszawskiego.

∞ The paper used in this publication meets the minimum requirements of the American National Standard for Information Sciences—Permanence of Paper for Printed Library Materials, ANSI Z39.48-1992.

For a listing of books published and distributed by Syracuse University Press, visit our website at www.SyracuseUniversityPress.syr.edu.

ISBN: 978-0-8156-3334-1 (cloth) 978-0-8156-5245-8 (e-book)

Library of Congress Cataloging-in-Publication Data

Person, Katarzyna.

Assimilated Jews in the Warsaw Ghetto, 1940–1943 / Katarzyna Person. — First edition.

pages cm. — (Modern Jewish history)

Includes bibliographical references and index.

ISBN 978-0-8156-3334-1 (cloth : alk. paper) — ISBN 978-0-8156-5245-8 (ebook)

1. Jews—Persecutions—Poland—Warsaw. 2. Holocaust, Jewish (1939–1945)—Poland—Warsaw 3. Jews—Poland—Warsaw—History—20th century. I. Title.

DS134.64P47 2014

940.53'1853841—dc23 2014014564

Manufactured in the United States of America

To Antonia.

Katarzyna Person has a PhD in History from Royal Holloway, University of London. She held postdoctoral fellowships at Yad Vashem and the Center for Jewish History in New York and is currently a researcher in the Jewish Historical Institute in Warsaw.

Contents

Acknowledgments

This book is a result of my doctoral research conducted in the History Department of Royal Holloway, University of London.

I am indebted to the department and organizations from whose generous grants and help I have benefited while conducting the research for this book: the Center for Advanced Holocaust Studies, United States Holocaust Memorial Museum, Helen Shackleton Fund, American Society for Jewish Heritage in Poland, Yad Vashem, and the Jewish Historical Institute in Warsaw.

This book would not have come into being without the work of all the scholars whose research has been invaluable for my own. I am particularly grateful to Professor David Cesarani who supervised my thesis and with patience and extremely hard work made a historian out of a drama student. I will also always be indebted to Professor Andrzej Żbikowski from the Jewish Historical Institute, who gave me enormous support in every step of my work, beginning with my MA dissertation.

I would also like to thank my PhD examiners Professor Antony Polonsky and Dr. François Guesnet, whose invaluable comments on my thesis and generous advice helped to shape this book. I am grateful for the support of my PhD advisers at Royal Holloway, Professor Dan Stone and Dr. Zoë Waxman, whose comments on my early work helped to save me from errors and guide my way.

Finally, I would like to thank my family for making this work possible. My parents have continuously inspired me and given me confidence. Heather, Eric, and Kristina Wooddin gave me a home in England. Roger and Kot sat with me and provided emotional support.

Finally, Jonathan read countless drafts, and was with me from the very first steps of this journey. This book would not exist without his help.

My work belongs to the Warsaw Ghetto survivors and their families who spoke to me about their experiences. This is their story.

Timeline

1939

September 1: The outbreak of the Second World War. Beginning of the German air assault on Warsaw.

September 23: Adam Czerniaków becomes the Chairman of the Jewish Community.

September 28: Capitulation of Warsaw.

October 7: Establishment of the Jewish Council (Judenrat) in Warsaw.

October 26: Introduction of compulsory labor for Poles aged 18 to 60 and Jews aged 14 to 60.

December 1: All Jewish men, women, and children over 10 years of age are ordered to wear a white armband with a blue Star of David. Jewish shops and enterprises also have to be marked.

1940

January 1: Jews are forbidden from changing their place of residence without permission.

January 14–25: Repressions against Jewish intelligentsia after the escape of Andrzej Kott.

February 8: Jews in the Generalgouvernement are forbidden to travel by rail.

July 23: The first issue of "Gazeta Żydowska" is published.

October 12: Decree establishing a ghetto in Warsaw is announced over the street megaphones.

November 16: Warsaw ghetto is sealed off.

November 25: The first concert of *Żydowska Orkiestra Symfoniczna* (pol. Jewish Symphony Orchestra).

December 6: The first theater performance in the ghetto.

1941

July–September: Height of the typhoid epidemic.

October 1: Elementary schools are opened in the ghetto.

October 23: Reduction of the ghetto's borders. About 75,000 Jews are required to relocate.

October 29: The opening night of *Miłość szuka mieszkania* (pol. Love Seeks a Lodging).

November 10: Introduction of death penalty for leaving the ghetto without permission.

November 7 and December 15: Twenty-three Jews are shot in the prison at Gęsia Street for illegally leaving the ghetto.

December 25: Ghetto inhabitants are required to hand in all fur coats.

1942

January 26: Foot bridge over Chłodna Street is opened.

April 17/18: Gestapo murders 52 people in the ghetto. Among them are Gestapo collaborators as well as members of the underground.

July 22: The beginning of the great deportation action. First transports leave from the Umschlagplatz to the Treblinka killing center.

July 23: Adam Czerniaków commits suicide.

August 5 or 6: Janusz Korczak is deported to Treblinka together with the children and personnel of his orphanage.

August 20: Attempted assassination of Józef Szeryński.

September 6 to 12: Roundup ("cauldron") at Miła Street.

September 21: The end of the great deportation action in the Warsaw ghetto.

October: Establishment of *Żydowska Organizacja Bojowa* (pol. Jewish Fighting Organization). Establishment of contact with Armia Krajowa (pol. Home Army).

1943

January 18 to 21: The second deportation action in the Warsaw ghetto, interrupted by the first armed resistance.

January: Józef Szeryński, the head of the Jewish Order Service, commits suicide.

April 19: Outbreak of the Warsaw Ghetto Uprising.

May 8: Mordechai Anielewicz, commandant of Żydowska Organizacja Bojowa, commits suicide in the bunker at 18 Miła Street.
May 16: Demolition of the Great Synagogue of Warsaw and the symbolic end of the Uprising.

1944

August 1: Outbreak of the Warsaw Uprising.
October 2: Capitulation of the insurgent forces.

1945

January 17: The Red Army enters Warsaw.

Assimilated Jews in the Warsaw Ghetto, 1940–1943

1

Introduction

It was March 1, 1940, and Arnold Szyfman, the director of *Teatr Polski* (pol. Polish Theater), one of Warsaw's most illustrious stages, was finishing his work for the day. Like many other theater employees who lost their apartments in the bombings of September 1939 he was now living permanently in his office. It was only a few minutes past 9 pm, but, as he wrote in his memoir, because of the cold and the curfew imposed on the streets of Warsaw, he was used to going to sleep earlier than before the war. Suddenly, Szyfman heard a bang on the door and in the doorway appeared the building's janitor followed by six Gestapo functionaries. The Germans searched the room thoroughly, asking him about the theater bonds, money, and jewelry. They were just about to leave, when, as Szyfman recalled, they saw his fur coat hanging on the door. Inspecting it, one of the Gestapo men asked why he did not wear an armband. Szyfman noted his answer in his memoir: "I explained that I am not a Jew neither from nationality nor religion and that is why I do not wear it. They asked me if I know that this risks the death penalty. I replied that they threaten me unnecessarily."[1]

Szyfman was ordered to report to the Gestapo the next morning and was promptly imprisoned. Freed in the autumn of 1940, he left Warsaw for the countryside, where he survived the war. Thousands of others like him, Polish Jews or Poles of Jewish origin subjected to Nazi anti-Semitic legislation, followed in his footsteps, fleeing Warsaw or going into hiding. However, the vast majority of those who remained in a state of suspension, on the border of national and cultural identities, were not given this choice. In November 1940, with the closure of the Jewish Quarter in Warsaw, their fate became entwined with that of all of the victims of the Holocaust.

The Concept and Classification of Assimilation

The concepts of assimilation and acculturation evade clear definition. The borders separating assimilated and acculturated groups from other parts of the Jewish community are hazy, unclear, and ever changing. Nonetheless, at least as a starting point, some definition must be undertaken and such borders must be defined. Robert E. Park and Ernest W. Burgess, in one of the first and most influential works on assimilation, define it as "a process of interpenetration and fusion in which persons and groups acquire the memories, sentiments, and attitudes of other persons or groups, and by sharing their experiences and history, are incorporated with them in a common cultural life."[2] Numerous other definitions, more or less rigid, have been proposed by those working on the history of Polish Jewry in the nineteenth and twentieth centuries. Yet, the murkiness of the concept and the difficulty of applying it to the specific context of the Polish-Jewish community have resulted in the term "assimilation" being less commonly used in more recent scholarship. Instead, the process of assimilation is broken down into various components discussed separately. Historian Todd Endelman defines four changes in Jewish behavior and status, which are usually encompassed by the term assimilation: acculturation (the acquisition of the cultural and social habits of the dominant non-Jewish group); integration (the entry of Jews into non-Jewish social circles and spheres of activity); emancipation (the acquisition of rights and privileges enjoyed by non-Jewish citizens/subjects of similar socio-economic rank); and secularization (the rejection of religious beliefs and the obligations and practices determined by these beliefs).[3] As a result, Jonathan Frankel notes, the discussion of assimilation has shifted "from the extremes, from the dichotomous archetypes, to that middle ground where it is no easy task to distinguish the exceptions from the rules."[4] This statement is especially viable when applied to the Jewish community of interwar Poland, where full integration could not take place because of factors such as weak economic development, the dense concentrations of traditional Jews who opposed the emancipation process, and the negative attitude of the non-Jewish community. However, at the same time a new generation of Jews who were educated in Polish schools, were fluent in Polish, and were increasingly familiar with the environment outside traditional Jewish quarters were becoming ever more visible in Polish social, political, and cultural life. Some of these Jews retained a Jewish national consciousness; others, who felt connected to a Polish or predominantly Polish national and cultural affiliation, formed a group that remained in the middle, "the caste" of assimilated Jews.[5]

Some of those who feature in this book were simply born into assimilated families; others were brought up in two cultures. For some assimilation was a personal choice, not influenced by their family background. Others became assimilated through processes of modernization and laicization, which was gradual and often went unnoticed.[6] What they all had in common, and what will be my main point of reference, is the predominant identification with Polish culture and language, even though some of these individuals also cultivated certain aspects of their Jewish identity. The identity of Polish Jews at this time was in no way static and remained dependent on numerous external and internal factors. The only way to define "Jewish Polishness" is to see it as a set of expressions of constant changes in various components of self-identity, a journey undertaken by almost all of those who will feature in this book.

The individuals presented in this book encompass very different life stories and paths toward assimilation. The first group consists of very young people, who in 1939 were still children or teenagers. One such individual was Marcel Reich. Born in 1920 to a lower-middle class family, he was sent by his mother to attend school in Germany after his father went bankrupt in 1929. Forced to relocate to Poland in 1938, Reich made a living giving German lessons until the outbreak of the war. Another, Antoni Marianowicz, born in 1923 and baptized at birth in the Protestant church, was a son of an assimilated wealthy merchant and a graduate of one of the most exclusive Warsaw gymnasiums. Mary Berg, a year younger than Marianowicz, was a native of Łódź, the daughter of a well-known art dealer and an American mother. The family only arrived in Warsaw after the beginning of the war.

The demographic of individuals in their 20s and 30s will be mainly represented by artists and professional intelligentsia. Poet Władysław Szlengel was born in 1914. A native of Warsaw, he was the son of a painter, and graduated from a Polish secondary school. From a young age he was a fixture of the Warsaw literary scene, regularly publishing in the most prestigious Polish literary magazine and writing texts and popular songs for literary cabarets. Though influenced significantly by Polish poetry, he nonetheless remained a complex figure, located on the Polish-Jewish border, who devoted some of his poetry to topics of Jewish identity. Jerzy Jurandot, three years older, was already a very established name in the immediate pre-war years. He came from an assimilated family and was a graduate of Warsaw University. Jurandot wrote his first hit song at eighteen and in the next ten years he wrote the biggest hits of interwar Warsaw, which were sung by the greats of the Polish stage. From 1935 he was a director of literary cabarets. He too wrote solely in Polish. Władysław Szpilman, who was the same age as Jurandot, also came from a family of assimilated intelligentsia. He was a pianist and graduate of the Warsaw and Berlin conservatorium. Szpilman worked in Polish radio and was the composer of film scores and popular songs.

The first representative of the older generation to feature in this book, Roman Kramsztyk, was born in 1885 into one of the most illustrious assimilated families of Warsaw. Baptized as a child, he always considered himself to be Polish. From 1909 he lived and gradually gained fame as a painter in Paris and was caught up in the outbreak of the Second World War during a visit to Warsaw. Helena Szereszewska was born in 1891 to a progressive Jewish family. She was a graduate of a university in Geneva and was married to a successful engineer working in the yeast industry. She considered her family to be assimilated, but twice a year, on the Jewish New Year and Day of Atonement, her daughters did not attend school. Szereszewska did not work and devoted most of her time to reading Polish and French literature.

Professor Ludwik Hirszfeld, born in 1884 in Łódź to a thoroughly assimilated family, was one of the most famous Polish scientists. A graduate of German and Swiss universities he returned to Poland to become a professor at Warsaw University. His illustrious career in microbiology and serology was partially possible because of the fact that as an adult he was baptized. He was married and had a daughter who was, however, not baptized. Finally, engineer Adam Czerniaków was a typical representative of late nineteenth-century assimilation. He was born in 1881 into an assimilated Warsaw family and went to university both in Poland and abroad. He spoke Polish as his first language and wrote Polish poetry but remained active in Jewish communal life, serving on the boards of several Polish and Jewish institutions. In 1931 he was elected to the Polish Senate. In 1939 he became the head of the German-created Warsaw Jewish Council—the Judenrat. It is the experience of these individuals and many others like them that form the story of the assimilated, acculturated, and baptized Jews in the Warsaw Ghetto.

It is also necessary at this point to underline the fundamental difference in the use of the term "assimilation" between the Eastern and the Western and Central European contexts. During the nineteenth century in the United States as well as in Western and Central Europe, acculturation and social integration as a result of emancipation, along with the retention of some form of Jewish identity, were prevalent among urban and, later on, small-town Jews. In Eastern Europe conforming to the norms of non-Jewish society was a more highly charged issue. The Assimilationist movement in Poland remained marginal and, as will be shown throughout this study, among the majority of Jewish society in Poland the term "assimilation" had predominantly negative connotations. Such an attitude toward this cultural and political program was shared by both the members of youth movements, even those coming from polonized homes where Polish was their first language, and the Orthodox, Yiddish-speaking community. This division has to be kept in mind, if we are to discuss the specific situation of this group in pre-war and wartime Poland.

Assimilation of Jews in Poland until World War I

In the multiethnic state of the Polish-Lithuanian Commonwealth, Jews formed an autonomous, very traditional community that to a significant degree remained separate from the external social framework. Their only possible mode of assimilation was through conversion, a path highly favored by the Polish state, which saw it as "a living proof of the triumph of the Catholic faith, and thus deserving of special benevolence."[7] As historian Magdalena Teter shows, most neophytes came from lower strata, and the most famous case of Jewish conversion was that of Jacob Frank (1726–1791), leader of a Sabbatean sect known as the Frankists.[8] After Frank converted to Catholicism, thousands (although not all) of his followers did the same. The most prominent Frankist families were rewarded for this step by the Polish *Sejm* and ennobled in 1764. They later integrated into Polish society and by the end of the nineteenth century were widely intermarried within the nobility, often gaining prominence in Varsovian society.

After the partitions of 1772, 1793, and 1795, the Polish-Lithuanian Commonwealth was divided among three absolutist states: Prussia, Russia, and the Habsburg Empire. Following the decisions of the 1815 Congress of Vienna, Warsaw became the capital of the Russian-ruled, semi-autonomous Kingdom of Poland. The main force shaping the assimilation of Polish Jewry in this part of Polish lands was the Haskalah—an enlightenment-related Jewish modernization movement that emerged in Germany in the 1770s. The Haskalah began as a current of the intellectual renewal of Judaism, but later became a tool for the political emancipation of the Jews. The first leading Polish *maskilim* (followers of the Haskalah) were almost all gathered around the Kingdom's government and public institutions and had given themselves the task of modernizing the Jewish community. As in Germany, the Haskalah was also supported by wealthy merchants, bankers, and industrialists. Warsaw, as the regional center of the movement, played an integral role in its development. Among the three main social groups that emerged from the Polish Haskalah were traditional maskilim who wrote only in Hebrew, a group of radical assimilationists who postulated severing all ties with Judaism, and finally the largest and most important group, who promoted pro-Polish acculturation while preserving the status of Judaism and its religious traditions.[9] According to its ideology, Jews should become "Poles of Mosaic Faith," that is, Poles differing from others only in their religion. Full integration into Polish society was to be achieved through acquiring secular knowledge and full acquisition of the Polish language. This worldview combined rejection of separatism (understood as differences in culture, clothing, and language), loyalty to the Polish state, and reinforcement of a Jewish religious identity. The combination of Polish patriotism, often taking the shape of an enthusiastic devotion to the cause of oppressed Poland, and Jewish religion, was shaped in a significant way by the tradition of Polish Romanticism.[10] The height of this current of assimilation came with the "Polish-Jewish Fraternity" of 1861–63, peaking with the participation of some young Jews in the January Uprising of 1863.[11] The next generation of assimilationists focused on a type of assimilation similar to that in Western and Central Europe, underlining the need for education and conforming to the non-Jewish way of life. Its result was to be the creation of the urbanized Jewish middle class.[12] This model, leading to assimilation as a political program, flourished after the Emancipation Act of 1862.

The assimilation process in nineteenth-century Warsaw was strengthened by emerging capitalism. The rich industrialist Jewish families—such as the Kronenbergs, Wawelbergs, or Natansons—started playing a very important part in both Polish and Jewish community life, many of them gaining social prominence through financing the Polish fight for independence. Some of their members converted to Christianity, some remained close to Judaism, but basically all became integrated into Polish society, which was in many cases confirmed by intermarriage with Polish noble families. Conversion was also a growing phenomenon at that time among Warsaw's lower-middle class, many of whom changed religion to elevate their economic status.[13]

Another result of the introduction of the capitalist economy was the establishment of the urban intelligentsia—the social group that was most open to assimilated Jews and into which, through university education or professional contacts, they most often integrated. The pioneering group of Jewish intelligentsia that emerged from the followers of the Haskalah gathered around the Warsaw Rabbinical School, a secular, secondary-level school, which functioned between 1826 and 1862, inculcating the spirit of Polish patriotism into more than a thousand young men from wealthy Jewish families.[14]

Assimilation in Interwar Poland

Interwar Warsaw, with its Jewish population ranging between 320,000 and 370,000, was undoubtedly the European center of Jewish life. Even though the vast majority of its Jewish inhabitants remained traditional, Warsaw was also the most assimilated city in a newly independent Poland. Since the 1919 Versailles Treaty, Polish Jews were guaranteed full civil rights, which included retaining their national identity, language, and religion, and the freedom to set up religious and social organizations. Even though these rights were infringed upon by the Polish government and often by Polish society, there is no doubt that the interwar period witnessed a surge in all aspects of artistic, cultural, and social Jewish undertakings. Warsaw became the dynamic center of new Jewish life, attracting young talented people from the whole of Poland. Historian Israel Gutman, describing the interwar city, wrote:

> Warsaw had neither ancient buildings nor the aura of glorious memories, the vestiges of an influential past. There were no ancient synagogues such as the one in Cracow; none that had been the home of world-renowned scholars. There was no tradition of greatness. . . . Nevertheless, there was ample opportunity for newcomers to make their impact and the city had the feel of a community coming into its own. Warsaw's comparatively new facades and its fast-growing strength were a source of openness. New inhabitants and casual visitors could feel welcome. Social change was more prevalent than stability. . . . In these two decades of naïve expectations and short-lived hopes Warsaw, with its variegated textures and contrasts, became the

> focus of unlimited and wide-ranging Jewish activity. In those days of confusion on the brink of an abyss, it was virtually the capital of the Jewish people. . . .[15]

Jewish Warsaw, brimming with newcomers—scholars, political activists, aspiring writers, and theater makers—became the site of extensive cultural and political activity. It was the seat of all major Jewish parties, youth movements, and trade unions, the location of theaters and research centers, and home to Jewish journalists and publishing houses. It was clear that assimilation was no longer the only way to escape the ghetto of traditional Jewry. Zionism and socialism was increasingly the ideology of choice among the young Jewish intelligentsia.

All this did not mean, however, that assimilation as a social process was stopped in its tracks. Its progress could not be halted by either the growing anti-Semitism or the negative attitudes held by the greatest part of the Jewish community. As already shown, the milieu of Warsaw's assimilated Jews at the beginning of the twentieth century was composed mainly of Jewish professionals, bankers, publishers, scientists, medical doctors, and industrialists. Unlike in Western Europe, where assimilated Jews in the nineteenth century participated in the creation of arts and literature, in Poland assimilated Jews were mainly prominent in technical and scientific literature.[16] In the twentieth century this group expanded to include artists and intellectuals. As historian Lucy Dawidowicz remarks: "that which one chooses to be, must also be able and willing to be chosen."[17] The groups "willing to be chosen" in interwar Warsaw can be confined almost exclusively to the liberal intelligentsia and artists. The process was, however, spreading through all strata of society, a phenomenon that can be clearly seen when looking at the backgrounds of those involved in the assimilationist movement. The leadership of the assimilationist society of veterans—*Związek Żydów Uczestników Walk o Niepodległość Polski* (pol. Association of Jewish Participants in the Struggle for the Independence of Poland)—consisted mainly of traditionally assimilationist groups: lawyers, industrialists, and army men.[18] Children in the assimilationist youth movement already represented the whole range of Jewish middle and lower-middle class backgrounds.[19]

Writing about the Warsaw environment of assimilated Jews, Todd Endelman describes it as a heterogonous mix of converted and unconverted (but indifferent) Jews, with a sprinkling of unconventional Poles.[20] Most scholars of this period underline the "caste" status of the assimilated Jews in interwar Poland—a group stuck between the Polish and Jewish community and, with a few exceptions, not fully accepted by either. Assimilationist groups were universally rejected by anti-Semites, who saw them as threatening and a source of competition, and also by the majority of Jews who often considered assimilation to be a form of apostasy. Interwar Jewish assimilation should therefore be seen not as a movement over the generations from one form of group identity to another, but rather as a movement into a state of ambivalence, where no one culture or identity can be considered to be one's own and where one's position in society remains ambiguous.[21]

Language

The most visible aspect of progressive acculturation was undoubtedly linguistic polonization. As Yiddish scholar Chone Shmeruk shows in his seminal text on Jewish languages in pre-war Poland, interwar Jewish Warsaw was a city of three languages—Polish, Hebrew, and Yiddish—which interlinked in various configurations.[22] While the older generations of the Jewish intelligentsia grew up in multilingual environments—most often consisting of Polish-Yiddish but also Polish-Yiddish-Russian or Polish-Yiddish-German—those who reached adulthood in the interwar period were increasingly likely to come from purely Polish-speaking homes.[23] Although the exact linguistic tapestry of the Jewish community on the eve of the Second World War is impossible to establish, it can be assumed that the norm was bilingualism. As a result, by the end of the interwar period, Polish was no longer the language spoken only by the assimilated strata. The group of Jews speaking Polish as their first language crossed all cultural and national affiliations.

The group most commonly associated with Polish cultural activities was made up of famous writers of Jewish origin. Antoni Słonimski, Julian Tuwim, and Boleslaw Leśmian, who were born into assimilated families, helped create the thriving poetic scene of interwar Warsaw. This group rarely if ever touched upon Jewish themes in their work. They created works for a Polish-speaking audience and collaborated artistically with non-Jewish writers. Describing their creative input Aleksander Hertz writes:

> In the way they looked at Jews and Jewish affairs, those poets did not differ fundamentally from other Polish poets. No doubt personal factors were much alive in their poetry. There was a note of bitterness about the anti-Semitism that denied them the right to call themselves Polish poets. But their basic approach was in accord with the general mode prevailing among Polish poets.[24]

Despite their self-identification those authors remained Jewish in the eyes of many of the interwar anti-Semites who thrived by writing about the "Judification" of the Polish literary scene.

At the same time, the growing linguistic assimilation combined with the awakening of Jewish national consciousness led to artistic creativity in Polish by people with a distinctive and openly demonstrated Jewish identity. Probably the most eminent of them was Marek Arensztajn (Andrzej Marek), an established director of Yiddish theater who took on the task, or what he considered to be his duty toward the Jewish community, of putting on translated Yiddish plays in Polish theaters for a mainly Jewish audience. Polish-Jewish literature also came into being, created by a number of illustrious writers such as Jakub Appenszlak, Maurycy Szymel, and Roman Brandstaetter, who all wrote in Polish for the Jewish reader and about matters connected with the Jewish community. A growing number of books were being translated from Yiddish into Polish, most often targeting a readership of Polish Jews who spoke Polish as their first language.[25] Probably the most visible and important sign of this trend was the rapid growth of interwar Polish-language Jewish newspapers aimed at the acculturated intelligentsia, such as *Nasz Przegląd* (pol. Our Review) or *Nowy Dziennik* (pol. New Journal). These were often openly affiliated with Zionism, and became champions for the modern Jewish national consciousness aimed at, in the words of Brandstaetter, "Jewish intelligentsia which could function only in non-Jewish languages but felt responsible for Jewish culture and wanted to shape it."[26] Polish-Jewish theater, literature, and the press were, in the eyes of their creators, a historical necessity. Because linguistic assimilation could not be stopped, the Polish language had to be employed to serve the needs of the Jewish national revival.

With its clear Zionist standpoint, *Nasz Przegląd* was in constant ideological conflict with assimilated writers who were gathered around a famous literary weekly—*Wiadomości Literackie* (pol. Literary News).[27] From the point of view of the Polish-Jewish milieu, assimilated Jews were traitors to their nation and culture. They were accused of rejecting their Jewishness and of opportunistic conversions, assimilatory complexes, and even of being Jewish anti-Semites. For *Wiadomości*, the Polish-Jewish writers represented backwardness, and their insistence on Jewish separateness was seen as fueling the anti-Semitic stereotypes that the assimilated writers struggled to disassociate themselves from.

The majority of Polish-Jewish writers will remain outside of the framework of this study because of their clear Jewish identification. Yet, the group was far from homogeneous and the borders between Polish writers of Jewish origin and Polish-Jewish writers are sometimes very murky. One of the *Nasz Przegląd* contributors to feature in this book is Władysław Szlengel, a young poet with both strong Polish and Jewish affiliations.

Education

The driving force behind the acculturation of interwar Jewry was the Polish-language state school system. Despite ratification of the Minorities Treaty, which offered access to primary school education in the national languages of minorities, the Polish government at both the national and local levels increasingly refrained from providing adequate funding for Jewish schools.[28] Graduates of Yiddish- and Hebrew-language schools also had problems with access to university-level education.[29] This situation was further complicated by the controversies within the Jewish community over the language of instruction (whether it should be Yiddish or Hebrew), the level of secularization, and the problem of political and ideological orientation, with proponents of all options actively trying to influence the government with their own conceptions of Jewish education.[30] In consequence, a large proportion of Jewish youth in the interwar period, as much as eighty-seven percent in 1937,[31] went through Polish-language primary education. Many of them did so through so-called *szabasówki*—state schools that respected Jewish holidays, set up in predominantly Jewish communities. The large percentage of Jewish youth attending these schools could be attributed to a number of factors, such as that Polish schools were the only free schools in the vicinity, that most private Jewish schools were heavily ideologically oriented, or that the Polish educational system seemed to facilitate the future professional careers of the students. As a result, all of these children acquired a fluent knowledge of Polish. At the same time, it was at schools, and particularly universities, that the youth from assimilated backgrounds first experienced anti-Semitism. It was anti-Semitism, combined with pauperization, that led to the increasing decline of the numbers of Jewish students at Polish universities throughout the interwar period. To combat this, many took radical steps, either by undertaking baptism and attempting to merge with the Polish community or by embracing Jewish nationalistic movements.

After more than a hundred years of partition, Poles finally had their own free educational system, through which they were allowed to teach the Polish language alongside a syllabus imbued with patriotism. Concurrently, private Jewish schools were gradually submitting to the growing current of acculturation and introducing into their curriculum an increasing amount of Polish literature and culture. One interwar Jewish student remembered: "Schools brought us up to be patriots and patriotism was undoubtedly the most important aspect of our education. There is no doubt that in this sense school had much more influence on us than our homes."[32] In many cases this patriotic education was strengthened even further by the family tradition that championed a "romantic" vision of assimilation.

Romanticism

Despite rejection by the liberally oriented circles of the intelligentsia, the ideals of romanticism and neo-romanticism are nonetheless crucial to any understanding of mass national identity in interwar Poland. In the newly independent state romantic heroes and mysticism were as much alive as they were in 1830s. *God, Honor, and Fatherland,* taken from the banners of nineteenth-century uprisings, were the founding principles which provided a basis for the new historiography and shaped the consciousness of young inhabitants of Poland—Jews and Poles alike.

The key figure that should be discussed when assessing the role that romantic culture played in the lives of Polish Jewry is undoubtedly Adam Mickiewicz. Mickiewicz, the great *wieszcz* (pol. prophet) of Polish romanticism, remained "our book of common prayer, our bedtime story, our national anthem."[33] He was the most widely read poet in interwar Poland and an icon of Polish romanticism. For the Polish Jewish community his work had a special significance as the poet's Jewish affinities made him a symbol of Polish-Jewish unity.[34] While interwar publicists debated whether Mickiewicz's mother was, or was not, a descendant of a Frankist family, much more important were his links to messianic prophesies. Mickiewicz was strongly influenced by these, and in his works described the existence of Jews in Poland as a sign of a mystical-messianic union that was to lead to national liberation. This idea of the mystical union of the two nations peaked during the Polish-Jewish brotherhood of the January Uprising, when, as historian Magdalena Opalski writes:

> The fall of insurrectionary Warsaw was commonly compared to that of Israel. Poland was referred to as Zion; the Polish freedom fighters were identified with the Maccabees; the pain and humiliation of the defeat found their equivalents in biblical imagery such as the

> Babylonian exile and the destruction of the Temple. Even the scenes sculpted on the arch of Titus, commemorating the destruction of the Jewish state, were reinterpreted as portrayals of the sufferings of the Poles as "Jews of the New Testament."[35]

In 1855, at the outbreak of the Crimean war, Mickiewicz set forth to Istanbul to organize Polish forces against Russia. Fighting alongside Poles were to be the Jewish legion the Hussars of Israel, comprised of Russian and Palestinian Jews, an undertaking thought to be highly influenced by the Frankist concept of "messianic militarism." After Mickiewicz's sudden death in the same year, his plans never became reality, yet his concept of a multicultural, multi-religious Poland remained a recurring theme in the public discussion on the place of national minorities in the Polish fight for independence and later in the resurrected country.

While widely read among the educated strata, the complex philosophical ideas of Mickiewicz could hardly fill the needs of interwar popular culture. In order to fully participate in the historical discourse of interwar Poland, Jews needed a romantic hero who could fully compete in the public imagination with Polish independence fighters. Such a symbol became Berek Joselewicz, a Jewish colonel in the failed 1794 Kościuszko Uprising and a creator of a 500-strong Jewish regiment, which was wiped out in a heroic fight against the Russian attack on the right flank of Warsaw. Joselewicz's proclamation encouraging Jews to fight for the independence of Poland, in which he stimulated their patriotic feelings by referencing motifs from the Old Testament, became one of the foundation stones of a national identity for Poles of Mosaic faith.[36] Joselewicz, a man who came from a shtetl, rose to become a hero of assimilation. In the interwar period his story illustrated the concept of the "national assimilation" of Jews through their participation in the fight for the defense of Polish independence.

The embodiment of Jewish romantic hopes in independent Poland was First Marshal Józef Piłsudski, the authoritarian leader of the Second Polish Republic, who gained cult status among the assimilated Jewry. With his Lithuanian background Piłsudski embodied the idea of the "Jagiellonian" federalist, multicultural Poland and stood against the ethnicity-based vision of nationhood proclaimed by his main political adversary, the founder of right-winged National Democracy, Roman Dmowski. After his death, universally mourned by the Jewish community, Piłsudski became a subject of romantic worship. In a symbolic gesture, earth from Berek Joselewicz's burial place was transported to the Marshal Piłsudski mound in Krakow. Thus, as historian Maria Janion writes, Colonel Berek Joselewicz became a part of the eternal glory of the Polish army, connected to its greatest legend—that surrounding Józef Piłsudski.[37]

The influence of this patriotic-romantic narrative was not limited to the assimilated circles. Katrin Steffen in her work on Zionist-oriented Polish-Jewish press discusses how nineteenth-century romantic ideals of tolerance and the right of independence were absorbed and transformed by Polish Jews and served as the basis for the new identity of Polish Jewishness. The discourse of Polish-Jewish circles was indeed often fiercely patriotic, with Kościuszko, Mickiewicz, and Piłsudski seen as "geniuses of the nation," representing "independence, freedom of spirit and the defense of human dignity."[38] Yet, in this discourse, Joselewicz, rather than being upheld as a symbol of assimilation, was seen as an embodiment of the "Maccabean sprit," while Mickiewicz, along with his idea of Jewish legions, was seen as the precursor of Zionism. The diaries of young Polish Jews who grew up in interwar Poland demonstrate how these ideas were embedded in their upbringing. Although those young people were critical of Poland and often saw their future abroad, the Polish patriotic historical narrative was clearly a crucial part of their social consciousness.[39]

Politics

It can be safely stated that assimilation as a political movement lost its momentum by the end of the First World War. While the so-called neo-assimilators were still relatively successful in the 1916 local elections, they turned out to be defenseless when faced with the growing strength of Zionists, Communists, the Bund, and Orthodox parties. The assimilationist party eroded over the definition of assimilation and the extent to which it was possible. The wave of pogroms and the growth of anti-Semitism in newly independent Poland only served as a further proof that Jews could never successfully integrate in the Polish society. By the mid-1920s the assimilationists had lost all political influence. Though attempts to revive the movement were made with the creation of organizations such as *Związek Młodzieży Polskiej Pochodzenia Żydowskiego—"Żagiew"* (pol. Association of Polish Youth of Jewish Origin—"Torch"), *Związek Akademickiej Młodzieży Zjednoczeniowej* (pol. Association of Academic Youth for Unity), and the aforementioned *Związek Żydów Uczestników Walk o Niepodległość Polski*, these groups remained of marginal importance in the context of the broader Jewish community.[40]

At the same time, the middle and upper-middle class Jews were becoming increasingly involved with leftist Polish political parties—*Polska Partia Socjalistyczna* (PPS, pol. Polish Socialist Party) and the *Komunistyczna Partia Polski* (KPP, pol. The Communist Party of Poland). The PPS, initially led by Józef Piłsudski but later in opposition to his authoritarian tendencies, was a major center-left political power. KPP was an illegal, revolutionary party, which attracted mainly revolutionary youth. Yet despite their differences, both the PPS and KPP were the only parties in Polish political spheres to openly oppose anti-Semitism, offering their members a combination of socialism and full integration into society. Even though they did not have any concrete solutions for the everyday problems of Jews in Poland, and, as can be claimed, used the "Jewish question" mainly as a tool of attracting Jewish voters,[41] leftist parties often seemed to be the only environment in an increasingly anti-Semitic Poland where one's national background was, at least in theory, of no importance.

As a result both the PPS and KPP had among their members a disproportionate number of Jews, mainly from a middle-class background. While PPS remained a "safe" choice for the young middle class, joining the radical Communist party was regarded as a complete break with traditional Jewish society and religion. Jaff Schatz describes becoming a Communist at that time in Poland as "the most radical of all possible rebellions. It meant rebellion against the traditional Jewish world, the values of one's parents, and the values of general society."[42] By joining the party one became a Communist and a revolutionary, and was no longer a Jew or a Pole.

Another option for those willing to engage in secular, socialist politics was to join the Bund. The ideology of the General Jewish Labor Bund in Poland was based on Marxism. By using Yiddish as the main way of reaching the Jewish working class this group proposed a Jewish concept of nationhood where religion was replaced by class. Firmly set in the Diaspora, it promoted the principle according to which Jews should seek "national-cultural" autonomy in the places where they lived, rather than pursue mass emigration. Even though it rejected cultural polonization, the Bund undoubtedly developed local patriotism. According to historian Gertrud Pickhan, the most outstanding characteristic of all those who came together in the Bund was the belief "that one could feel bound to a country and yet be consciously 'different,' that it was possible to live out a dual loyalty to one's own ethnic group and to the country that was also regarded as one's homeland."[43]

Other options for Jews with dual Polish-Jewish affiliations were the parties and movements connected with Zionism. What they offered was a chance of embracing one's Jewishness without going back to the cultural "ghetto" and the need to learn Yiddish. The development of a Polish-Jewish press made this offer especially attractive to Polish-speaking Jews. When emigration to Palestine seemed unrealistic, combining Zionism, especially in the form presented by General Zionism, with complete cultural assimilation or even Polish patriotism, became a fairly common occurrence among the intelligentsia. According to Erza Mendelsohn, in the cases of those coming from especially assimilated backgrounds Zionism was sometimes "the second-best choice" after Polishness, which could never be fully attained.[44] Some of its creators can indeed be safely described as "drawing-room Zionists"—people who despite their support for Zionism saw their future in Poland.[45] The clear pattern of ideological changes in subsequent generations of Jewish families, with assimilated parents and Zionist children, allows us to speak of dissimilation currents in the interwar Jewish intelligentsia.

Religion

Another result of the growing acculturation was a gradual secularization of the Jewish community. The history of interwar assimilated families often reveals the appearance of syncretism of religious customs, with acculturated Jews celebrating both Jewish and Christian holidays. This was especially common in assimilated intelligentsia families, where children went to secular Jewish or Polish schools and wanted to conform to their peers. As a result, children brought up in atheist homes, or those that did not pay much notice to religion, often had much more contact with the Polish Catholic faith than with Judaism.

Undoubtedly, the most radical expression of assimilation was conversion. This is true when referring to all of interwar Europe, but is especially pertinent in Poland where national identity was at that point inseparable from Catholicism. The most common reasons for conversion seemed to be, aside from genuine religious belief, either advancing one's career (which was often dependent on being Catholic) or intermarriage. The latter, requiring conversion because of a lack of institutions for civil marriage, could have been excused, albeit very rarely and mainly in case of highly assimilated families. However, overall, the attitude toward converts can be described as universally negative. Even the assimilationist circles condemned "the corruption of social ethics by insincere conversion for opportunistic reasons."[46] Baptism was seen as an act of denying one's Jewishness and almost always as a sign of opportunism. Those undergoing conversion were condemned as rejecting their culture, tradition, and nation, and sometimes were even accused of anti-Semitism. As a result, some parents who chose to baptize their children did so in secret, keeping their choice hidden from other members of their family.[47] The vast majority of those who did choose to convert were either members of families already assimilated for generations, or, as one baptized Holocaust survivor wrote, "laicized, leftist intelligentsia, who were not bothered much with God."[48]

Sources and Methodology

Because the aim of this study is to uncover the personal experiences of assimilated and acculturated Jews, principally the inhabitants of the Warsaw Ghetto, the main sources for my research will be personal, autobiographical documents—diaries, memoirs, and testimonies.[49] The majority of those quoted in my work came from the archive of the Żydowski Instytut Historyczny (ŻIH, pol. Jewish Historical Institute) and the Yad Vashem Archive in Jerusalem. I will also rely extensively on documentation from the proceedings of the Social Courts of the Central Committee of Polish Jews, as among those tried between 1946 and 1950 for collaboration and other acts against the Jewish community was a clear overrepresentation of Jews with assimilated or acculturated backgrounds—people who had held high-level positions in the ghetto administration and the police. The testimony of those who stood trial should of course be treated with caution. For the purpose of my research, greater importance is placed on the testimonies of impartial witnesses who were called in front of the court to describe various aspects of the functioning of the ghetto and general attitudes toward its authorities.

Important sources for my work were also collections of oral testimony, especially the Shoah Foundation Visual History Archive. Even though those interviewed were asked to recall events from more than fifty years before, the archive is undoubtedly a very valuable source for the history of the assimilated community of the Warsaw Ghetto. This is mainly because the majority of interviews has a pre-planned structure and covers survivors' lives before, during, and after the war, allowing us to trace their changing national and cultural affiliations. Just as importantly, among those interviewed are often people who chose not to speak publicly immediately after the war and did not wish to have their experiences published, including members of the Warsaw Ghetto's Order Service and employees of the ghetto administration. The great educator Janusz Korczak wrote in his Warsaw Ghetto diary:

"Long after the war, men will not be able to look each other in the eyes without posing the question: How did it happen that you survived? How did you do it?"[50] To no one is this statement more pertinent than to the so-called "victims of privilege"—those remaining on the verge of collaboration, policemen and members of the ghetto authorities, actors in German-licensed theaters. In the eyes of the public, the stories told by the ghetto elite could not match those of the underground fighters. They were more likely to be tried for collaboration than hailed as heroes. Moreover, those assimilated Jews who published their testimonies shortly after the war often chose to highlight the Jewish aspect of their ghetto experience. They were writing as "Jewish Holocaust victims," not as Poles or Poles of Mosaic background. The reason was, according to Zoë Waxman, that the survivors had to deal with the issue of "how the representation of their experiences relates to the *modus operandi* of collective memory, the concept of the Holocaust, and the accepted role of the witness."[51] It can be claimed therefore that most authors of early post-war memoirs, notwithstanding their affiliations during the war, took on the role of a *Jewish* survivor.

Diaries, memoirs, and testimonies will be supplemented by documents, which will allow me to place the personal experiences of assimilated Jews in the context of the wider ghetto society. The most famous collection dealing with the Warsaw Ghetto is undoubtedly the Ringelblum Archive—the Underground Archive of the Warsaw Ghetto.[52] Even though the aim of the Ringelblum Archive was to collect information from every strata of the ghetto community, the majority of essays and reviews of life in the ghetto written for the archive represent the views of the politically committed left-wing Zionists.[53] In consequence, the tone of the texts in the collection is overwhelmingly against assimilation and sometimes even openly hostile toward it.[54] This collection will therefore form a counterpoint to the diaries and memoirs written by assimilated inhabitants of the Warsaw Ghetto.

An important source both for Polish-Jewish relations during the Holocaust as well as for reports concerned with the situation of Jews in Poland can be found in the archives of Polish clandestine institutions, the most important source for which are two collections in Archiwum

Akt Nowych—*Delegatura Rządu na Kraj* (pol. Government Delegation for Poland) and *Armia Krajowa* (pol. Home Army). Especially interesting are reports from the Polish underground authorities to the Polish government-in-exile in London about the situation in the Warsaw Ghetto, which are included in the Delegatura Rządu na Kraj collection.

The final source for my research will be newspapers, both official and clandestine. The Ringelblum Archive remains the primary and almost exclusive source of the Warsaw Ghetto's underground press. The majority of Polish underground newspapers are in Biblioteka Narodowa in Warsaw (500 titles) and Archiwum Akt Nowych in Warsaw (approx. 100 titles, mainly from the Warsaw Uprising). When it comes to sources of German origin, the main source for the social history of the Warsaw Ghetto is *Gazeta Żydowska* (pol. Jewish Newspaper), a German-controlled, Polish-language newspaper published two or three times a week in the ghettos of the *Generalgouvernement*. Though censored and very heavily biased, *Gazeta* nonetheless contains an enormous amount of information about everyday life in the ghetto, which will often be considered in this book. Also of importance (especially for the period before the creation of the ghetto) are Nazi-controlled publications from occupied Warsaw, particularly *Nowy Kurier Warszawski* (pol. The New Warsaw Courier).

On the basis of the above sources I will attempt to reconstruct the multitude of voices of the assimilated and acculturated ghetto inhabitants. My first aim will be to avoid the traditional discourse of the history of the assimilated community in the Warsaw Ghetto, which tends to be viewed either from purely "Jewish" terms, or from a purely "Polish" perspective, as nothing more than the Jewish angle of Polish history. In order to strike a balance between the "Polish" and "Jewish" aspects of the identity of assimilated Jews, it will be particularly useful to adopt a postmodern approach to history, which focuses on the historical context of Jewish existence. Explaining this approach, Moshe Rosman writes:

> In each historical context, Jewish society and culture are not seen to be cells of some worldwide Jewish community "in dialogue" with

> "surrounding" or "host" societies and cultures, as the acculturationist school had it, but to be a "hybrid" component of the "hegemonic" society and culture whose frameworks set the templates according to which, and the parameters within which, Jewish identity, culture, and society are "constructed."[55]

This approach will allow me to look at the Warsaw Ghetto not only as part of the history of the Holocaust but also to place it in the context of the particular history of Polish Jews.

Since a particular historical period can be described only in categories of its own language, I will also employ the terminology that was used at the time. I will therefore refer to the "Aryan" side of Warsaw, and divide the inhabitants of Warsaw into "Poles" and "Jews," even though I am fully aware that such division is in many cases against the self-identification of these individuals. So far, however, scholars of the period have not found another way of dealing with this terminology.

When it comes to the internal life of the ghetto, I will not attempt to show a comprehensive picture of the ghetto community, nor do I presume to think that I am capable of doing so.[56] On the contrary, I will concentrate on the story of a very marginal group, which can in no way be seen as representative of the Warsaw Ghetto community. In his memoirs, Antoni Marianowicz, a member of a well-off converted family, who was in the ghetto as a teenager, wrote: "I owe my survival not to any personal qualities, but to my ancestors, chance and luck. I did not spend a single minute in a concentration camp. No one shot at me and, no less fortunately, I shot at no one. My memoirs are not memoirs of horror. I want to tell my own truth about the Occupation, to describe that period from my own point of view."[57] This story, just as every voice of the Holocaust, deserves to be told.

2

In the Warsaw Ghetto

Between September 1939 and the Closure of the Ghetto

In the summer of 1939 Warsaw readied itself for a German invasion. The newspapers reported on tens of thousands of volunteers from all walks of life digging trenches in various parts of the capital, while others began preparing to enlist. On September 1, 1939, Hebrew scholar and future chronicler of the Warsaw Ghetto, Chaim Kaplan, noted that "all classes and all nationalities, even those who suffered persecution at the hands of the Poles in the time of peace, volunteered to fight in defense of the country."[1] Jewish newspapers called the community to fight for "our most sacred concern, for the Fatherland, for Honor, for our glorious future, for the freedom of all peoples, and the Rebirth of Humanity,"[2] and diarists noted the "patriotic ecstasy" with which they published photographs of gray-bearded rabbis and leading Jewish representatives digging trenches.[3] Yet it seems that the atmosphere of patriotic frenzy did not last long. Already in the first days of the war many Jews encountered severe problems when trying to enlist for military service. Many of them openly blamed these problems on anti-Semitism.[4] This view was shared by the most diligent chronicler of the Jewish experience in occupied Warsaw, historian Emanuel Ringelblum, who noted that "Anti-Semitic saboteurs" imposed obstacles to recruiting Jews into active service.[5] It is hard to establish to what extent this was the case, as the problems with enlistment in the chaos of the September campaign also appear in war diaries of non-Jewish Poles. There is no doubt however that as a direct result of the restriction placed on Jewish students entering the officers' school in interwar Poland, only a small number of non-commissioned officers of Jewish origin, limited to specialists, were called up in Warsaw.[6] On September 7, Polish radio announced the evacuation of the city and urged all men to flee east. Among those who left Warsaw were a large number of Jews, including the leaders of the main Jewish political parties and youth movements. Those who stayed in Warsaw were commanded to dig trenches and raise fortifications to prepare for the defense of the city. As Ringelblum noted, Jews, who before the war were felt to be second- or third-class citizens, finally achieved equal rights when "asked to render help to the common fatherland."[7] However, those Jews who wanted to involve themselves in the civilian defense of Warsaw in more prominent ways than through digging trenches encountered difficulties. According to Ringelblum, the *Stołeczny Komitet Samopomocy Społecznej* (SKSS, pol. Metropolitan Committee of Mutual Social Aid) accepted Jewish candidates only very reluctantly, and those who were accepted were often harassed to such an extent that they were forced to resign.[8] The Jewish equivalent of SKSS, *Komisja Koordynacyjna Żydowskich Instytucji Społecznych* (pol. Coordinating Committee of Jewish Social Institutions, was created on September 14 to deal with the problems of the Jewish population, yet this organization, formed by interwar Jewish community leaders, was alien to most of the assimilated and acculturated Jews who lacked experience and contacts in the environment of Jewish community work. Similarly, the Jewish communal body—*Żydowski Komitet Cywilny Miasta Stołecznego Warszawy* (pol. Jewish Civilian Committee of the Capital City of Warsaw), which later became the Jewish Council, the Judenrat—included mainly prominent pre-war public figures. They were experienced leaders of Jewish political parties and directors of economic and social institutions.

On October 1, German military rule was imposed in the city. The Warsaw region became part of the *Generalgouvernement für die Besetzten Polnischen Gebiete* (G.G., ger. General Government for the Occupied Polish Territories). From the beginning of the occupation Jews were the ones singled out for forced labor. Their property was plundered and the Germans began gradually excluding them from the most important branches of the economy.[9] One of the first Nazi decisions in the occupied city was the creation of the Judenrat. Set up on October 6, the Council consisted of twenty-four members of the former Jewish Civilian Committee and was immediately employed to carry out a census of all Warsaw Jews, on the basis of which Jewish workers were called up for forced labor. On November 23, 1939, a decree of Governor-General of the Generalgouvernement, Hans Frank, ordered all Jews over the age of twelve to wear an armband with the Star of David. The decree was the end to any Jewish-Polish brotherhood that might have been formed during the defense of the city as it not only differentiated the Jewish community but also escalated instances of violence against Jews, both by Poles and by Germans, and led to the beginning of blackmailing and denunciations—*szmalcownictwo* (pol. popular expression for extortion of money from Jews in hiding). The question of who was to wear the armband was very far from clear. According to the decree anyone who belonged or had belonged to the Jewish community and anyone whose father or mother belonged or had belonged to the Jewish community was to be considered Jewish. On the next day, however, the German-licensed newspaper for Warsaw, *Nowy Kurier Warszawski*, defined as Jewish "anyone whose both parents were Jewish. Those who on the 1st of October, 1939, did not belong to the Jewish religious community are not considered Jewish."[10] The confusion caused by the conflicting official messages and the changing attitude of assimilated Jews toward armbands can be traced in the diary of an economist of Jewish origin and a member of the Polish underground, Ludwik Landau. On December 8, two weeks after the introduction of the order, Landau, who himself never wore an armband or moved into the ghetto, noted that Jewish armbands are in general worn, "even though some people try not to wear them. So far nobody checks."[11] On January 10, 1940, he wrote: "wearing armbands is for assimilated Jews and people of Jewish origin still an unsolved problem,"[12] and two days later repeated gossip that for 500 złoty one could be freed from wearing them.[13] On February 1, he noted: "The order does not provide a definition of a Jew, which leaves scope for speculation and doubts—starting with first generation baptized Jews.

The definition of a Jew has not yet been provided anywhere."[14] It was only in August 1940 that a clear definition of who was a Jew was given. "Jews are stuck between Scylla and Charybdis," explained Landau, "as not wearing armbands makes them susceptible to imprisonment, or more often, necessitates recourse to bribery. By wearing them they are likely to be beaten up and subjected to mugging."[15] Many assimilated Jews nonetheless chose not to comply. One of them was Arnold Szyfman. After he was released from prison, Szyfman spent the rest of the occupation in hiding outside Warsaw, first in Podkowa Leśna, an affluent suburb of Warsaw popular among the Polish educated middle class (intelligentsia), and later in the countryside. Another war-time inhabitant of Podkowa was Irena Krzywicka, a well-known writer of Jewish origin, whose Polish husband was deported to the USSR. Krzywicka lived openly in Podkowa, never considered wearing an armband, and was not bothered by the Gestapo until May 1941. She left the town the next day and went into hiding. Both Krzywicka and Szyfman shared the fate of Polish intelligentsia and their memoirs barely mention the fact that according to Nazi regulations they were both Jewish. The decision to wear or not to wear an armband also led to rifts within the Jewish community. Those who ignored it were often criticized or even ridiculed, their decision seen as a sign of renunciation of their Jewish identity. An ardent Zionist, Chaim Kaplan, noted on November 30, 1939, his satisfaction in wearing a badge of Jewish national colors, even if as a result of Nazi ruling.[16] Another person, however, wrote honestly that "the armbands were worn with pride but only when we were not scared of being beaten up."[17]

The armband edict was only the first of an escalating number of anti-Jewish laws, which gradually separated Jews from Polish communal and cultural life. In his diary Landau painstakingly enumerates and discusses restrictions on walking on the most affluent Polish streets, sitting on the public benches outside the Jewish quarter, entering the public parks, taking books from libraries, and buying books in bookshops.[18] Another group of restrictions were those aimed at the professional segregation of "Aryan" and non-"Aryan" parts of the society. The Jewish intelligentsia functioning in a mixed Polish-Jewish environment thus became the first victims of the Nazi objective of pauperizing the Jews. Describing the situation, an attorney of Jewish origin, Adam Starkopf, wrote:

> Lawyers were no longer permitted to appear in court; doctors were forbidden to have non Jewish patients; journalists, writers, artists, musicians, and teachers were now all superfluous because practicing their professions had been declared illegal. The pauperization of these professional groups meant that many of them had to turn to trade. The most energetic intellectuals got into trade in the early stage of German occupation. They became dealers in foreign currencies, gold, dry goods, wrist watches, flour . . . anything they could lay their hands upon and that could still be traded.[19]

In consequence, when street vending was forbidden in January 1940, Landau noted that the decision not only targeted the Jewish working class but also the impoverished intelligentsia.[20] Unsurprisingly therefore, a manufacturer of wooden shoes organized by former employees of the Warsaw's Institute for Social Affairs at one point employed over fifty academics, writers, and artists, who were mainly Jewish.[21]

During this time Warsaw was filled with gossip and hearsay about the creation of the ghetto. From January 1, 1940, Jews were not allowed to change a place of residence without authorization. On January 23, the Resettlement Department of the Governor's Office of the District of Warsaw was created in order to hold civil authority over the future ghetto. From January 26, they were not allowed to travel on trains. On March 27, the Judenrat received an order to build at its own cost a wall around what was officially referred to as the *Seuchensperrgebiet* (ger. territory threatened with epidemics), which roughly covered the territory of the pre-war "Jewish Quarter" in the northern part of central Warsaw. The wall was finished in June. In August 1940 Ludwig Leist, the newly nominated municipal district governor, ordered all Jews to move out of the German part of the city, while all Jews moving to Warsaw were only allowed to settle in the newly defined Jewish Quarter. Even though Jews were still allowed to stay in their apartments on the Aryan side, this was widely regarded in occupied Warsaw as a step toward the enclosure of the ghetto. On October 2, Warsaw district governor Ludwig Fischer signed an official document ordering the creation of the ghetto; the order was made public ten days later and 113,000 Poles and 138,000 Jews were given until the end of the month to move into their respective quarters.[22] People reacted with panic, and the vast majority of even the most assimilated Jews, including many of those who never wore armbands, decided to move into the ghetto. Fear of repercussions is cited in many diaries as the principal motivating factor, but there was also undoubtedly an element of safety offered by enclosure within the ghetto walls. Describing the reaction he witnessed in his environment, acculturated medical doctor Henryk Makower wrote: "As the looting did not let up and more and more marauding gangs roamed the streets, people actually began to hope that the rumors about establishing a ghetto which would seal off the Jews from the rest of Warsaw were true. 'Let them go ahead and close us in. . . . Things couldn't possibly get worse than they are right now' people said."[23]

When assimilated Jewish families decided to move into a ghetto, they entered into an environment that, as Landau highlights, they often felt they had nothing in common with.[24] Yet it seems that this realization of insurmountable cultural differences was often recognized only after the enclosure of the ghetto, as the sheer speed of events between the announcement of the ghettoization decree on October 12 and the end of resettlement on November 15 did not give them much time for reflection.[25] In September 1940 Landau commented on the events unfolding around him that "It is hard to imagine what hell will break in Warsaw if the Germans attempt relocating the Jews."[26] Subsequent events fully confirmed his observation. Despite that, only a few Jews, mainly from intellectual or artistic circles, decided to risk an illegal existence with forged papers bearing "Aryan" names. Some of them were assimilated enough into the Polish society to remain living "on the surface," while others went into hiding in Warsaw or left the city. These were mainly people who were very strongly linked to the Polish environment, most often by marriage. A survivor, whose mother was of Jewish origin, described what happened after the family learned about the enclosure of the ghetto: "We decided to stay where we were. The only thing that happened was that my mother took out the family album and removed out of it photographs of family members with so-called 'bad looks.'"[27] She also recalled that the majority of her friends of similar backgrounds never entered the ghetto. She explained: "It is difficult to go into a ghetto if you consider yourself to be a Pole."[28] Even Ringelblum, who rarely showed compassion for the fate of the assimilated community, noted that Polish families, irrespective of their worldview, as a rule tried to safeguard their Jewish relatives.[29] According to Landau, this was especially valid if it was the wife who was of Jewish origin and the family name was not conspicuous.[30] Only a very small group of converted Jews and foreign citizens were allowed to legally stay on the "Aryan" side.[31] The rest, irrespective of their national and cultural identity, began their lives as citizens of the "closed quarter."

Assimilated Jews in the Ghetto: Main Groups, Social Position, Life Conditions

There is no doubt that assimilated Jews' pre-war professional standing, financial situation, and especially contacts on the "Aryan" side created the impression that they were in a much more fortunate position than other inhabitants of the Warsaw Ghetto. Testimony and memoirs from the Warsaw Ghetto demonstrate that this was not the case, as the vast majority of assimilated and acculturated ghetto inhabitants fully shared the general fate of impoverished intelligentsia. There were, however, among this group those whose living standards were indeed, even if only at the beginning, starkly different from the poverty of the ghetto street.

In the best situation were those who were well-off before the war and were not cut off from their pre-war assets. These were adequate to sustain them through two years of living in the ghetto. Some of them managed to smuggle a large part of their pre-war assets into the ghetto; others lived off what they left for safekeeping with trusted people on the other side of the wall. In the ghetto, the majority of these individuals remained within their small circle of acquaintances of similar backgrounds and had very little contact with other ghetto inhabitants. They were part of the small minority who even in those circumstances could still keep up the pretense of the pre-war way of living. One of these "ghetto elites," who shared her apartment with the illustrious baptized painter of Jewish origin, Roman Kramsztyk, described her home as "a blossoming oasis in the middle of the desert," complete with a marble fireplace, paintings of notable painters on the walls, a brilliant library, and "soft sofas and chairs where you could chat with a glass of wine and a cigarette in your hand."[32] This group was undoubtedly marginal, yet it did exist. Although they were not forced by living circumstances to work, a number of members of the elite nonetheless did choose to take up employment. More often than not, they did so in order to secure exemption from forced labor, but also as a way of filling spare time, or in the case of work in social welfare or education, as a way of contributing to the community. There were also cases, though probably not numerous, when members of this part of the society set up ventures with smugglers and the new-rich and further expanded their wealth.[33]

The most prominent members of the assimilated and acculturated community were members and employees of the Jewish Council led by its chairman, Adam Czerniaków. The Judenrat, described by Ringelblum as a "nest of disgusting assimilation,"[34] was to become, as a result of its overblown bureaucratic structure, the most prominent job provider for the educated assimilated strata of the ghetto. Attorney Stanisław Adler wrote that most of the people in his situation and with similar qualifications worked for the Jewish Council,[35] and as if to confirm his statement almost all of the assimilated diarists were either employed by the Council themselves or were closely related to or acquainted with one of its 6,000 employees. Stefan Ernest, himself a high-level clerk in the Judenrat, described the employees of the Council as lawyers left without practice, teachers with no teaching positions, high-level civil servants, university students, and employees of pre-war social help institutions.[36] The widespread opinion in the ghetto, confirmed by those employed there, was that the main prerequisites for getting jobs in the Council were pre-war contacts and bribes. As a result, the majority of Judenrat clerks had no previous experience in office work and were generally thought to be arrogant and incompetent.[37]

Those with adequate contacts were also able to find employment in other branches of the ghetto administration overseen by the Judenrat. One of those who managed to get a highly coveted job at the post office described her co-workers as "a few elegant ladies and gentleman, very intelligent, cultured and nice people."[38] Another post office employee described those working there as "some incredible people," among them "the first violinist from the Warsaw Philharmonic and Erna—wife of the chairman of a bank."[39] Another illustrious post office worker, after his uncle's recommendation, was the nephew of the prominent Judenrat member and industrialist Abraham Gepner.[40]

Members of the assimilated intelligentsia, officers from the Polish Army, and lawyers were also over-represented among recruits to the ghetto police—the Jewish Order Service. The highest ranks of the Service were filled exclusively by converts and highly assimilated Jews, led by Józef Szeryński, a pre-war colonel in the Polish police and a convert to Catholicism. Following a brief period when the Jewish Police were seen as proof of the autonomy of the ghetto, the Order Service became synonymous with bribery and abuses of power and even before its involvement in the 1942 deportations was widely regarded as "a mob of gangsters."[41] However, the vast majority of members of the assimilated community who authored recollections of life in the Warsaw ghetto mention a member of the family or at least a friend or acquaintance in the Service. As Stanisław Gombiński, himself a policeman in the ghetto, wrote in his diary: "Everyone had brothers or sons in the service but they were thought to be the exception; as a rule members of the Police were thieves, blackmailers and sadists. The Jewish Police were the enemy."[42]

Among the fortunate inhabitants of the ghetto's assimilated and acculturated community were also those who despite new living circumstances were still able to continue in their pre-war profession. These people included mainly manual workers and craftsmen but also those employed in health care and education. In the best situation were the medical doctors, among them a significant number of converts. Once in the ghetto, qualified doctors of pre-war renown usually had no problems obtaining well-paid jobs and securing comparatively good living conditions. Describing his life in the ghetto the doctor Henryk Makower wrote: "Aside from a lack of freedom I could not complain . . . I had a nice, well located flat . . . I had plenty of work in the hospital and a well-functioning private practice."[43] Although this view can be widened to representatives of other professions connected with health and hygiene, the vast majority of them, especially those employed in lower-level positions in chronically underfunded, overcrowded hospitals, were in nowhere near as good a position as doctors with thriving private practices.

The situation of teachers on the whole was more difficult, yet the assimilated were again in a generally better position. Despite high unemployment among teachers in the ghetto, the vast majority of those without work were primary school teachers from Jewish schools. Those who before the war taught in Polish-language schools were undoubtedly favored as they could find employment in the Polish-language elementary schools maintained by the Council. Former teachers from Polish secondary schools and former university lecturers could also make a living teaching secondary level clandestine classes or the Judenrat-run vocational courses, many of which served as de facto preparatory courses for university.

Another group that remained active in their pre-war professions were Polish-language actors and musicians. After April 1941, when the German authorities allowed the opening of theaters, five theaters were established in the ghetto—two showing Yiddish-language performances and three showing Polish-language performances. Even though the salaries of actors and musicians were often not high enough to safeguard them from hunger, they had many opportunities to make money on the side by gaining employment in one of the cafés mushrooming in the ghetto. Some of them also started teaching, most often children from their own social circles.

Contacts on the "Aryan" side were an important source of money for the majority of the assimilated intelligentsia. As already stated, those who could still access their assets that were left outside the ghetto were in the best situation. Others were helped financially by their Polish friends, colleagues, associates, or family members as well as by Jews who did not move into the ghetto. Members of the assimilated community with contacts on the "Aryan" side had a higher chance than most of the ghetto society of finding someone trustworthy to take care of their belongings and provide them with access to their money, ensuring a degree of steady income.

The comparatively good living situation of the most fortunate members of the assimilated community started to change in mid-1941. As time passed, the proportion of people in the ghetto able to live off their pre-war assets shrank. Simultaneously, the price of food was constantly growing while wages remained at the same level. By then only the highest-level Judenrat workers could live off their salaries alone.[44] As historian Israel Gutman, who spent his teenage years in the Warsaw Ghetto, noted, from that point there was no longer a class system in the ghetto, only an overall slide toward poverty.[45] Helena Szereszewska, wife of the Judenrat member and wealthy pre-war entrepreneur Stanisław Szereszewski, described in her memoir how members of the relatively well-off part of the ghetto society were increasingly forced to sell their belongings:

> The kitchen door was used by professional hawkers. The front door was used by society ladies, who had taken up hawking because of circumstances. The kitchen door hawkers said "goodbye" and closed the door. We didn't have to fuss over them. The front door hawkers were offered tea and sometimes soup. They could use the toilet. We saw them to the door and sometimes continued our conversation when the door was already open.[46]

The financial situation of assimilated Jews was worsened by the general poverty surrounding them. Antoni Marianowicz recalled that his comparatively well-off father fully supported eighteen people—members of the family and close friends.[47] Describing this problem, educational activist Janusz Korczak wrote:

> Anyone who is a little better off must help his family. A family means him and his wife's brothers and sisters. Their brothers, sisters, old parents, children. They give between five and fifteen zlotys and so it goes, day in, day out. If someone is starving and happens to find relatives willing to acknowledge kinship and ensure two meals a day, he will be happy for two or three days, not more than a week, he will then ask for a shirt, shoes, a decent place to live, some coal. Then medical treatment for himself, his wife and children.[48]

With the changing situation, even factory workshops owned by German companies were becoming an attractive form of employment for many members of the assimilated strata. Marek Edelman noted that: "ladies who until now have been sitting in the coffee houses, are now turning into overworked seamstresses, menders and civil servants with a vengeance."[49] In consequence, in the Többens tailoring workshop, eighty percent of the employed were described as "snooty women from bourgeois homes."[50]

Most diaries of members of the assimilated community reflect the gradually worsening financial situation of the ghetto inhabitants and the distress caused by it. In his report on the ghetto intelligentsia one of the collaborators of *Oyneg Shabes*, the group gathered by Emanuel Ringelblum to work on the Underground Archive of the Warsaw Ghetto, wrote: "Money ends, one finds some more stuff to sell. One day there will be nothing left though. This is the end. This is what awaits most, as nothing lasts forever. It is only a question of order. We are all standing in the queue."[51] As if to confirm his words, in the winter of 1941 an *Oyneg Shabes* report on social help pointed out that "one-time professionals—engineers, lawyers, teachers, artists, intellectuals—people who worked all their lives, were unable to beg, and succumbed to hunger, sickness and death."[52] In May 1942 Ringelblum described the new wave of beggars on the streets as "a better class of people, their breeding being obvious from their faces and manner" and noted their "good, sometimes excellent Polish."[53] Another picture of an impoverished, formerly well-off group was painted by prominent social activist and writer Rachela Auerbach, who described once-affluent families begging on the streets, set up as if posing for a middle-class family photograph.[54]

However, when looking at the history of the Warsaw Ghetto it is important to bear in mind that despite their progressive pauperization, assimilated Jews, unlike the rest of the community, still retained access to positions in the Judenrat or the Order Service. In many cases they had just enough savings to buy a place in the workshop and often kept some contacts on the "Aryan" side. During the final period of the ghetto history these became factors that could ensure survival.

It can be safely stated that the vast majority of the ghetto population had a decisively negative attitude toward assimilated Jews. In many documents preserved in the *Oyneg Shabes* Archives, converted, assimilated, and highly acculturated Jews are put in one category, signifying a view of assimilation as an apostasy and the last step before baptism.[55]

This negative attitude seems to have been returned by at least a significant part of the assimilated group. The testimony of many of the assimilated offers proof that the division between the two parts of the society remained as deep as before the war. One of the assimilated ghetto inhabitants stated: "As things turned out, we shared a common fate, but what was the community supposed to consist of? Do two pigeons sitting on the same roof form a community? . . . How can one feel communion with half a million people in the ghetto?"[56] This attitude is mirrored in other testimonies, such as that of the famous bacteriologist, who converted to Catholicism, Ludwik Hirszfeld. Throughout his memoirs Hirszfeld maintains a distinction between "them" (Jews) and "us" (Poles).[57] Marian Małowist, a historian working in the ghetto with the assimilated youth, summed up this attitude by noting: "I believe they did not grow closer to the Jewish society. They encounter now the darkest aspects of Jewish life and in many cases extend their dislike to the whole of Jewish society. I believe that after the war, many of them will undergo baptism to fully break their links with Jewishness."[58] This opinion is repeated by many others.

Yet, at the same time, the small size of the ghetto meant that traditional, nationalist, and assimilated Jews were forced to remain in much closer contact than was the case before the war. An especially important factor in this respect was the existence of house committees, which gathered all socially active inhabitants of the apartment blocks irrespective of their background.[59] As time passed, the growing contacts between the two groups clearly led to a change in the attitude of nationalists toward the assimilated ghetto inhabitants. Many of the late 1941 and 1942 documents show growing differentiation between the main group of alienated assimilationists and those who could be "induced, through quiet, objective and restrained persuasion, to re-establish ties to the nation from which they stem."[60] These included mainly personal friends of the authors of the documents. As social activist and Hebrew teacher Abraham Lewin put it: "In the course of time the sense of brotherhood conquers all the feelings of alienation that time and differences of culture have given rise to. . . . We still feel estranged from each other, but this estrangement will soon disappear and we will be at ease with one another like brothers once more."[61]

There were undoubtedly those who while in the ghetto acquired a new Jewish, national, and cultural identity. This, it seems, is typical of those who entered the ghetto with some degree of dual identity, even if Polish remained the principal one. The majority noted a gradual, yet perceptible, integration with the wider Jewish society. In the words of one of the ghetto inhabitants:

> There were many people among us who felt more Polish than Jewish. They didn't turn themselves into stereotypical Jews, but only a few rejected the community. The majority found a bond with Jewishness in the ghetto because of the common destiny. That didn't lessen the feeling of Polishness, but it increased the feeling of belonging among people sharing a common fate.[62]

One of the most striking examples of this common fate is the content of the Underground Archives of the Warsaw Ghetto. Even though the Archives had a clear ideological orientation and made a point of not cooperating with either members of the Judenrat or of the Jewish Order Service, among *Oyneg Shabes* collaborators were assimilated and acculturated Jews who before the war had no contact with the general Jewish community or with the nationalist movement. Commenting on this phenomenon, Ringelblum noted in February 1940 that the "completely assimilated Jewish intelligentsia is coming to join us."[63] Among members of the Polish-speaking intelligentsia who wrote prolifically for the Archives were popular writers Gustawa Jarecka and Henryka Łazowert. Jarecka's coworker in the correspondence department of the Judenrat, Marcel Reich, who provided the Archives with copies of documents exchanged between the Jewish Council and the German authorities, not only considered himself to be completely alienated from the Yiddish-speaking community, but also wrote music reviews for the German-controlled *Gazeta Żydowska*.

What undoubtedly brought these two groups together in spite of stark ideological differences was the fact that they were both clearly distinct from the rest of the ghetto's inhabitants. In the eyes of many ordinary ghetto dwellers the assimilated Jews and nationalist activists were to the same extent part of the ghetto's privileged strata. Differences in political affiliations might have been crucial to Ringelblum or to his assimilated opponents, but, to quote the words of a worker in one of the large ghetto workshops, they were all regarded by the ghetto street as "lazy good-for-nothings, sycophants, petty politicians, associates and friends"[64] and therefore clearly different from the impoverished majority of Jews in the ghetto.

Christians in the Warsaw Ghetto

Few aspects of social life in the Warsaw Ghetto were as heavily restricted as religious practice. As of January 1940, all forms of public worship, both in synagogues and in private dwellings, were forbidden.[65] Even before the closure of the ghetto, religious Jews were especially at risk of oppression, and religious objects and artifacts were routinely desecrated. Once in the ghetto, religious members of the society quickly organized underground religious practices. There were a number of clandestine prayer houses and talmudic schools operating in the Warsaw Ghetto and at least four illegal *mikvaot*.[66] In the spring of 1941 Jews were again allowed collective prayer. The Great

Synagogue was re-opened, followed by two other synagogues. In the spring of 1942 the Germans allowed for two mikvaot to open. While the official religious life of the quarter was overseen by the Department of Religious Affairs and the Rabbinate by the Judenrat, another stream of religious life continued operating under the patronage of illustrious rabbis and *tzadikim*, among them a significant number of refugees from the most important religious communities in pre-war Poland. The head of the Jewish Social Self-Help religious department was Rabbi Shimon Huberband.[67]

There is very little information on the religious practices of assimilated Jews. As was already noted, the vast majority of them came from homes that were not overtly religious, and religious practice was limited to celebrations of High Holidays, often only for the sake of the older generation. There is a lack of testimonies of assimilated Jews attending underground houses of prayer or any other form of collective religious practice, even though there are descriptions of family gatherings linked to Jewish holidays. Such descriptions are usually emotional as in many cases they reminded the authors of a past celebration and of those family members and loved ones who were no longer with them. Sometimes they served as a reinforcement of the Jewish identity of those attending.

A completely different situation applied to Christians of Jewish origin. The number of Christians living in the Warsaw Ghetto is hard to establish. According to the Statistics Department of the Judenrat as of January 1, 1941, among 380,740 ghetto inhabitants there were 1,540 Catholics, 148 Protestants, 30 Russian Orthodox, and 43 other Jews of non-Mosaic faith in the ghetto—altogether 1,761 "Christian Jews."[68] Still, Peter Dembowski, author of the only comprehensive study of the subject, estimates their number to be closer to 5,000.[69] According to Dembowski, this is also the number that is preserved as part of oral tradition in the former ghetto parishes. This claim is undoubtedly supported by numerous witness reports of churches filled to their capacity during the ghetto masses. One of the former ghetto churches, the All Saints Church, is the largest church in Warsaw and when full can accommodate 4,000 people.[70] The estimate of more than 6,000 baptized Jews in the ghetto is also suggested by one of the pioneering researchers of the Warsaw Ghetto—historian Philip Friedman.[71] Another argument supporting the thesis is that the figures from the Statistics Department would not have included any of the 66,000 Warsaw District refugees who arrived in the ghetto between January and March 1941, nor the 3,000 mainly highly assimilated German refugees who arrived in the spring of 1942. Chaim Kaplan, describing the German refugees, wrote that many of them "were born into the Christian faith, their parents or grandparents having converted years ago. Many were children of mixed marriages. Some of the wives are pro-German. In other words, in practice they are Christians in every way, full-fledged Germans."[72] It can be safely assumed that these groups included a proportion of converts. A significant addition to the initial number of Christians must have been made by a wave of baptisms in the ghetto. According to Rev. Czarnecki, a priest in the ghetto, before the baptism of Jews was forbidden in October 1942, the churches conducted a few courses in preparation for baptism with up to twenty students at each.[73] Diarists speak of at least several hundred, if not thousands, baptized in the ghetto.[74] Ringelblum mentions over 200 Jews baptized in Warsaw until March 1940, and a year after the enclosure of the ghetto refers to the wave of conversions in the quarter as a "psychopathological phenomena."[75] Ludwik Hirszfeld recalls the baptisms of "many people—older and younger, sometimes whole families."[76] The constantly updated list of those who converted was meant to be kept in the Judenrat.[77]

The first clear sign of Nazi intentions toward baptized Jews came in January 1940 with the so-called Kott Affair. Andrzej Kott, coming from a long converted family, was one of the members of the Polish intelligentsia who was arrested by the Nazis for involvement in *Polska Ludowa Akcja Niepodległościowa* (PLAN, pol. Polish People's Independence Action)—an underground freedom movement. He managed to escape from the Gestapo Headquarters on Szucha Avenue in Warsaw, leading to a very intensive and widespread search. Even though Kott was baptized at birth, he was described on the search warrants as "the Jew Andrzej Kott" and it was the Jewish community that was ordered to find him. Because this proved impossible, as a form of collective punishment, the Nazis executed 225 Jews, the vast majority of them coming from the intelligentsia. Understandably, converts reacted to Kott being considered a Jew with panic. According to a Jewish diarist, many medical doctors and lawyers (i.e., the most assimilated groups, often including converts) left Warsaw and escaped to the Soviet zone.[78] The Kott affair was probably the main incentive for a group of Christians of Jewish origin to address the *Rada Główna Opiekuńcza* (RGO, pol. Main Welfare Council), a branch of the *Naczelna Rada Opiekuńcza* (NRO, pol. General Welfare Council), an organization established in order to coordinate charity activities and distribute aid from foreign organizations in occupied Poland and the only representative of Polish authorities considered legitimate by the Germans. In their appeal to clarify their legal status, they were backed up by the authorities of both the Protestant and Catholic Churches. On November 25, 1940, the Superintendent of the Protestant Church in Poland, in a letter to Adam Roniker, the head of the RGO, described converts as:

> People who out of their free will undertook the sacrament of baptism, according to the teaching of our savior Jesus Christ, and became completely spiritually estranged from the Jewish nation and its religious-ethical worldview, while becoming one with the life and worldview of the Polish nation. They are pushed by force into an environment which is religiously and nationally alien to them, and which regards them as renegades.[79]

Five days later, on November 30, 1940, Archbishop Adam Sapieha, the war-time leader of the Polish Catholic Church, pointed out that

> Our brothers in faith are undoubtedly undergoing a great misfortune. They are being pushed back into an environment which they have broken with out of their own free will and which had become alien to them. This environment meets them with mistrust and hatred; their situation is exceptionally difficult and morally painful. We have to stand by their side. Catholics converted from Mosaic faith cannot be considered to be members of the Jewish community. Their family

> relations, perceptions and customs are completely different to Jewish ones. I am surrounded by the complaints of these people and as a bishop I cannot remain deaf to them.[80]

As a result of these letters, those baptized before September 1, 1939, were exempted from forced labor, resettlement into the ghetto, and the obligation to wear armbands.[81] Such preferential treatment did not however last long. In February 1941, the list of converted Jews prepared by the RGO was used by the Gestapo to track down families of assimilated Jews from Warsaw who did not move to the ghetto.[82] As the group of the so-called "Ronikers" included prominent intellectuals, scholars, lawyers, physicians, and top-ranking officials, the RGO affair was widely seen as a German trap set against those who could have easily stayed on the "Aryan" side, through support from their non-Jewish family members and friends.[83]

We do not know how Adam Czerniaków reacted to Ronikers being brought into the ghetto, as the pages covering this period are missing from his journal. A description of what Ringelblum ironically describes as a "welcoming ceremony"[84] and of the reaction to it of probably the vast majority of the ghetto society can, however, be found in the diary of Chaim Kaplan. He wrote about "the cream of the Polish society, people who always showed their hatred for the Jews and who adhered closely to the customs they had adopted," who were brought back to the ghetto in front of Jewish passersby "like members of the rabble caught in crime and sentenced to severe punishments."[85]

Even though Christians formed only 0.5–1.0 percent of the ghetto population, they were very much the center of attention in the quarter. Many of them belonged to the professional and social elite of pre-war Warsaw, and the group included a significant number of scientists, doctors, artists, and attorneys.[86] Due to their pre-war professional standing and contacts on the "Aryan" side, converts almost automatically penetrated the top layers of ghetto life, creating the feeling of a mutually supportive Catholic "clique." Among the most prominent baptized Jews were Dr. Mieczysław Kon, director of the Health Department; Major Dr. Tadeusz Ganz, medical officer in the Polish

Army, commissioned to direct the battle against epidemics; Gomulnicki; Maciej Czarnecki, one of the directors of the Fuel Commission and the owner of Café Sztuka; Dr. Jerzy Landau, director of the Health Center; Dr. Józef Stein, director of the Czyste Hospital; Dr. Wilhelm Szenwic, department head of the Czyste Hospital; and Dr. Stanisław Tylnbor, Deputy Head of the General Secretariat of the Judenrat.[87] In September 1941, Emanuel Ringelblum reiterated what seems to have been the opinion of the ghetto street when he wrote about how converts occupied the most important posts in the Jewish quarter: "They look after one another. They push their way into every situation and are very successful."[88] The best example of converts' prominence in the district was Józef Szeryński, the head of the Jewish Order Service. Szeryński was widely thought to give preference to Catholics applying for the highly coveted work in the Service and was accused of attempting to "make the Jewish Order Service Headquarters into a Christian island in a Jewish sea."[89] It is difficult to say to what extent this situation was indeed proof of existence of a "Catholic clique" or if Catholics were simply better qualified than the rest of the society.

Adam Czerniaków, who himself did not have a high opinion of converts, believed that when applying for posts in the Council they should be given equal treatment to other residents of the ghetto, even though such a stance was widely criticized by the general ghetto society.[90] Important posts being awarded to even the most deserving converted Jews aroused intense protest. Such was the case of Professor Mieczysław Ettinger, a distinguished pre-war attorney of generally acknowledged moral authority, who was appointed as the Disciplinary Magistrate. According to his opponents Ettinger as a convert could not be regarded as an exponent of the "highest ethics," necessary for that post.[91] In his diary Adam Czerniaków noted a four-and-a-half hour "fruitless" meeting of the Council devoted to the issue of converts in the Judenrat. Despite stormy exchanges, nothing was decided.[92] Such instances were the reason why some converts purposefully shied away from undertaking important positions in the ghetto. Hirszfeld claimed for example that some converted doctors did not take up posts in the ghetto hospitals out of fear of the reaction of nationalists. Even Józef

Szeryński was meant to have initially rejected the position of the head of the Order Service for the same reason.[93]

The high visibility of Catholics in the ghetto was also connected with the Church's prominent infrastructure. Even though, as already mentioned, until the spring of 1941 there was a ban on collective prayer in synagogues and private houses, churches functioned without disturbance. The Nativity of Blessed Virgin Mary Church at Leszno Street and the All Saints Church at Grzybowski Square, the largest parish in the city led by the most prominent figure in the Catholic life of the quarter, former right-wing activist, priest Marceli Godlewski,[94] both celebrated widely attended Sunday masses.[95] There were reports of Catholic weddings taking place in the quarter,[96] as well as funerals, after which the bodies were taken outside the ghetto and buried in the Catholic Powązkowski Cemetery.[97]

The large gardens adjacent to the church at Leszno Street, among very few places of greenery in the ghetto, were a meeting place for the elite of the quarter—professors, engineers, teachers, and their families. Many of them sent their children to the parish-run clandestine primary school.[98] There were also extra-curricular classes for Catholic children, including sports as well as dance classes held by the famous ballet teacher Irena Prusicka. In his memoirs Stanisław Adler describes the unsuccessful attempts of many ghetto mothers to get permission for their non-baptized children to play in the parish gardens. His own nephews, who looked "like typical Aryans," received permission without any difficulty.[99]

It was, however, the All Saints Church that became the center of Catholic life in the ghetto. Its adjacent buildings housed many prominent converts and offered them living conditions starkly different from those in the rest of the ghetto. According to an inhabitant of the parish, Ludwik Hirszfeld: "From Twarda street and Grzybowski square, through the depth of Hell, disgusting odors, and screaming people, one would enter the church's quad. It resembled the quads of Italian monasteries. The windows of our flat were facing a small but very pretty church garden. We felt that we are in an oasis of reflection, silence and good will which existed in Hell."[100] His friend and coworker Henryk Makower, who often visited Hirszfeld, described it as "so quiet and peaceful that you felt like there was no ghetto and no war."[101] According to the tenants list which was deposited after the war in the Jewish Historical Institute, among the inhabitants of the parish were five medical doctors; two professors of medicine; five attorneys; two judges, including a judge of the High Court; two architects, one of them the very famous engineer Maksymilian Goldberg; an economist; a director of *Qui pro quo*, the most elitist Warsaw interwar literary cabaret; a film maker; and an owner of two famous hotels in Kraków.[102]

Aside from receiving provisions from the Judenrat, Catholics in the ghetto remained under the additional social care of *Caritas* (a Catholic charity organization), which provided them with extra food from the "Aryan" side. Even though the Caritas kitchen was meant to provide also for a number of non-converted Jews in need, its existence was seen as another sign of the favored position of the converts in the ghetto society.[103] Commenting on the situation of Catholics of Jewish origin Ringelblum noted: "They get so many free lunches, that even the rich get them," adding later that "As regards food provisions, the Supplies Office favored the converts to such an extent that it was giving them large rations at a time when there was no food for the children in the orphanages."[104] This "illusion of privilege" was thought to be the main reason for the wave of conversions in the quarter.[105] This opinion was clearly shared by the Church authorities, as even Rev. Czarnecki admitted that it was hard to establish what was a genuine conversion and what formed an effort to facilitate survival.[106] Despite these doubts, in both of the churches the preparatory period before baptism was shortened from the customary six months to six weeks. In some cases priests conducted baptisms even without the necessary preparations, *in articulo mortis* (lat. at the point of death).[107]

The reasons for the dislike of converts in the Warsaw Ghetto were of course much deeper than just their privileged position and the alleged "conversionist mindset" of the Catholic Church. The ghetto society, notwithstanding their level of assimilation, saw converts as traitors betraying Jewish heritage and culture. It seems that not many in the ghetto believed in conversion for genuinely religious reasons. Converts were accused of a lack of morality, of having spiritual complexes, of megalomania toward Jews, and of having an inferiority complex toward Christians.[108] "I will laugh aloud at the sight of their tragedy," wrote Chaim Kaplan in his diary, concluding: "This is the first time in my life that a feeling of vengeance has given me pleasure." Later he added: "I don't know what their end will be, but one thing I know for a certainty. Their enmity to Israel will never cease."[109] A slightly less outspoken though not much more sympathetic picture of converts can be found in the diaries of assimilated Jews. They, however, seem to draw a clear line between conversion for self-interest, which was outwardly condemned, and conversion out of belief or in order to get married, which in certain cases could be if not excused, then understood. The fate of mixed marriages was generally viewed in the ghetto with pity verging on sympathy.[110]

Much less sympathy was reserved for those thought to have converted in order to advance their careers. The most famous such case was that of Ludwik Hirszfeld, the world-renowned bacteriologist. Hirszfeld, the head of Judenrat's Health Council, was, if we believe the diarists, an embodiment of all the negative traits associated with converts. Even though he was a great scientist, who undoubtedly contributed very significantly to health care in the ghetto, the assimilated and secularized ghetto inhabitants accused him of "defending the anti-Semitism of the government and society," showing scorn for non-assimilated Jews,[111] "never showing remorse for converting,"[112] and "ostentatious conversion to the Catholic church."[113] There is no doubt therefore that notwithstanding their professional position converts were considered to be at the bottom of the moral hierarchy of the ghetto society. Stanisław Adler, a member of the Order Service, accused them of "hating Jews," while Mary Berg, one of the so-called "golden youth," a group of well-off young people alienated from and generally despised by the wider ghetto society, saw converts as "more resentful against the Jews than the Nazis."[114] Many diarists claimed that the Jewish converts were also rejected by the Polish-Catholic community, underlining the view of converts as a separate "caste" who were not accepted by either national group. Zionist poet Yitzhak Katzenelson, who was one of the most outspoken critics of assimilation, wrote:

> The Gentiles have a positive dislike of Jews who disown their Jewishness; who are flatterers, cringers, servile, and imitate everything in their neighbors. . . . It is easy to understand why intelligent Gentiles have a natural dislike for Jews who try to efface their Jewishness. "These so-called Jews who have betrayed their God, their nation, their father and mother, will certainly betray us. Our spirit is alien to them and not easy to acquire. They have no real desire for our values; it is just a matter of convenience for them."[115]

Those accusations were also demonstrated practically. One of the Czyste Hospital employees remembered that some of the patients did not want to be treated by baptized doctors.[116] The ghetto's attitude toward converts was also reflected in the widespread discussion over the appropriateness of disguising oneself as Christian as a way of saving one's life on the "Aryan" side.[117]

A different view of this issue comes from the memoirs of converts themselves. Aside from a few unpublished short testimonies,[118] the only memoir written by an adult Christian survivor of the Warsaw Ghetto is that of Ludwik Hirszfeld. Even though Hirszfeld was widely thought to have converted purely for self-interest, his memoir written in hiding in 1943 is that of a devout and ostensibly Catholic man. It is filled with religious references and imagery, with Hirszfeld portraying himself as a Catholic missionary in the alien world of the ghetto. Probably the most important issue that emerges in Hirszfeld's diary is that of the links between the Catholic Church and Polish national identity. Hirszfeld considers the main motivation of those converted in the ghetto as "the appeal of the religion of the nation to which they felt they belonged."[119] Just as it can be claimed that for Jews traditional religious rituals reinforced their national identity, according to Hirszfeld, converts in the ghetto, many of them veterans of the Polish struggle for independence, were drawn to the churches by the nationalistically Polish character of Catholic masses. He recalls the emotions evoked among the congregation by patriotic sermons, and quotes Reverend Godlewski speaking in church about "the love for motherland creating a community more profound than that of shared heritage."[120] One such patriotic mass was described for the *Oyneg Shabes* Archives by journalist Yekhiel Górny in June 1942. He wrote: "Separated from their 'Aryan' brothers, christened Jews by all means try to hold on to the Catholic church. The hymns are getting quiet and only with difficulty can one hear quietly sung 'God who for centuries.' The spirit of patriotism, the spirits of freeing oneself from the Hitlerite choke, is alive in every corner here."[121]

The ghetto's Jewish Christian community as such ceased to exist after the 1942 *Gross Aktion*. Though it is impossible to establish, it can be assumed that the survival rate among Catholic Jews was higher than among the general population of the ghetto. There is no doubt that an important factor was the web of support within the Catholic community, which kept functioning during the deportations. One of the Czyste Hospital employees recalled its director Dr. Józef Stein handing out work certificates which functioned as a safeguard against deportations. Stein was believed to take account of two factors: the professional quality of the employee and whether he was baptized—and, according to the testimony, "baptized was to always have precedence over non-baptized."[122] Moreover, Catholics of Jewish origin had a better chance of escape and survival on the "Aryan" side and were often significantly aided by the Catholic Church.[123]

The Role of Polish Language in the Ghetto: Official and Underground Use, and the Changing Attitude toward Polish

Even if a constantly growing number of Warsaw's Jews possessed a working knowledge of Polish, it was Yiddish that at the moment of the enclosure of the Jewish quarter was the language most widely spoken on the ghetto street. Pre-war Warsaw was the largest Yiddish-speaking community in Europe and this was fully reflected in the ghetto's everyday life. Yiddish was the language "of the street merchants, small grocery store owners, artisans, tobacco industry workers, booksellers and Warsaw droshka drivers," as well as a group of intelligentsia gathered around the *Aleynhilf* (yid. Self Help).[124] For the latter group, Yiddish represented a new secular culture which could be created in the ghetto to form a base for the new, post-war Jewish society, whether in the Diaspora or in Palestine. According to activists, Yiddish as the true language of the masses had every right to replace Polish, a language associated with the snobbery of the assimilated classes. And, indeed, in the first months of the ghetto's existence it seemed that Yiddish might become the national language of Polish Jewry. Together with a Jewish policeman and a Jewish postman, it became one of the signs of the new community being created behind the walls of the ghetto, with some ghetto inhabitants recalling being told off for speaking Polish in public spaces.[125]

Yet, despite the best efforts of the activists—and the presence of signs that read "We speak Yiddish" put up in public institutions—Polish remained the only language of the ghetto bureaucracy. As a large number of the Judenrat clerks spoke no Yiddish at all, or at best at a very basic level, Polish was the only language of internal correspondence and clearly prevailed during the meetings. It was also the main language of dealing with the patrons, even, according to Ringelblum, those who did not understand it.[126] Similarly, in the Jewish Order Service, where knowledge of Yiddish was meant to be a prerequisite for employment, none of the high-ranking officials spoke it.[127] As already discussed, a similar situation was evident in other public institutions of the ghetto, where most of the employees came from among the assimilated circles. Adina Blady Szwajger, who worked as a nurse in the ghetto, remembered "using the few paltry Yiddish phrases I'd picked up from the children so as to be able to talk to them."[128] In the ghetto education system, the Judenrat's council schools, though ostensibly operating on a tri-lingual system, in practice ended up teaching mainly in Polish. Almost all secondary-level private classes, the so-called *komplety*, were conducted in Polish. All occupational courses run by the Judenrat were also run in Polish.[129] Additionally some of the students from assimilated families followed the Polish school curriculum, studying alone at home in the ghetto, passing from time to time to the "Aryan" side to sit their exams.[130]

Jewish nationalists identified the use of Polish in Jewish institutions with: "ignorance, disdain and ill-will towards the common man and his needs, and with lack of understanding, in the literal sense of the word, of the Yiddish masses."[131] As a result both the Bund and Left Poale Zion mandated the use of Yiddish in the Judenrat's offices. More surprisingly perhaps, in September 1940 the Nazi-controlled *Gazeta Żydowska* reminded the Judenrat officials that they were to use Yiddish, stating that "in the nearest future there will be compulsory Yiddish language courses organized for all Community employees who will later on have to prove their oral and written knowledge of the language."[132] There are no records of such courses ever taking place. If they did, they clearly had no effect on the work of the Judenrat. By early 1942 the yiddishization of the Warsaw Ghetto was a thing of the past. In the words of one diarist: "One could have expected that once Jews find themselves only among their own, they will get back to Yiddish. Nonetheless, aside from small tri-lingual placards enforced by the Germans, I never found anywhere a placard in a language other than Polish. Polish single-handedly ruled in everyday life."[133] The principal reason for this phenomenon was clearly the gradual dying out of the poorer strata of the society and the refugees, that is, the backbone of Yiddish speakers. However this factor alone cannot explain the fact that among Jews separated from the Polish community, linguistic polonization not only did not stop, but on the contrary was progressing.

It is clear that speaking Polish was a highly emotional issue for assimilated Jews, many of whom were brought up in an environment where Yiddish was stigmatized as jargon, a symbol of low status and low culture. In the ghetto it was a symbol of the new society assimilated Jews found themselves in, and of their alienation. Polish, on the other hand, was one of the few links to their pre-war life and as such had to be preserved. In a letter written from the ghetto to a Polish friend eighteen-year-old Wanda Lubelska saw "keeping her accent intact"[134] as something of the utmost importance for her family, and she complained about the manner in which the ghetto society spoke Polish. Yet the ghetto's Polish speakers did not only comprise the assimilated community. There was also a very large number of ghetto inhabitants who had a Jewish identity and rejected assimilation, yet were brought up speaking Polish and continued to do so in the ghetto. Zionist youth leader Yitzhak Zuckerman, describing the linguistic affiliation of the principal underground activists, recalled that those young people, despite the affinity for Yiddish, were graduates of Polish schools and among each other spoke almost exclusively Polish.[135]

The use of Polish among youth groups is reflected by the underground periodicals published in the ghetto. Between mid-1940 and mid-1942, there were fifty-six titles published in the ghetto. Out of these, twenty-six were published in Yiddish, twenty in Polish, and ten in Hebrew. However, when we look only at publications of the youth groups, which soon after formed the backbone of the armed underground, the proportions change; the majority of these publications were published in Polish. Among the twenty Polish-language newspapers only one, the Bundist *Za naszą wolność i waszą* (pol. For our freedom and yours), can be seen as potentially directed at the Polish reader. All the rest were part of the internal discussion within the ghetto community, with the Polish language chosen to express Jewish identity.[136]

The decisive moment in the battle between Polish and Yiddish in public life came in early 1942, when Jonas Turkow, the head of the Central Entertainment Committee and one of the major figures of the pre-war Yiddish theater in Poland, together with the illustrious Yiddish actors Diana Blumenfeld and Miriam Orelska, decided to move to the Polish-language theater. This decision caused outrage within Yiddish cultural circles. In an open letter addressed to the ghetto society, cultural leaders described it as "desertion" and "an expressive betrayal of the Yiddish language and cultural movement."[137] According to Ringelblum, Turkow's action led to many "heated discussions" among intellectual circles.[138] Some of the views of the ghetto's leading personalities are evident in the *Two and a Half Years* questionnaire—a survey conducted in the spring of 1942 by the *Oyneg Shabes* members among the intellectual elite of the ghetto. All of the respondents noted that polonization was progressing at a fast pace and classified it as a negative development. The illustrious Yiddish-language writer Yehoshua Perle stated: "In our institutions there are only people who always spoke Polish and hated Yiddish . . . Who speaks Yiddish with us here, in the Ghetto? Only the smugglers, those people for whom one feels ashamed."[139] Other intellectuals gave different reasons for the progress of assimilation. Hillel Seitlin, a religious thinker, saw the polonization of the ghetto as "plain spite . . . they want to isolate us by force from other peoples, cultures and languages. Therefore we will persist in speaking other languages and spit on our own language, our own culture and spiritual values."[140] The issue was viewed similarly, albeit more sympathetically, by the Zionist journalist Shaul Stupnicki, who claimed, "It all began with pretending not to understand German, people preferred it this way, it was more convenient. So Jews started to speak Polish so they could answer when spoken to by a German, 'nie rozumiem' [pol. I don't understand]. In this way one could isolate himself from the enemy."[141] Emanuel Ringelblum himself saw polonization as a straightforward continuation of the pre-war linguistic assimilation.[142] Finally, an anonymous religious respondent described the Polish language as a "straw clutched by people forcibly isolated from the external world."[143] This applied in an obvious way to the assimilated part of society, but also to many others who spoke Polish as their principal language and associated the Polish language with the world left behind on the other side of the ghetto walls. For many ghetto inhabitants, the feeling of abandonment and longing for the past was stronger than any ideological affiliations they might have had. For those who had no contacts on the "Aryan" side and no other links with their past left, the Polish language did indeed become the last link with the outside world.[144]

Contacts and Links of the Ghetto Population with the "Aryan" Side

Despite physical separation, Poles and the "Aryan" side of Warsaw were omnipresent in the life of the ghetto and had an immense impact on the inner dynamics of life in the quarter. One of the assimilated ghetto inhabitants described her emotional state in the ghetto: "I was never 'Here' [in the ghetto], I was always 'There' [on the "Aryan" side]."[145]

For many of the inhabitants of the ghetto, both assimilated and not, pre-war Warsaw became the symbol of their lost pre-war life. This idealized Warsaw of the past was presented in clear contrast to the reality of the ghetto: "an overflowing, stinking prison, where we stopped being human, where anyone can hit us and where we are nothing more than part of the despised masses."[146] Interestingly, ghetto diarists very rarely wrote about an urge to be in another country or "on the other side of the world." They did, however, constantly return to the images from the other side of the ghetto wall.[147] Yet, for the vast majority of ghetto inhabitants, the streets of "Aryan" Warsaw remained unobtainable, to quote one letter from the closed quarter, as far away as the Champs Élysées or Piazza San Marco.[148] The poet Władysław Szlengel encapsulated the mood of the ghetto's elite in a poem about the lucky few Jews who managed to obtain foreign passports and were thus initially not forced to live in the Jewish quarter, but allowed to "live peacefully in Warsaw . . . the most beautiful of lands."[149] The only sight of Warsaw that the vast majority of ghetto inhabitants could obtain was from the top of the bridge connecting the two parts of the Warsaw Ghetto. As people were not allowed to stop on the bridge, some of them crossed it many times a day, just to cherish a glimpse of the other side of the wall.[150]

Although there was a nostalgia for pre-war Warsaw, the city under Nazi occupation was viewed with fear and loathing. The majority of diarists saw the "Aryan" side as an increasingly threatening place and, at least until mid-1942, felt safer staying in the ghetto.[151] One of the ghetto inhabitants described occupied Warsaw as "some strange German city, where I should feel afraid of the stones under my feet, afraid of the air and afraid of the sky."[152] Barbara Berman, a social activist and a Warsaw native who had a pass enabling her to legally leave the ghetto, recalled feeling in her home city "like Hansel and Gretel lost in the woods."[153] The rare exceptions to these sentiments can be found almost exclusively in the testimonies of highly assimilated Jews. Teenager Wanda Lubelska, who ventured to the "Aryan" side to meet up with her school friends, referred to it as "time spent in paradise."[154] Doctor Henryk Makower, who from time to time left the ghetto on professional duties, spoke of feeling "like a free man" outside the ghetto walls.[155]

Movements between Warsaw and the ghetto were not only the preserve of Jews, as Poles also crossed into the ghetto, even after it was hermetically sealed on November 16, 1940. In November 1940 alone, 15,000 individual and monthly passes were issued to Poles entering the Jewish quarter.[156] Those with passes included the priests of the Catholic churches in the ghetto, various municipal workers, workers in the Polish enterprises within the ghetto, and officials of the welfare agencies. Many more, however, entered the ghetto illegally, bribing their way into the quarter either for business or for personal reasons. Personal contacts between the ghetto and the "Aryan" side were of various types and intensity. The most obvious ones were those resulting from pre-war personal relationships. For the assimilated Jewish community, contact with Polish friends and acquaintances was, in the early stages of the ghetto, a part of everyday life. Just before the ghetto was sealed off many diarists recorded a wave of visits by their "Aryan" friends. One of them noted that "they brought food parcels and what we needed even more: expressions of sympathy."[157] After the ghetto was hermetically sealed, such visits became very difficult and expensive. Nonetheless, contact between the two sides remained possible with the use of telephone and mail.

Aside from the purely personal, an important type of Polish-Jewish contact was that kept by professional circles. For example, a large amount of scientific material, literature, and underground newspapers was sent to teachers in the ghetto by friends from the other side of the wall.[158] Thanks to this underground network some of the ghetto teachers found refuge on the "Aryan" side and worked in underground Polish schools. Contacts between those on the opposite sides of the wall were also based on a shared political ideology, such as those of the Polish Socialist Party and the Bund or the Polish scouts and Hashomer Hatzair. Such contacts, resting on pre-war friendships and similar ideological affiliations, formed the backbone of later cooperation between the Polish and Jewish underground.[159]

It must be emphasized, however, that all these types of relations could not be representative of the whole Jewish community. According to Israel Gutman, such visits were "not popular in the ghetto as it concerned the group of assimilated Jews and they were never liked."[160] For the vast majority of the ghetto the relationship with Poles was strictly economic, with the pre-war economic co-dependency between the Jews and the Poles continuing after the creation of the ghetto. The most obvious sign of this were Polish smugglers, who through their presence offered a major morale boost to the Jewish society and a chance to recuperate from the interwar economic boycott. According to Ringelblum Archive collaborator Peretz Opoczyński:

> The bridge that linked Jew and Gentile was made of bad material—speculation, but it served a good purpose, to save many Jews from starvation. . . . These Polish smugglers [worried about their pockets] but still served a national purpose to maintain the ties between the loyal citizens of Poland and to stretch out a brotherly hand to the persecuted. Thereby they sow the seeds of morality in a time of major moral degeneration.[161]

Emanuel Ringelblum also described smuggling as a milestone in building Polish-Jewish relations.[162] It is important to note that Polish smugglers fulfilled not only the ghetto's physical but also spiritual needs. They provided the ghetto with ritually slaughtered meat and some of them came to the ghetto on Saturdays to serve as *Shabbos goyim*.[163]

However, not all contact with Poles was as positive as this. Probably the most widespread form of encounters with the other side was through the so-called *placówki* (pol. placements)—labor groups that were employed to carry out various works outside the ghetto and that in May 1942 employed 3,000 Jews.[164] According to many diarists, such Jewish labor groups often encountered hostility from hooligans, which for many in the ghetto served as proof of continuing Polish anti-Semitism. Gutman remembered: "When we were walking down the street we would see people looking at us, some were looking because it was an interesting sight, sometimes you could see pity in their eyes, but mainly you heard laughter."[165] As a result of such instances most of the ghetto society seemed to share the sentiment that while there were individuals or even environments that were well-disposed toward them, the majority of Poles remained anti-Semitic. Most diarists highlight the contrast between the anti-Semitic masses and individual members of the intelligentsia who were actively helping Jews.[166] This view was also spread by the underground newspapers.[167] The Bundist and Communist press often portrayed Poles as equal to Jews in suffering, and anti-Semitism as a betrayal of Polish national values and an element of Nazi policy.

This positive perception of Poles ended in 1942 as the situation in the ghetto worsened and contact with the "Aryan" side declined. In June 1942 Abraham Levin, commenting on recent developments in the ghetto, noted that "not a Christian is seen, with the exception of a few tax officials and collectors of gas and electricity payments."[168] With no physical contact possible, the main source of information about the "other side" was tales and rumors, and these were mainly concerned with the spread of *szmalcownictwo*. Devoid of first-hand information, ghetto inhabitants would draw conclusions on the basis of gossip and haphazard stories.[169] The growing distance between communities on the two sides of the wall is also evident in the diaries of assimilated Jews, who in the earlier stage of the ghetto had frequent contact with Poles. One of them, a teenage girl, reflected in a letter to a former teacher on the lack of contact with her former school friends:

> I sometimes think that I grew up on a different planet—that's how differently our lives developed and made different people out of us. And it's not even five years since we left the same nest, from the care of the same people and the same ideas. We had much in common, even similar marks in the final exams. We have the same mother tongue; we were shaped by the same books, the same school bench, the same city. Now, each of us thinks differently as if we grew up in different hemispheres and there is even some enmity between us. I can't help feeling that they are all happy with the fate that has befallen us.[170]

The growing accusations of the indifference of the "Aryan" side toward the Jewish citizens of Poland peaked during the Deportation and later the Warsaw Ghetto Uprising. In post-war memoirs the merry-go-round on Krasicki Square spinning on the other side of the wall of the ghetto became a symbol of the abandonment of the Warsaw Jewry. Marek Edelman explained: "For us it seemed that despite the terror in Warsaw, there on the other side is to be found a normal everyday life. Because people walk on the streets, enjoy themselves, the fairground is spinning. We could not understand that. We felt abandoned, angry and bitter that the whole world does not want to see what is happening to us."[171] As Samuel Kassow remarks in his work on Ringelblum and his collaborators, had the war ended in mid-1941, then the picture of Polish-Jewish relations conveyed by the *Oyneg Shabes* Archive would have been of complex ambiguity but not of "unbridgeable national hatred."[172] After the Warsaw Ghetto Uprising, for the vast majority of survivors, the slogan *For your freedom and ours* rung hollow, and even the brotherhood of Polish and Jewish smugglers had become a thing of the past.

3

The Judenrat, Self-Help, and the Fight for the Soul of the Ghetto

The Judenrat

The Jewish Council and the Jewish Order Service probably had the most profound influence on the general perception of the assimilated community. Their overblown structure provided jobs for the Polish-speaking unemployed intelligentsia who could not find any place in Jewish grass-root organizations. However, the vast majority of them were completely unprepared for the task and lacked the ability, or sometimes the will, to understand the needs of the quarter, from which they felt strongly alienated.

The Warsaw Jewish Council (the Judenrat) was established alongside other Judenrate in the *Generalgouvernement* by a decree of Hans Frank on November 28, 1939.[1] Its chairman, engineer Adam Czerniaków, had been appointed head of the Jewish community on September 22, 1939, by the Civilian Commissar of Warsaw, Stefan Starzyński. He replaced the former head of the community, Maurycy Mayzel, who fled Poland in the first days of the war. Czerniaków presented the occupation authorities with twenty-four councilmen, among them all of the members of the pre-war Council who were still in the capital. Those of them who later fled Warsaw were replaced, so that the number of councilors always equaled twenty-four.

The main role of the Judenrat in the ghetto was to oversee and administer life in the quarter and to carry out the directives of the occupational authorities. The growing number of tasks expected to be fulfilled by the Jewish Council led to a growth in the apparatus—an extremely complicated structure of commissions and departments with often vague or overlapping areas of responsibility. These included the postal service, police, supervision of primary and vocational education, and an elaborate health organization that included two hospitals. The administration was expected to organize censuses and gather statistical data for the Nazi authorities. It was also responsible for issuing a growing number of passes to go to the "Aryan" side (in the initial stage of the ghetto's existence), labor cards, exemption certificates, permissions, and food ration cards, all of which proved an immense task given the constantly changing population. As a result, between July 1, 1940, and August 1942 the number of people engaged in the apparatus of the community grew five-fold—from 1,741 to 9,030 employees.[2]

The position of the Warsaw Judenrat in relation to the German authorities was one of complete subservience, of forced cooperation, devoid of any voluntary actions or autonomous decisions. Yet, for the majority of ghetto inhabitants, the Judenrat was the only legitimate government that they experienced in their everyday lives. In their eyes the institution was fully responsible for their tragic situation. One of the diarists, describing the mood prevalent in the quarter, wrote:

> All the evils that have befallen Jews in Warsaw: forced labor, roundups, arrests, the Kott affair, beatings on the street, muggings, confiscations of goods, furniture, clothing, being forbidden to help the arrested, no news from them—for all this it was the Judenrat that was responsible. The atmosphere of dislike meant that many people preferred to keep away from it, limiting their contacts to personal matters or social help issues.[3]

Fully aware of how he was perceived, Adam Czerniaków often complained in his diary about being "blamed without end" for strings of decisions that were completely outside of his control.[4] The most painful of these for the everyday lives of the ghetto community were labor camp roundups, anti-typhus measures—the so-called *parówki*—and taxes.

Forced labor for all Jewish men aged between fourteen and sixty was introduced in Warsaw on October 26, 1939.[5] Until August 1940 it was to take place locally, in *placówki*—such as military or police stations and private firms. From August 1940, over 15,000 Warsaw Jews were sent to forced labor camps—initially in the Lublin and Kraków areas and from the spring of 1941 in the surroundings of Warsaw. The second wave of forced labor roundups took place in the spring of 1942. Aside from very few camps where Jewish laborers were treated in a relatively humane way, most were places of torture, and as the first forced laborers began returning to Warsaw, harrowing news about the work conditions began circulating in the ghetto. In a letter to the Jewish Council in Warsaw, prisoners of the Tyszowice labor camp wrote:

> We are beaten and maltreated and, added to this, we are in mourning for three of our colleagues who died a tragic death—executed by shooting . . . Here the freezing temperature falls as low as minus 10–12 degrees, and we stand waist-high in water. We have been eaten alive by lice and an epidemic is unavoidable. We are half dead with hunger. It is high time to end this torture. We now face a winter camp, which we are not likely to survive. It is you who will bear responsibility for this.[6]

As a result of such news and letters, the Judenrat was accused of ignoring the needs of those in the camps and of not providing them with adequate help. In this respect, their actions were contrasted with those of Jewish Councils from smaller towns, who, it was alleged, visited the camps to exercise protection over the prisoners, bringing them medication and setting up deals with the SS guards.[7]

The Council tried to place responsibility for ensuring the quota of forced laborers was met on the shoulders of the house committees. It was accordingly the house committees that were held accountable for the failure of registered laborers to show up for work. Describing one confrontation between house committee members and a representative of the Judenrat, Ringelblum reported on the official speakers being continually interrupted during the meeting by protesting listeners. As a result, the meeting was swiftly concluded, with no discussion permitted.[8] At the same meeting one of the house committee chairmen was arrested for protesting against Order Service corruption, but was released soon after because of the stormy protest of the audience. During such meetings, the representatives of the Judenrat portrayed service in the labor camps as a national duty, and were keen to point out the potential consequences for the rest of the ghetto if not enough people volunteered.[9] Indeed, a lack of volunteers led in time to forced roundups conducted by the Jewish Order Service. These were conducted in an increasingly brutal way, often in the middle of the night.

Unaware of the German sanctions on the Judenrat should they fail to meet the quota of workers, the majority of ghetto inhabitants blamed the Jewish Council for the roundups.[10] On September 29, 1940, Adam Czerniaków noted: "The moment I arrived at the Community [the Judenrat] at 8am, I was surrounded by a group of women—mothers of the workers in the camps. Weeping and shouting. Recriminations as to why I am not obtaining their releases."[11] A few days later the mothers and wives of the camps' workers carried out a demonstration in front of the Council building.[12]

The main accusation leveled against the Jewish Council was that not all ghetto inhabitants were equal when it came to forced labor. Firstly, exemptions from work duty were given to those who were legally employed—mainly in the Judenrat. In April 1941 Ringelblum noted that: "the rich boys are working in the police force, in community organizations, or are registered with the sick fund, and supposedly employed by various firms—but, most importantly, they can always buy their way out of work-camp duty."[13] Additionally, in the beginning, those who could afford it could pay for a replacement. Both parties profited from such practice as those replacing better-off people would usually get more money than they would from the Judenrat if they volunteered for work. In response the Judenrat stopped this procedure—substitutions became illegal, and those who chose not to go had to pay directly into the Judenrat's coffers. From May until December 1940 altogether 33,000 people paid to be exempted from forced labor.[14] The cost of the exemption fee was from 60 to 100 złoty, but those who were hard up or especially active in social welfare or community activities were allowed reductions.[15] As Ringelblum writes, the Council was so busy issuing exemptions to those who paid that there were problems with providing those who were already in work camps with adequate documentation, and they were often seized to go to camps again.[16] The system of releasing people from forced labor for a fee was seen by the majority of the society as deeply unjust. Indeed, according to doctor Henryk Makower, who participated in health checks of those designated for labor, virtually no members of intelligentsia were among those who were sent to camps.[17]

Similar controversies were triggered by *parówki* (pol. steaming)—large-scale disinfections of houses with known cases of typhus—the principal though completely ineffective way of stopping the spread of the disease. The house in question would be quarantined, sometimes for a very long time, while all the belongings of its inhabitants were sprayed with a disinfection substance. This led to the devastation of apartments and more often than not theft. As a result, some described the anti-typhus measures as worse than the epidemics itself. The most notorious case was the disinfection action at Krochmalna Street, one of the most disreputable and shabby parts of the ghetto. In August 1941 18,000 inhabitants of the street were kept outside for twenty-four hours with no food, in many cases with their clothes lost or destroyed in disinfection following mandatory baths. Some people died. After coming back to their apartments Krochmalna inhabitants found many of their belongings were stolen or destroyed. As in the case of forced labor, those targeted were almost exclusively the poor. The rich apartment blocks simply bribed the disinfection squad to go away and were left untouched. Additionally, similarly to other employees of the Council, members of the disinfection squads were recruited almost exclusively from people with contacts in the Judenrat, including the acculturated and assimilated intelligentsia, which only added to the social tensions caused by *parówki*.

Another significant cause of conflict within the ghetto society was the taxation system. The finances of the Judenrat were stretched to the limit by German-imposed expenditure such as the wages of forced laborers and the building of constantly shifting ghetto walls. The Judenrat came into the war not only with their pre-war assets confiscated but also heavily indebted with unpaid salaries. The money to cover this came from loans from private banks (one of them against the mortgage of the Council's buildings), from blocked Jewish accounts, and finally an endless stream of taxes and fees directed at the ghetto inhabitants. The most controversial of these was the "bread tax" introduced in June 1940, which taxed everyone, except the very poorest, for their bread ration cards. As a result, according to a Polish Underground report, in March 1942 20,000 bread cards were not collected due to lack of funds.[18] Altogether, ghetto inhabitants were subjected to over forty different taxes, imposed per capita as opposed to by ability to pay. As those without income did not have to pay, this system was seen as favoring not only the poorest of the ghetto society, but also basically all of the new-rich, who had made their fortunes illegally, as well as those who made their living from selling their property and from help from the "Aryan" side. Even though there were attempts to change this policy, the system remained the same until the liquidation of the ghetto.

For those who got closer to the bureaucratic machinery of the Judenrat, the incompetence, bribery, and protectionism prevalent in its structures were even more readily visible. It was established knowledge in the ghetto that jobs in the Judenrat, at all levels, were available only to those with contacts. As a result, many of those employed lacked the skills to deal with their new duties. The Judenrat was also undoubtedly negatively affected by the fact that many of those who before the war had experience in the civil service and in administrative work chose to keep away from the Council.

The incompetence of the new clerks was, however, not as marked as their corruption, which was endemic in all the major fields of work. Some instances could be explained, and indeed often were, by the impoverishment of notoriously underpaid Judenrat clerks, who treated their job as a safeguard against forced labor. As the highest monthly salary of a Judenrat clerk in 1941 was roughly equivalent to four kilograms of lard on the black market,[19] it is not surprising that, according to countless testimonies, whoever had the opportunity to take bribes would take them. At the same time, as historian and Holocaust survivor Isaiah Trunk noted: "Corruption was the kind of scandalous news which, when revealed, became the topic of the day in the ghetto. And what was there to talk about concerning the activities of honest functionaries who devotedly performed their tasks? Little was known about them, and they were of little interest to gossip-prone ghetto inmates."[20]

Even so, the Council was riddled with high-level bribery and protectionism that could not be justified by the poverty of individual clerks. The widespread toleration of corruption was undoubtedly strengthened by the attitude of the German authorities. All interventions of the Judenrat on behalf of the Jewish society had to be accompanied by extortionate bribes. On March 11, 1940, Czerniaków noted a demand for "an extraordinary quantity of furniture, bed linen, 15 grand pianos, boot removers etc."[21] A week later the voluntary collection resulted in "one upright piano and hundreds of pieces of all kinds of furniture, beds etc. Nonetheless we are far short of the quota."[22] According to Judenrat employee Marcel Reich: "for [Hans] Frank it could be a special Turkish coffee maker, an expensive night pot for some dignitary, sometimes a coupon for clothing or three to ten meters of wool material. The most common were golden watches—this was a classic present."[23] Unsurprisingly, in such an atmosphere, corruption in the Jewish Council was omnipresent. As Stanisław Adler, a ghetto policeman and later a Judenrat official, wrote: "Bribers roamed unfettered and only when their affairs became excessively public were they transferred to other posts."[24] The most notorious were the councilmen themselves, as some of them were silent partners in cafés and nightclubs. One of the Judenrat members, Beniamin Zabłudowski, head of the corruption-ridden Personnel Section and the Department of Fuel, which dealt with coal allocation, was particularly known for his contacts with the underworld, and according to the gossip of the ghetto died of excessive drinking after a particularly heavy night in a ghetto nightspot.[25]

However, the most infamous cases of corruption were in the Labor Department, which dealt with labor exemption, as well as the all-powerful Housing Bureau, which decided on handing over apartments to those who needed them. An Underground report describing corruption in the Bureau stated:

> The Councilmen did not spare effort and intervened almost en masse. Undoubtedly the Order Service and the Supply Department fully used the goods of these interventions. But there were also interventions on behalf of individual people who had nothing in common with the Council (night club owners, journalists, attorneys etc.). All requests of the Councilmen were in the vast majority accepted.[26]

Such a situation understandably provoked the wrath of the ghetto population. The general attitude of the street, voiced by Kaplan, was that among the sea of growing poverty, some members of the society were making their living "from the misfortunes of Israel."[27] These included smugglers, bakers, traders in produce, and, above all, the functionaries of the Judenrat and those who revolved around it.

The image of the Council was not improved by the growing megalomania of some of even its most honest members. Indeed, Czerniaków himself, whose behavior at times bordered on the grotesque, was the butt of jokes within the ghetto society.[28] In November 1940, describing his sixtieth birthday celebration, Czerniaków candidly wrote about detachments of the Order Service lining the Council's corridors as he passed, speeches and orations by staff delegates, and "a profusion of flowers."[29] According to an underground newspaper, the flowers mentioned by Czerniaków cost a few thousand złoty and were paid for from the budget of the Judenrat.[30] Another trademark of Czerniaków was his elaborate, bombastic speeches, which he would deliver on public occasions. Those of the ghetto inhabitants who did not hear them in person could read the speeches, or at least their most flowery fragments, in the underground press, which keenly reproduced them with appropriately ironic comments. Finally, the fact that Czerniaków was the only person in the ghetto who was allowed to retain his car was another symbol of the delusion of power among the Judenrat members. According to Marcel Reich, "The scruffy vehicle was the most visible and the most striking symbol of his power and dignity."[31]

At the same time, however, contrary to the gossip circulating on the ghetto streets, Czerniaków and many other Judenrat members lived in conditions not dissimilar to those of other members of the intelligentsia. According to the memoirs of Helena Szereszewska, wife of Councilor Stanisław Szereszewski, the couple's two younger daughters attended vocational training courses; the oldest worked as a clerk in the Judenrat and made hats in the evenings, while Helena Szereszewska herself learned corset making. The family did employ domestic help and were relatively well off, but their standard of living could not be compared with that of nouveau-riches in the ghetto. Szereszewska wrote in her memoir: "My husband couldn't get used to horseflesh for a long time. We cheated him and told him it was beef. Then he got used to it. The whole ghetto ate horseflesh, only people who were very rich ate other meat. Everyone adapted to necessity quickly."[32]

Yet in the eyes of the vast majority of the ghetto inhabitants, the Judenrat was a symbol of the power that wealth commanded, clearly favoring the rich over the poor. Even though the Council did undertake a number of objectively very useful actions—such as medical research conducted by the health department, help for children or patronage of the symphonic orchestra—these were known to only a small part of the society. Typical of such undertakings were university-level courses, disguised as vocational training, by all means very valuable but due to high fees only accessible to the youth from the richest part of the ghetto society. Those who participated in the courses testified later that, aside from money, their admission was often dependent on having considerable contacts.

Aware of the negative image of the Judenrat, already by the beginning of 1941 Czerniaków managed to convince some of the prominent social activists, including historian Yitzchak Schipper and politician Szachne Sagan, to join a commission aimed at resolving its problems. They resigned in June 1941, informing Czerniaków in a letter that they lacked any influence over the functioning of the commission.[33] There is no proof of any steps undertaken later on to control the proceedings of the Council. And even if something was changed, it is doubtful whether it significantly altered the ghetto street's perception of the Judenrat, and its chairman. Those dying of hunger and disease, homeless, in quarantine, and tortured in labor camps could not care less about the good will and internal doubts of Adam Czerniaków. For them he was simply the one responsible for the fate of the ghetto and their own suffering.[34]

It is important to emphasize that the increasingly unhappy ghetto street was not the only population within the quarter that had to be taken into consideration by the Judenrat. The other was the growing number of informers, German agents, and all types of extortionists who continuously attempted to influence its actions. Describing the situation in the ghetto, Rabbi Simon Huberband, one of the major contributors to the *Oyneg Shabes* Archive, wrote: "The Talmud permits the killing of informers . . . in the days of R[abbi] Shachna of Lublin, Jewish informers were drowned in the *mikveh* [baths used for ritual purification]. But today there aren't enough *mikvehs* to suffice for all the Jewish informers."[35] There is no doubt that many of these people (exact numbers or even estimates are hard to establish) did infiltrate the Judenrat. This point was made by Councilman Israel Milejkowski, who in an interview conducted by an *Oyneg Shabes* member openly stated that "the authorities demand of us dirty work which, under duress, must be executed. Not everyone can perform such work and, like it or not, we must turn to those of the underworld. In this respect, I see the positive role played by this element in life."[36] And, indeed, at least two of the high-level Judenrat officials—Alfred Nossig, the head of the Emigration Department, and Israel First, director of the Economic Department—openly doubled as middlemen between the Council and the Germans, though both were later executed by the armed underground as collaborators.

The most open representative of the Gestapo in the Warsaw Ghetto was the "Office to Combat Usury and Speculation," often referred to as "The Thirteen," headed by Abraham Gancwajch. The office, the only institution in the ghetto not subordinated to the Judenrat, was set up in the autumn of 1940 with a very murky area of responsibility, which was vaguely defined as fighting profiteering. In reality the organization focused on extortion from the ghetto businesses and controlled smuggling. If in the majority of testimonies the Judenrat is not seen per se as a collaborationist institution, it is because of the conspicuous, clearly collaborationist character of the Thirteen. Stanisław Adler, a member of the Jewish Police and later a Judenrat official, wrote: "The Thirteen was an open and suppurating abscess. It is difficult to imagine anything morally decaying at a faster rate, but then how can one even speak of moral decay in relation to an institution of brigands to whom the populace of the quarter had been handed over as prey in return for their own special services?"[37] Unlike the Judenrat, the Thirteen was not straightforwardly associated with the assimilated strata of the ghetto; most often diarists described its members as influenced by German culture. The head of the Thirteen was as shadowy as the office he represented. Ringelblum described him as "Once a Communist, a Zionist, he speaks Hebrew well, Polish and Yiddish too. Very talented, but ready for anything."[38] Gancwajch reportedly made a number of attempts to take over the leadership of the Judenrat, and at some point the Council was apparently considering making him vice president. According to Judenrat clerk Stefan Ernest, when gossip started spreading around the ghetto that Czerniaków might be replaced by Gancwajch, some saw this as a positive development, as the Thirteen undoubtedly could have more influence over the Gestapo than Czerniaków and the rest of the Council.[39] The Thirteen was dissolved for unknown reasons, most probably as a result of a power struggle between German offices, in June 1941.

Most of the witnesses, whether they approved of the Judenrat's actions or not, did nonetheless make a clear distinction between the Jewish Council and the Thirteen (though Czerniaków did record receiving letters addressed to him at "Leszno 13"—the seat of the Office to Combat Usury—and there are cases of association between the Thirteen and the ghetto police).[40] Nonetheless many assumed there was some connection between the two, although these were thought to be involuntary on the part of the Judenrat. Many shared the view of Yitzhak Zuckerman, who stated: "I am not asserting that the members of the Judenrat were of the same ilk as Gancwajch. But he had hundreds of confidants in the Judenrat. Czerniaków was surrounded by agents of Gancwajch and the police captains were all his men."[41] For others however the very existence of the Thirteen proved that the Germans did not have a strong enough net of informers and collaborationists in the Judenrat.[42]

The image of the Judenrat was also severely affected by the only newspaper legally distributed in the ghetto—*Gazeta Żydowska*. In the eyes of many of the ghetto society this thrice-weekly Nazi-controlled propaganda periodical was the "loudspeaker" of the Judenrat. In reality, however, it is clear from Adam Czerniaków's diary that he himself had no control over the contents of the newspaper. Indeed *Gazeta*, which propagated itself as the voice of the "true people" of the ghetto, often criticized the nepotism, corruption, and lack of order in the Council, while at the same time openly supporting the Thirteen. Assimilated Stanisław Adler described its Warsaw reporters as "some obscure characters, mostly Jewish, who knew more German than Polish, or no Polish at all."[43] There is no doubt, however, that through an assumed guilt by association, the newspaper's existence did significantly harm the image of the Jewish Council.

It seems that the Judenrat was perceived by the majority of the ghetto as an alien, German-induced body, composed almost entirely of the assimilated strata. Yet it is important to emphasize that while many clerks or Order Service functionaries were recruited from among the Jewish professional intelligentsia—a group that was usually very assimilated and that lacked ties with the traditional religious community which constituted the vast majority of the ghetto society—the same cannot be said about the actual Councilmen. The question of whether Czerniaków was assimilated or not is open to debate. The Judenrat's archivist Hillel Seidman characterized him as a devout Zionist,[44] but others saw him as a fully assimilated Jew, linked almost exclusively to the Polish culture.[45] These conflicting images were poignantly encapsulated by Raul Hilberg who, describing the head of the Warsaw Judenrat, noted: "Too non-observant for religious orthodoxy, he was also too pragmatic to embrace socialism and too 'assimilationist' to evolve into an ardent Zionist. Indeed, he is more often characterized for what he was not than for what he was."[46] Czerniaków undoubtedly came from an assimilated home, and was closer to Polish than to Jewish culture. At the same time, however, he remained active in Jewish society and undoubtedly never attempted to cut his ties with it. On the contrary, he had a rather impressive record of engagement with Jewish pre-war society life. He was active in the General Association of Jewish Craftsmen, he was a representative of Jewish artisans in the Warsaw Municipal Council, and he was on the Executive Council of the Warsaw Jewish Community. It should be stressed that contrary to popular preconceptions Czerniaków even spoke, or at least read, Yiddish.[47] The same cannot be said of many youth activists who saw him as a symbol of the dangers of assimilation.

The backgrounds of other Warsaw Judenrat members varied considerably. The Council was initially formed by such personalities as industrialist and philanthropist Abraham Gepner, established medical doctor Israel Milejkowski, industrialist and head of TOPOROL Stanisław Szereszewski, and well-known Orthodox leaders Meshulam Kaminer and Zisha Frydman. Also among those who joined later were many with distinguished track records of leadership positions in the Jewish community—including the director of Polish ORT Józef Jaszuński. All of them, even those who were strongly acculturated like Czerniaków, undoubtedly retained a Jewish identity and can be seen as representatives of traditionally understood assimilation— "Poles of Mosaic Faith." Yet the diaries, especially those written by those who were more nationalistically inclined, often see members of the Judenrat as equal to those who abandoned their Jewish identity for purely utilitarian reasons. In the words of Chaim Kaplan they were: "Strangers in our midst, foreign to our spirit, sons of Ham who trample upon our heads, . . . musclemen who were put on our backs by strangers."[48] And indeed, the most common accusation against Czerniaków, as well as against other members of the Judenrat, was that they served in a Nazi-induced body, and thus were not fit to represent the ghetto society. This issue was clearly crucial to Czerniaków himself, and he constantly returned to it in his diary. The rationale repeatedly brought up by Czerniaków was simple—the members of the Judenrat, whether assimilated or not, were the true leaders of the Warsaw Jews as they were drawn from among those of the pre-war leadership who decided to stay in the capital.[49] Many of them, Czerniaków included, were offered ways of leaving the country, yet they chose instead to remain with their community. In a very emotional entry of February 20, 1940, Czerniaków noted the story of a certain Kirszblum, who decided to leave for Palestine. He fumed: "You louse, I will not forget, you louse, how you pretended to act as a leader and are now running away with others like you, leaving the masses in this horrid situation."[50] In May 1940 he wrote in his diary fragments of a speech he made in the Judenrat about "those Jews who run away, or are about to run, about the Jewish activists . . . who moreover promised hypocritically that they will send us assistance from abroad (money)."[51] In October 1941 he related a conversation with Yitzchak Schipper, one of the leaders of the Jewish Self-Help, an organization which opposed the Judenrat and which saw itself as the true representative of the ghetto streets. Czerniaków wrote bitterly: "Since he contrasted those present with the 'true mentors of the people' I asked him where those 'mentors' were? Should we not look for them among those who had fled or among those who tried to leave but did not succeed."[52] Moreover, it is clear that as it was Stefan Starzyński who had chosen him to head the Jewish society, Czerniaków saw himself as fulfilling a Polish rather than a German appointment.

Czerniaków and his councilors did indeed stay with their people until the end. The head of the Judenrat committed suicide on July 23, 1942—on the second day of the deportations. The Council clerks, even though initially exempted from deportations, shared the fate of the ghetto. During the course of the Aktion, the number of workers of the Judenrat was reduced from 9,030 to 2,527 people.[53] After the deportations its role, under the new leadership of former deputy chairman Marek Lichtenbaum, was much restricted, finally reduced only to controlling supplies to the ghetto.[54] None of the councilors escaped the ghetto and survived the war. The majority was murdered on January 18, 1943. One of the assimilated diarists witnessing the execution noted that the death of the councilors symbolized for many from his environment the true end of the closed quarter.[55]

The Jewish Order Service

The Jewish Order Service, the formation so strongly associated with the assimilated strata, was preceded by Jewish guard units set up by the Germans to fulfill certain duties connected with the Jewish society in Warsaw. These included the 200–300-strong guard which escorted those enlisted for forced labor as well as the *Instandhaltung der Mauer im Seuchengebiet* (ger. maintenance of the wall in the infected area), set up to help build and protect the wall around the closed quarter. On September 20, 1940, Adam Czerniaków was ordered to form a 1,000-strong Jewish police force that would take over the duties of the Polish Police, commonly referred to as the "Navy Blue" Police.[56] The intake of new recruits generated great interest in the ghetto. Thousands of candidates turned up to the recruitment point and underwent a lengthy process of verification. Aside from adequate physical qualities and education, those applying had to be free of criminal convictions and submit positive references from their house committees. As with other initiatives of the Judenrat, news quickly spread that the only sure way of getting into the Service was either through a hefty bribe or personal contacts.[57] This opinion was reinforced by the fact that recruitment was overseen by Councilor Leopold Kupczykier, who was famous for his corruption and nepotism. The wife of Councilor Stanisław Szereszewski remembered in her memoir that even though her husband had nothing to do with the formation of the Service, immediately after the beginning of the intake, their apartment was visited by a string of friends looking for ways to get into the police force.[58] Even though those joining the police signed a declaration of the honorable (free) character of their work, for masses of unemployed ghetto inhabitants enlistment was a very attractive prospect. From the first days of the Service, the property of the policemen was safe from requisition and confiscation and the forces were entitled to extra supplies of food and health care.[59] Later on, with the growth of smuggling and bribery, the perks from the Service became even more considerable.

But it cannot be assumed that these advantages were obvious to all of those joining the Service in the autumn of 1940. A crucial factor for those deciding to join the Jewish Order Service was that policemen were to be exempted from forced labor. There were even claims that Czerniaków purposefully decided on enlisting members of the intelligentsia to the Service, to protect those who in his eyes were the most valuable members of the society.[60] As a consequence, the newly created police force was regarded as "riddled through with egoistic aims," where "eighty percent of them are rich men's sons trying to avoid labor camps."[61] Indeed, a number of testimonies confirm that among the policemen were many young men from privileged backgrounds. Those of them too young to join the actual Order Service were placed in various forms of improvised "auxiliary forces."[62]

With the creation of the police the divide between the assimilated and non-assimilated truly became an institutionalized part of the everyday life of the ghetto. Among the 1,700 policemen admitted into the Service was a definite over-representation of members of the assimilated intelligentsia, including 107 lawyers, the vast majority of them attorneys.[63] Against the background of the traditional, religious ghetto street, the Jewish policeman represented the quintessential outsider. The personification of the assimilationist character of the Order Service was its first superintendent, Colonel Józef Szeryński, a baptized member of the pre-war Polish police. It should be mentioned here that contrary to the rumors circulating in the quarter, Szeryński himself was probably one of the very few members of the Service not appointed through bribes or personal contacts in the Judenrat. According to Czerniaków's personal secretary, Leon Tyszka, and other diarists who were well acquainted with the situation, Szeryński was simply the only candidate qualified enough to take the position.[64] After assuming his post, Szeryński sought to surround himself mostly with converts. Jonas Turkow voiced what was probably the opinion of the majority of ghetto inhabitants when he wrote that "this he easily managed to do, since corrupt souls saw in the newly established 'institution' a road to their career, a source of profits and an opportunity to satisfy their lust for power. . . ."[65] A common view was that Szeryński likened himself to Józef Piłsudski, and his greatest ambition was to turn the Jewish police into Jewish legions subordinated to the future Polish army.[66] Interestingly enough, he was not alone in this ambition. At least three members of the Order Service testified after the war that they were informed that the police later played an active role in the Polish uprising against the invader.[67] One of the policemen was to be informed about it personally by Adam Czerniaków.[68]

There is reason to believe that also for others from the assimilated circles joining the police might have been much more than a way of escaping forced labor. According to the memoir of policeman Stanisław Gombiński, the Order Service was the only way for assimilated Jews to actively participate in the life of the ghetto society. As he writes, participation in the Order Service allowed such people to: "become active, cooperative and involved Jews, without having to give up on the values and passions that were put in their souls through their education and environment."[69] The most notable example of such attitudes was the involvement in the Service of two illustrious attorneys with assimilated backgrounds—Maksymilian Schönbach and Leon Berenson—both of them unquestionable moral authorities. According to one testimony Berenson was highly critical of those who avoided involvement in the newly created ghetto authorities. He was reported to have told assimilated candidates for the Service: "Keeping away will change nothing for you. . . . you will always have friends and relatives in the Judenrat. It is the men from the street that will suffer as there will be fewer decent men in the offices."[70]

Obviously not all members of the assimilated intelligentsia saw the Order Service as "a vanguard, a civic militia based on service to the public, assistance to the poor and the unfortunate."[71] The proof that such an attitude was not commonplace can be found in the fact that joining the police led to major rifts in even the most assimilated of families. For a significant part of the intelligentsia, *not* joining the police was part of a moral code, stemming from a tradition of distrust toward the police prevalent in Poland through the partition and interwar period.[72] Additionally, joining a formation that was de facto an auxiliary force of the occupational authorities was seen as morally questionable. Reporting after the war, one of the assimilated ghetto inhabitants noted: "I had certain rules which did not change—one of them was that in those circumstances one does not join the police."[73]

Notwithstanding the controversies surrounding its creation, it seems that the initial attitude of the ghetto society toward the newly established Order Service was quite warm. They were seen by many to be a positive development—a replacement of sometimes anti-Semitic "Navy Blue" policemen[74] and the first ever Jewish police force. To highlight this phenomenon, *Gazeta Żydowska* published an article in which it placed the new police in the history of the Jewish armed forces.[75] Alongside Jewish postmen and Jewish janitors, the police signified the autonomy of the quarter, and to an extent, the safety of Jews locked away from the dangers on the "Aryan" side. Mary Berg, a teenager from a polonized family, noted in late December 1940: "I experience a strange and utterly illogical feeling of satisfaction when I see a Jewish policeman at a crossing—such policemen were completely unknown in pre-war Poland."[76] A crucial factor in the ghetto society's attitude toward the police was that the Order Service was unarmed, and as such, unlike the Polish Police, posed no real threat. As Bundist activist Marek Edelman later claimed, nobody was really ever scared of them.[77] This opinion was confirmed by a former member of the Order Service, who described the police force as: "yesterday's students, attorneys, clerks, artisans or sons of a merchants, 'armed' at most with a rubber or wooden club, with no idea of fighting criminals, unable to face up to any crook, pickpocket or burglar."[78] Yet, at the same time, it cannot be forgotten that for those linked to underground parties, the attitude to the police was from the beginning a reflection of their attitude toward the Judenrat. These groups saw the police primarily as a foreign growth on the Jewish street.[79]

The initial input of the Service into ghetto life was also notably positive. According to the order from December 23, 1940, the initial duties of the Order Service were meant to be rather limited and mainly concerned with technicalities connected to regulating the traffic on overcrowded ghetto streets, dealing with illegal trade, ensuring cleanliness of courtyards and staircases in apartment blocks, streets, and pavements, and dealing with misdemeanors.[80] As cases of common criminal activity were dealt with by the Polish courts, and those involving "attacks against the German people and the Reich" by the German system of justice in the *Generalgouvernement*,[81] fighting crime was not within the mandate of the ghetto police. In practice, however, there were cases of Order Servicemen taking part in solving simple crimes. According to one policeman, up to ninety percent of the cases were solved by the Jewish Police, as otherwise they would have to be directed to the Polish or German courts.[82] A common rationale was that this was the only way of preventing "Navy Blue" policemen from involvement in the internal matters of the ghetto. However, soon enough the authority of the Order Service was widened. In practice their duties also included fulfilling the orders of the Chairman of the Judenrat, mainly in terms of keeping order in the Judenrat and collecting payments. The most important assignment, however, involved guarding the inside walls of the closed ghetto. On the outside, the gates of the ghetto were guarded by the German gendarmes—members of the *Schutzpolizei* (ger. protection police)—a city formation of the *Ordnungspolizei* (ger. Order police), and were patrolled by the "Navy Blue" police.

The first clearly negative change in the perception of the Order Service came with their deployment in the roundups for labor camps, first in the spring of 1941 and later in the spring of 1942. During the roundups the police acted very violently—catching men on the streets, surrounding apartment blocks, and dragging people out of their homes in the middle of the night. According to pianist Władysław Szpilman: "During the human-hunt in May they surrounded the streets with the professionalism of racially pure SS men. They strode about in their elegant uniforms, shouting in loud and brutal voices in imitation of the Germans and beating people with their rubber truncheons."[83] Aside from violence during the roundups, the police were accused of beating the detainees and not passing on parcels with food that were handed to them by the families of those who were rounded up. As an exemption from labor could always be ensured by a well-placed bribe, at that point the ghetto society also learned for the first time about the extent of corruption in the Service. One of the most popular songs in the ghetto, sung both on the streets and in musical theaters, proclaimed: "The Jewish policemen, such scoundrels they are/ They grab you and send you to camps in a truck/ Oh money, with money how happy you are!"[84] At the same time, however, some members of the Service refused to participate in roundups and at that point left the police.[85]

In November 1941 the ghetto was shaken by the execution of seventeen Jews caught illegally crossing the ghetto wall. The sentence was passed on the basis of Fischer's November 10 order of capital punishment for illegally leaving the ghetto; yet those sentenced were already imprisoned before the order was made public. Even though the execution was carried out by the "Navy Blue" police, it was the Order Service that was ordered to bring and tie down the prisoners before the execution and to remain with them until the moment of their death. Yet, in this extreme case, no testimonies have come to light blaming the Jewish policemen. A rabbi who was present at the executions testified that a few policemen "wept profusely" during the preparation for the execution and two fainted while tying the convicts down.[86] Even Ringelblum stressed that Szeryński agreed to participate in the executions only under severe pressure from the German authorities[87] and that he threatened to commit suicide if the Order Service was actually ordered to execute the prisoners.[88]

Physical violence was not the main accusation leveled against members of the Service. The main plague eating away at the Service was immense corruption. Reporting on the behavior of the police for the *Oyneg Shabes* Archive Yachiel Górny exclaimed: "Whoever made them throw drinking orgies with the money robbed from hard-toiling Jewish homes? What justification against this charge will the command of the Warsaw Jewish Police find for these excesses?"[89] There is no doubt that employment in the Order Service offered plenty of opportunities for extortion from the wider ghetto society—ranging from exempting apartments from *parówka* to Mafia-like practices of "protecting" small businesses. Yet the most lucrative gains came from guarding the walls. One of the anonymous policemen claimed that if they wanted to, the Order Service "could have finished with smuggling in twenty-four hours or at least limit it a hundred fold."[90] Instead, the smuggling continued and the police took their share of all goods carried illegally through the ghetto border—ranging from a single loaf of bread to concealed human cargo.[91] Yet as smuggling sustained the ghetto society, this was not the issue. The main accusation leveled against policemen was that they shared the lifestyle of the smugglers they cooperated with. While the official regulations detailing the functioning of the Service were prepared and constantly improved by some of the best lawyers of interwar Warsaw, the unofficial ones were being settled in restaurants and nightclubs mushrooming all around the ghetto. Particularly infamous were the drinking bouts thrown by the leaders of the Order Service for the "Navy Blue" police. Stanisław Adler noted that 8,700 złoty had been spent on a drinking party in honor of the Polish Police at the Sztuka restaurant; money which had been taken from the common functionaries salaries fund.[92] This occurrence was meant to have prompted him to leave the Service. Members of the Order Service did not shy away from cooperation with even less honorable groups. Ringelblum's collaborator, Hirsch Wasser, noted that "The official Jewish Ordnungsdienst, which is, after all, legally constituted, trembles before the shadow of Leszno 13 like a fish."[93] The negative view of the social composition of the Service was reinforced in August 1941, when members of the dissolved Thirteen joined the Order Service. Ringelblum wrote of a well-grounded fear that any honest people still left in the Jewish police will (now be) completely demoralized.[94] Later on, the police was forced to accept into its ranks an infamous Gestapo informant, Josef Ehrlich, who despite a complete lack of military training was immediately promoted to the rank of officer. Moreover, many of the ghetto inhabitants simply did not distinguish between the very similar uniforms of the police and various branches of the Thirteen, and accordingly treated them as one group.[95]

The corruption was mainly attributed to the honorary character of the Service. Even Hirsch Wasser, who rarely showed sympathy to the police, noted in his diary that "not everyone in the Order Service can engage in crooked deals."[96] He later added: "How the Jewish police is to maintain itself is a true riddle."[97] Indeed, as the official income of the Service men was basically nonexistent, it can be claimed that all of those who were not involved in smuggling and bribery (from the post-war trials files, we know that such men did exist) were selling off their pre-war belongings and usually worked after hours in order to remain in the Service. As Stanisław Gombiński remarked, the Service might have freed its members from forced labor but had in effect sentenced their families to starvation.[98] As a result, according to Czerniaków's January 1942 report, on average 970 members of the police a day, that is, half of the Order Service functionaries, took advantage of the free or low-cost lunches provided by the Judenrat.[99] Taking into consideration the low quality of these lunches, it can be assumed that all those who could have in any way afforded not to eat them would have. To additionally help those in need the Judenrat set up *Sekcja Pomocy Rzeczowej* (SEPOR, pol. Section of Material Aid). Discussing SEPOR aid, Adler noted that any extra rations distributed were far from particularly attractive. He remembered them as "considerable quantities of old chopped beetroot in a liquid preserve which caused dangerous intestinal disorders of which we had not been warned. Later on, nasty smelling sausage and pickled cabbage were distributed in large quantities."[100] SEPOR also often paid for sumptuous dinners, where the "Navy Blue" police was entertained by the Order Service authorities.[101]

The most notable example of a policeman who did not make a fortune on illegal deals was Szeryński himself who, as many testimonies reported, maintained a relatively humble standard of living.[102] There were, however, many others like him. One such person was Gombiński, whose case is extensively documented in files from his post-war rehabilitation trial.[103] All testimonies indicate that Gombiński was in a very bad financial situation, and some suggest that he was starving. A cousin sharing a flat with him claimed that Gombiński "would leave for work early in the morning and come back after two to three hours. He mainly stayed at home. He was at that time imbalanced emotionally, broke down, often spoke of suicide."[104] Someone else said that he was on the verge of insanity during the deportation. The reason he stayed in the Order Service was thought to be the ill health of his mother. He had no material gains from the Service and lived very modestly from selling his belongings and with the help of his family. Neither did he go to cafés, nor keep social contact with other members of the Service. Supposing Gombiński was an exception to the rule, it would still be farfetched to believe that he was the only one to behave like this.[105] Proof for this may be the fact that among the policemen were members of the underground whose behavior was closely watched by their organizations. For example, while in the Service, Gombiński cooperated with PPS and distributed underground newspapers among other policemen.[106] Two other PPS activists and Order Service members—Tadeusz Witelson and Zygmunt Millet—were at the same time actively participating in the works of *Oyneg Shabes*. According to Marek Edelman, the Bund placed ten to twelve people in the Service.[107] One of the most famous underground fighters serving in the police was Izrael Kanał, who later on attempted to assassinate Józef Szeryński. A fellow member of *Akiva*—the youth wing of the religious Zionist movement *Mizrachi*—remembered that Kanał repeatedly attempted to leave the police but was ordered by the underground to remain in the Service.[108]

Evidence of the high moral standing of some ghetto policemen can be found in a document in the Ringelblum Archive. In a memorandum addressed to Adam Czerniaków, a group of members of the Service proposes solutions to what they perceived as the greatest faults of the Jewish Police. Among their demands was the introduction of a salary in the Service as a way to combat bribery; clear boundaries concerning the use of force by policemen; a reduction in the number of its members; and better control over its actions. According to the memorandum only such actions could rebuild the relations between the Service and the ghetto society. It is not known if the memorandum was met with any response, but it is doubtful that it would have. Even though Adam Czerniaków was fully aware of the extent of the demoralization of the Service, the relations between the Judenrat and the Order Service remained good and the Judenrat often used it for its own needs, such as dispersing demonstrations outside the Council.

Though free from forced labor, the ghetto policemen were not exempt from German hostility, and if anything, were even more at risk of being on the receiving end of random acts of aggression than regular ghetto dwellers. Even Ringelblum, who was generally very negatively disposed toward the Order Service, highlights cases of their sacrifices. On April 17, 1941, he noted a story of a policeman killed by a German guard after speaking out for a woman whose sack of potatoes was confiscated on crossing the ghetto gate.[109] Hirsch Wasser mentions in his notes instances of policemen being killed not only by German gendarmes but also by the smugglers. The risk from the smugglers was believed to be so great that there was talk of equipping the police with firearms.[110] No less threatening in the eyes of the ghetto society was the heightened risk of catching typhus. Policemen assisting the sanitary columns of the Health Department were especially vulnerable and one of the victims of the disease was Leon Berenson, the head of the section dedicated to fighting the epidemic.

However, the events that were to truly shape the image of the Order Service occurred during the summer 1942 deportations, and they became a symbol of one of the darkest aspects of Jewish communal life during the Holocaust. It is difficult to say if the Order Service members knew of the impending Aktion. According to one of the diarists, the ghetto elite, including the highest-level Order Service members, was aware of what was going to happen and a few days before the beginning of the Aktion sent their closest family members to the Warsaw suburban town of Otwock, considered to be a safe haven from deportations.[111] Once the deportations began, the Jewish Order Service became instrumental in delivering ghetto inhabitants to the Umschlagplatz. Most diaries and testimonies portray the extreme brutality of the policemen. Because the Order Service did not have firearms, they used sticks and axes to ensure delivery to the Umschlagplatz of a fixed quota of "heads." Many of the policemen completely ignored exemption papers, pocketing bribes instead. Those of the policemen who caught more people than was necessary often "sold" them to their less successful comrades. Some of the witnesses testified that the policemen were sometimes punished by the Germans for their overt brutality.[112] At the same time, the Order Service continued to extort money. Among the most common practices were stealing possessions left by those deported and taking fees from those at the Umschlagplatz for passing letters and parcels or bringing over objects left at home. Yet there are also numerous testimonies of policemen warning of roundups and thus protecting their own families, friends, or sometimes random passersby.[113] According to a high-level Order Service member, between twenty and thirty policemen were killed during the Aktion for attempting to help those gathered in the Umschlagplatz.[114]

In order to complete the picture of the involvement of Order Service functionaries in the first Aktion, it is necessary to establish to what extent it was possible for the policemen not to participate in the deportations. Firstly, there were policemen who remained in the Service throughout the Aktion, yet did not participate in "line" service but worked in police administration. Even though, according to a document in *Archiwum Akt Nowych*, those who did not want to participate in the Aktion were "terrorized" by their colleagues, there were many who survived the Aktion in the relative safety of the Order Service administration.[115] However, not all could get a job in the office. For them, the only way of avoiding the Aktion was resigning from the Service altogether. Even though many diarists recall policemen throwing their hats on the ground in the Umschlagplatz,[116] it is difficult to determine to what extent leaving the Order Service in July and August 1942 was indeed a viable option. One of those who did leave, Jerzy Lewiński, recalled that as a result he was degraded, imprisoned for two days, and later accused of sabotage. Only the help of an influential friend who managed to have him removed from the register of Jewish policemen allowed him to leave without major consequences.[117] Many others, however, exhibited claims to the contrary. In the chaos of the deportations, not fulfilling one's duties or even leaving the Service was a distinct possibility. According to Hirsch Wasser, up to fifty percent of all officers left during the Aktion.[118]

There is no doubt that the first two weeks of the Aktion was a time of relative independence in the proceedings of the Order Service. Some claimed that while the Judenrat was fulfilling its functions under clear pressure, the Order Service was diligent and even showed its own initiative.[119] This feeling was reinforced by the fact that after Czerniaków's death some of the public deportation announcements were signed by the Head of the Order Service. In the later stages of deportations, the involvement of the Order Service was gradually limited. According to Wasser the basis for this was not a lack of will on the part of the Jewish policemen, but rather the decision of the commander of the *Vernichtungskommando* (ger. Annihilation Detachment), a battalion-size unit of guards trained in the Trawniki SS labor camp, who had reservations as to the manner in which the Order Service fulfilled its duties.[120] In September, during the so-called "Cauldron" selection, the number of Order Service members, as was the case with other bodies, was significantly reduced. Only 300 members of the Service and an additional 200 closest family members were exempted from deportation. Abraham Lewin, watching the former policemen gather together with their families at the Umschlagplatz awaiting deportation, noted that ghetto inhabitants watching this scene "felt a definite satisfaction."[121] Another diarist wrote: "They were going down to Hades, cast down in spirits, but it must be admitted that Jews not only felt no great sympathy for the policemen's sufferings, but on the contrary, simply could not suppress their feeling of hatred and vengefulness towards those Jews who had served the murderers so faithfully and who had so many Jewish lives on their conscience."[122] Those policemen lucky enough to be sent instead to work in workshops were reportedly shunned by their coworkers, many of whom had to be forced by the workshop's leaders to even agree to work in the same room with them.[123]

Reflecting the mood in the ghetto, the newly formed armed underground started issuing death sentences for those deeply implicated in deportations—Jewish policemen and collaborators. One of the diarists remembered the effect that ŻOB leaflets about carried-out sentences had on the ghetto inhabitants:

> After every such occurrence I would go out on the street and when passing a policeman I would stare at him. I would straighten up and stare at him, convinced that he must be incredibly scared . . . I was waiting every day, if only they would kill one more traitor, just one more! If I had weapons, I would murder the Jewish policeman myself, even torture them. I was being eaten away by the hatred towards them.[124]

Similar sentiments were reflected in many other diaries and testimonies.

In the January 1943 Aktion the remaining members of the Order Service were used to a much lesser extent. According to one diarist they were meant to be used as shields by the German formation; according to others policemen participated in uncovering ghetto inhabitants hiding in bunkers. Many of the policemen were at that point already in hiding themselves. One ghetto survivor remembered that during his stay in the bunker there was a group of former policemen sitting off to the side, openly shunned by everyone around them.[125] After the January Aktion the policemen were seized with fear to such an extent that they started removing their caps and badges of rank.[126]

Despite the deterioration in the way in which they were perceived, members of the Jewish police remained friends, relatives, and neighbors of diarists as diverse as Abraham Levin, Emanuel Ringelblum, and Mary Berg. They also remained active participants in the ghetto's community life. The extremely successful police jazz band and cabaret performed in many café revues, mercilessly ridiculing well-known members of the Service. Leading personalities of the ghetto's cultural and social life—Władysław Szlengel and Jerzy "Jerry" Ryba, the musical director of *Femina* theater—were both members of the Jewish Police, even though they were not employed in everyday service. A number of policemen worked toward helping the abandoned children of the ghetto—the Service had achieved considerable success in setting up children's homes and extensively collaborated in that field with Centos (*Centralne Towarzystwo Opieki nad Sierotami i Dziećmi Opuszczonymi*—pol. Central Society for the Care of Orphans). They also collaborated with Janusz Korczak, and members of the Order Service repeatedly visited his orphanage.

After a few days of the Aktion the Service turned into undoubtedly the most hated group in the ghetto, despised more than the Judenrat Councilors, the new rich, members of the Thirteen, and, according to many, even more than the Germans. A witness to the Aktion explained: "People hated the Germans. But it was abstract hatred—to a great group of uniformed Wehrmacht soldiers or the SS. Rarely would anyone personally know some German murderer. And the Jewish policeman was an acquaintance, a man from your city, your courtyard—another Jew. Those people were not worthy of living."[127]

The uniformed group of the Order Service clearly contrasted with the rest of the ghetto. The policemen were not true children of the Jewish street; they were alien, in the words of Yehoshua Perle: "children of thieves and whores."[128] Their polonized character was held to be symbolic of their unfamiliarity. The behavior of the police was blamed on their assimilatory complexes and distance from the ghetto society, a reaction to the discrimination that the young lawyers encountered when trying to integrate into the Polish environment in the interwar period. This was, however, to be only characteristic of the assimilated strata. According to this theory, the Orthodox Jews had no dealings with Poles and no chance to develop an inferiority complex. The Socialists and Zionists both had a sense of Jewish dignity that kept them from succumbing to the feeling of inadequacy.[129]

For those coming from the same environment as the Order Service, the issue of their behavior was even more difficult to comprehend. Szpilman, who had many friends among the Order Service, explained: "They had been recruited mainly from young men in the more prosperous classes of society, and a number of our acquaintances were among them. We were all the more horrified when we saw that men with whom we used to shake hands, whom we had treated as friends, men who had still been decent people not long ago, were now so despicable."[130] This feeling of confusion and disbelief is prevalent in the vast majority of authors from a similar background. Even though, just like the wide ghetto community, most of the assimilated authors condemned the behavior of the police during the Aktion, they nonetheless often tried to explain this behavior as an attempt to save their families or as the result of a lack of choice when faced with German orders. "How else could the police have acted?" one of them asked. "They couldn't have all poisoned themselves."[131] Most importantly, however, diarists from the assimilated strata drew a clear line between the "decent" people from their closest environment and the hostile, threatening monolith of the Service as a whole.

Social Welfare in the Warsaw Ghetto: The Fight for the Soul of the Ghetto

No issue had more impact on the internal politics of the ghetto than the struggle over who really had the right to consider themselves its leaders, the "true mentors" of the society. The Judenrat and the nationalistically oriented community fought this battle over what was undoubtedly the most crucial of all aspects of ghetto communal life—social welfare.

The leading part in welfare work was played by the Jewish Self-Help, also popularly referred to in the ghetto as the *Aleynhilf* (yid. self help). The precursor to the Jewish Self-Help was *Komisja Koordynacyjna* (KK, pol. Coordinating Commission). The KK was created in the first weeks of the war, on September 14, 1939, at the initiative of the American Jewish Joint Distribution Committee (AJDC) to coordinate all the leading Jewish welfare organizations of pre-war Poland. The organization later changed its name to *Żydowska Samopomoc Społeczna—Komisja Koordynacyjna* (ŻSS-KK, pol. Jewish Self-Help—Coordinating Commission) and after that, in October 1940, to *Żydowskie Towarzystwo Opieki Społecznej* (ŻTOS, pol. Jewish Social Welfare Association) and in November 1941 to *Żydowska Opieka Społeczna* (ŻOS, pol. Jewish Social Welfare). ŻOS operated formally as the Warsaw branch of *Żydowska Samopomoc Społeczna* (ŻSS, pol. Jewish Self-Help)—a German-licensed social welfare organization, led by Michał Weichert from headquarters in Kraków. In reality, however, it retained far-reaching autonomy. To fulfill its aims the Jewish Self-Help developed a structure of commissions between which were divided various aspects of social welfare. In addition, a number of pre-war Jewish welfare agencies—organizations such as *Towarzystwo Opieki Zdrowotnej* (TOZ, pol. Society for the Preservation of Health),[132] ORT (Organization of Rehabilitation Through Training),[133] and Centos—functioned under its umbrella. All had a track record of successful work among Polish Jewry, and once in the ghetto would build extensively on this experience. By the end of 1941, both TOZ and Centos were formally incorporated into the Self-Help to become its Medical and Child Care Departments, respectively. The scale of the work was immense. The Jewish Self-Help took upon itself the task of running soup kitchens, refugee points, children's overnight shelters, day-care centers, and orphanages. It also supervised the work of over 1,100 house committees and sixty *landsmanshaftn* of refugees representing towns and villages, whose former inhabitants were now in Warsaw. This incredible effort was undertaken with the help of thousands of low-paid employees and volunteers, many of them who endured not much better living conditions than those who they were helping.

The Jewish Self-Help's social activism was interlinked with the commitment to spread Jewish identity. To a large extent these activities were undertaken in cooperation with Yikor (yid. Jewish Cultural Organization), but also with underground groups and other organizations. An important part of *Aleynhilf*'s activities was connected with research and documentation of life in the ghetto. The *Oyneg Shabes* Archive is the best-known undertaking, but other projects were also of great importance. Valuable research projects were carried out, for example, by the Evidence Department of the Self-Help, which collected data about all recipients of social help.[134]

A crucial part of the Jewish Self-Help's structure was the Group of Representatives of Political Parties, which assembled representatives of the largest pre-war parties and therefore assumed political representation of the ghetto society. Testifying as to how interlinked the world of the Self-Help and underground politics was, Adolf Berman, the head of Centos and a Left Poale Zion activist, wrote:

> During the period in which it carried out welfare activities on a large scale, Centos employed 1,000 persons. Several hundreds of them belonged to the various underground organizations, including communist organizations and Zionist and Halutzic ones. The first pistol brought in from the "Aryan" side for the Anti-Fascist bloc in the ghetto was handed over in the office of the director of Centos. Many of the key personalities of the underground movement in the ghetto were given "cover" in the children's institutions, where they find support for their activities.

Later on, Berman adds that the contact between the Polish and Jewish resistance was partially maintained through links between Centos and the Polish childcare institutions.[135]

The greatest proportion of funding for the Self-Help in the ghetto was provided by the American Joint Distribution Committee—until the end of 1941 openly, but later clandestinely. Other foreign institutions, such as the International Red Cross and the Commission for Polish Relief, sent their funds to the ghetto through the ŻSS headquarters in Kraków. The ghetto also received informal material help from the "Aryan" side, mainly from professional groups. However, the backbone of the Self-Help finances was formed by contributions from the ghetto society itself.

In comparison, the operations of the Judenrat's Department of Social Welfare were initially conducted on a much smaller scale and limited to help for children, the elderly, and the POWs, financed largely from indirect taxation. The main focus of the Council at that time was on the institutions that were already under its responsibility—especially the two hospitals, which, according to Adam Czerniaków, were in April 1940 eating up all the Judenrat's resources.[136] Yet, from January 1941, the Judenrat started gradually taking over responsibility for social welfare from the Self-Help. Its rationale, voiced by Council member Hillel Rosen, was to create a strong, broad administrative apparatus for providing genuinely effective social aid. According to Rosen: "the Jewish community ought to create the central administrative structure geared to provide the social help needed. A public-welfare institution does what it can but cannot force anyone, whereas an administrative organ does what it wishes, frequently with the help of some form of coercion."[137] Unsurprisingly, a completely different perspective on events was presented by the Jewish Self-Help, which saw it as an attack on its growing power by a German-imposed institution. According to Emanuel Ringelblum, the Judenrat saw in the *Aleynhilf* "a concentration of all social powers critical of the Council and its anti-social policy."[138] It is also likely that the object of the struggle was not so much the symbolic soul of the Jewish people, but their financial resources that were vital for the functioning of both the Judenrat and the Jewish Self-Help. The merger was quick and to an extent successful. In the summer of 1941 the Judenrat took over control of the soup kitchens. In the autumn of that year, the 148 refugee centers in the ghetto, three quarters of which were until then administered by the Jewish Self-Help, were taken over by the Judenrat's newly created Commission for Care of Refugees. The task of the Judenrat was made easier by the fact that the gradual decline in funding from the AJDC led to a significant impoverishment of the Jewish-Self Help.[139] Additionally, according to Michał Weichert, the Judenrat stopped *Aleynhilf* from obtaining internal loans in the ghetto in the spring of 1942, even though permission was already obtained from the German authorities.[140] In the spring of 1942, in its quest for power in the ghetto, the Judenrat did, however, come across an obstacle that it could not surmount. The attempt to impose control over house committees proved completely unsuccessful.

The Warsaw Ghetto's 1,100 house committees were the only bodies that could claim to be the voice of the ordinary people from the streets. Organized in almost all of the ghetto's apartment blocks, they were institutions of social help based on inter-tenant help, such as the organization of soup kitchens, day care for children, or loans. Many tenants additionally offered whatever skills they had to their neighbors, with doctors, for instance, working for free for those living within the same courtyard. Not all house committees were democratic in sprit—there were those where leadership was taken over by a group of social activists and those where all power was in the hands of a few (or sometimes even one) of the wealthy inhabitants of the block. Notwithstanding their democratic character, the house committees exerted extreme pressure on any individuals who did not wish to abide by their decisions. In the words of Chaim Kaplan: "If they encountered a 'stubborn pig' they softened his heart by various means, some ethical, some coercive."[141] Those who did not volunteer to help were often publicly shamed, with lists of non-payers displayed on the door of the apartment building.[142] The nature and extent of help in house committees differed according to the living standards of its inhabitants. For example, thirty-seven percent of the expenditure of house committees in the poor fourth quarter was taken up by funeral costs.[143] Even though the house committees legally functioned as part of the Public Sector of the Self-Help, the relationship between these two structures was anything but smooth. The Self-Help was an embodiment of the core values of the interwar youth and radical movements, which could be fulfilled only by complete subordination to the cause of solidarity and justice. At the beginning, the still reasonably well-off ghetto inhabitants were keen to help their brothers in need; yet this changed with the decline in their own financial situation. Despite *Aleynhilf*'s efforts, the majority of the house committees preferred to help their own inhabitants rather than to contribute to a central fund of the Jewish Self-Help. In his reportage, Peretz Opoczyński described his visit to a house committee that he tried to convince to join the *Aleynhilf* network. The inhabitants not only could not correctly identify the Self-Help but were also distrustful of giving their money away when at any point they might need it to bribe a disinfection squad.[144]

Portraying the attitude of the house committees toward the Self-Help, Opoczyński wrote that the welfare system was seen as "them," as a sort of tax office, and that the committees tried to avoid paying their due at any possible chance. Ringelblum himself was said to believe that the house committees had turned into some sort of *goylem* (yid. monsters) that diverted needed funds from the *Aleynhilf*.[145] As a result, in January 1942, in the poorest parts of the ghetto, only 14.2 percent of committees' expenditure was spent on "external" relief and 85.8 percent on "internal" help,[146] clearly showing how the charitable tradition of "caring for one's own" was gradually being limited only to one's own courtyard. Later on the situation worsened and the "circle of responsibility" of the vast majority of ghetto inhabitants shrank to their closest family and acquaintances. Instead of supporting their inhabitants, many house committees undertook steps toward evicting those who were the most in need. This attitude reached its peak in the first day of the deportations, when those with Judenrat's life tickets still felt relatively safe and the deportees included mainly refugees and volunteers. A witness to the events, Stefan Ernest, wrote that some of the working intelligentsia saw the deportations of the poorest to be a great advantage to the rest of the ghetto society, as they formed nothing but a burden on their resources and were bound to die anyway.[147] This observation was confirmed by others.

Relations between the house committees and the Judenrat were even more fragile. The Council needed the cooperation of the house committees to ensure compliance with its orders, especially when it came to taxation. The fact that the house committees were burdened with purely administrative or financial tasks essentially turned them into local administrative organs of the Judenrat.[148] This situation met with howls of protest from the house committee activists, who despite sometimes strained contacts with the Self-Help, felt much more affiliation with them than they did with the Judenrat. Michael Mazor, the president of the Commission of Instruction and Inspection in one of the sectors of the house committees, remembered that no employees of the Judenrat, even the technical officials, were allowed to attend the house committee meetings. Mazor recalled in his memoirs that when a speaker in one such meeting was unmasked as a Judenrat employee, "the indignation that mounted against him grew so threatening, it was all I could do to get him out of the meeting unharmed."[149] Unsurprisingly, therefore, the draft of a resolution subjugating house committees to the Judenrat met with such an instant and acute social protest that it was never realized.

Describing the conflict between the Judenrat and the Jewish Self-Help, Emanuel Ringelblum accused "anti-social elements" of attempting to "turn the social welfare action into typical pre-war philanthropy."[150] And, indeed, the Judenrat policy should be seen as a traditionally understood philanthropy relying on voluntary donations. It was a clear continuation of a traditional imperative for individualized *tzedakah* (heb. justice, charity), seen as a private matter, as opposed to the radical ideology of the Self-Help, where the community was to be completely subordinated to the "cause." Yet the policy of Judenrat activists, many of them with sound experience in pre-war philanthropy and community life, did not stand the test when faced with the extreme human poverty of the Warsaw Ghetto. Aside from a small group of pre-war philanthropists, such as Abraham Gepner and Shmuel Winter, the remaining ghetto inhabitants either could not pay, due to lack of money or fear about the future, or, as was the case of the new-rich strata, were not active enough in the community life to see it as their duty. For example, tenants in the relatively wealthy house where Hirsch Wasser lived would all together pay a rental of 25,000 złoty per month, but only a total of about 1,000 złoty monthly for various taxes and contributions, a mere four percent of the rental fee.[151] As another diarist, a Judenrat employee, noted poignantly, without any practical way of extracting taxes, their payment was dependent purely on the good will of those concerned, which due to circumstances, was non-existent.[152]

There were a number of actions designed to raise money for the poor, which were initiated by the Self-Help and supported, though sometimes reluctantly, by the Judenrat. These included the confiscation of bread ration cards from the richest 30,000 people in the society and later a compulsory collection for the poor organized in the spring and summer of 1941. These measures generally did not yield the results that were needed, and led the Self-Help circles to believe that success could be achieved only by much more radical undertakings. Yet, despite the best efforts of Adam Czerniaków, the Judenrat very strongly resisted any sort of progressive tax on income. Instead the Council remained steadfastly attached to the per-capita tax, the exemption from which, on the basis of lack of income, reached 150,000 people in January 1942.[153]

The taxation system formed the core of anti-Judenrat rhetoric in the ghetto. An example of this is evident in a report on a meeting of the Financial Committee of the Jewish Council Refugee Commission compiled by a prominent social activist Menachem Kon. He wrote:

> The fact that thousands of children—their bellies swollen with hunger—are dying, leaves them absolutely cold. They—these good-for-nothings, fat-bellies, gamblers—they lack for nothing. The doors of the night clubs of the Jewish Ghetto are always open to them—there, they can drink and gorge themselves stupid—as they did in peace time. And it is people like this that the [Jewish] Council is protecting . . . Allow[ing] thousands of dried out bodies of dead men, women and children to litter the streets. Allow[ing] the angel of death to wield his bloody sword and to lay about him, cutting down the children of the masses—all for the sake of not forcing those over-fed individuals to pay tax.[154]

Even though many of them might have shrunk away from paying taxes, the financial elite of the ghetto, the "overfed individuals," referred to by Menachem Kon, were doing their bit for charity by organizing extravagant fundraising events and sumptuous parties. As Władysław Szpilman wrote in his memoir: "This charity work was particularly enjoyable because it involved frequent balls at which people danced, amused themselves and drank, donating the proceeds to charitable purposes."[155] Another ghetto inhabitant confirms this view by writing candidly: "No one cared whether these things and the money had gone to deserving or non-deserving cases. What was important was that the gift was entered on the list, and that as a result of it, one could walk, head held high, past a half naked man dressed in a woman's torn blouse leaning against a sun-warmed wall and begging. It was easier to give than not to give." He added later that "One danced and flirted better with philanthropic ideals at the back of one's mind."[156] As a result, while the income from entertainment in the poorest fourth district formed 2.8 percent of the house committee revenue, in the rich third district that encompassed the well-off streets of Nowolipie, Solna, and

Elektoralna this amount rose to 21.2 percent.[157] Commenting on the situation, a Self-Help activist wrote bitterly:

> We used to laugh at the traditional charity of those Jewish mothers, those simple women who used to come to our house. It's a shame we don't have them anymore. They were the true Jewish mothers, women with warm hearts. . . . They themselves gave generously and forced others to do the same. How differently today's society ladies act. They come wearing elegant clothes and bring weak, thin children broken dolls, punctured balls, a few pencils, and this way, as a sort of entertainment, they fulfill their need for charity.[158]

For the ghetto street the symbol of such charity was the quasi-philanthropic undertakings of collaborationist institutions such as the Thirteen. Its best-known attempt at social welfare was the funding of the Jewish Emergency Medical Service, the real aim of which seemed to be providing various deserving individuals with employment. According to Stanisław Adler, the members of the Service "ran away . . . when they encountered somebody in need of assistance, since they had neither experience nor training in rescue operations; their coffee flasks and bread containers were empty, and their emergency kits contained only iodine."[159] Nonetheless, the Thirteen did organize some sort of help. As one of the diarists remembered, in front of the 13 Leszno Street apartment block every day one could see crowds of poor among whom was distributed soup or tea with a piece of bread.[160] Abraham Gancwajch himself financially supported many individuals from the fields of arts and science.

More successful, though also morally dubious, were the undertakings of Moryc Kohn and Zelig Heller, refugees from Łódź and two of the richest people in the ghetto. After a short collaboration with Gancwajch, Kohn and Heller received with the help of the Gestapo a number of concessions, including trade in vegetables in the ghetto, and maintenance of the only tram line. Though clearly collaborationists, Kohn and Heller were both very involved in charity, especially when it came to religious circles. Describing their conduct, Stefan Ernest wrote that "hundreds" of poorer ghetto inhabitants, particularly those hailing from Łódź, "credited them with their existence," adding later that the two entrepreneurs clearly "were not completely devoid of that proverbial 'yiddishes hertz', the Jewish heart about which so much was spoken of in the ghetto."[161] Later on, according to numerous reports, Kohn and Heller also warned ghetto inhabitants of the impending deportations.[162] Charity work was also undertaken by the Jewish Police, who very successfully organized and financed a network of shelters for street children. These undertakings were organized in cooperation with Centos, and as Adolf Berman—political activist and head of Centos—emphasized very strongly, it was the only case of cooperation between the underground and the Order Service.[163]

Describing the Judenrat's social welfare policy the assimilated doctor Henryk Makower wrote about tiny bandages of philanthropy that the Council was sticking on the massive wounds of the ghetto.[164] The most visible aspects of the Judenrat's social policy in the closed quarter were large one-off money collections, organized with considerable cost to the society. An anonymous informant from the ghetto, describing the "Winter Aid" charity collection, one of the largest undertakings of the Judenrat, wrote:

> In the coffee shops and other places, as well as in the streets, small blue-white printed tags were handed out bearing the inscription "Winter Aid" in Polish and Yiddish accompanied by a graphic design. Contributions varied greatly, but as a rule they were modest—most people gave only about 0.10 zloty, in order to receive the tag and be left alone. The total receipts, however, do not seem too bad. . . . People comment ironically that a Winter Aid collection is not held in spring; that the Jewish institutions do not publish figures; that nobody is ever shown the exact results of collections. . . . The collection was meant to continue over several days, but was already halted after the first day.[165]

The second highly advertized action—"Month of the Child"—was organized by the Judenrat and Centos twice (in late summer of 1940 and in the autumn of 1941), but ended amid suspicion of financial irregularities.

Social welfare initiatives organized by the Judenrat suffered from problems prevalent in all the other spheres of this institution—corruption and protectionism. In a very interesting testimony, an assimilated ghetto inhabitant remembered how his grandfather, as a pre-war senator and a well-known public persona, addressed the Judenrat for discreet material help. The Council immediately found a needle wholesaler who was obliged to pay a percentage of his profits to the former senator. He recalled:

> The needle wholesaler could not defend himself, because in the ghetto all merchants—including him—were acting against the law and the Judenrat could have destroyed him at any moment. . . . The story lasted till the end of the ghetto. He survived the Great Aktion, we survived—and we still lived off a percentage of his profit. Lolek [the author's cousin] checked his books every month to make sure that he is not "cheating on us."[166]

To the same extent that the Judenrat created in its structures an asylum for the polonized strata, the Jewish Self-Help openly supported the nationalistically oriented intelligentsia, providing employment for the cultural elite. According to one diarist the fact that the *Aleynhilf* was taken over by intelligentsia meant that the intelligentsia became the main benefactor of social aid in the ghetto and "only sometimes mentioned were refugees, all the other groups—shopkeepers, artisans, workers—were pushed down to tenth place."[167] Symbolic of such an attitude was the Self-Help's Individual Assistance Section, the aim of which was to assign funds for the impoverished members of intelligentsia—lawyers, teachers, engineers and medical doctors.[168] This policy was continued until the last days of the ghetto as in September 1942 Ringelblum strongly supported the controversial plan to use money from the AJDC and other organizations to create a reserve fund to save the "core"—the intellectual and creative elite.[169] Similarly, leadership of the Self-Help was composed according to political affiliations. According to one diarist: "Rabbis, Zionists, Mizrachists, Bundists, Folkists, Augudhists, all took their share—the only ones missing were those who did not belong to any parties."[170] As a result, the Self-Help was accused of assigning key positions in its structure to people who despite the best intentions often lacked experience in conducting large-scale aid undertakings.[171] At the same time there must have been people who, similarly to their counterparts in the Judenrat, treated their job mainly as a way of getting exemption from forced labor. One of the survivors remembered her work in the *Aleynhilf*: "All of us young were filling in some sort of forms. What these forms were all about and what they were for, nobody cared—the only important thing was that we were not rounded up for forced labor."[172] Additionally, the sheer number of people involved in the Jewish-Self Help meant that not all of them even shared the basic ideology of *Aleynhilf*. Kopel Piżyc, who was responsible for a *Tarbut* folk kitchen serving 800 children, noted in his testimony that among fifteen kitchen staff, only six were "working in the spirit of the *Tarbut*. Out of the nine remaining, two were assimilated and the rest had a negative attitude to the upbringing of children in national spirit."[173] Even in the tragedy of the ghetto life, the pre-war alliances seemed to be of key importance.

Similarly to the Judenrat, the Jewish Self-Help was also not free from various forms of theft and embezzlement. Chaim Kaplan noted in his diary that before long public opinion began to notice problems with the Self-Help; "that they were stealing and embezzling; that the soup kitchens were spending a lot feeding a very few; that there was no overall control; that 'the whole business is not worthwhile' etc. etc."[174] Even if the leaders of the Self-Help could not be accused of dishonesty, some diarists went as far as to claim that when it came to the feelings of the ghetto street, the *Aleynhilf* was not much more liked than the Judenrat and the Thirteen.[175] There is also evidence that many of the recipients of social welfare saw the Self-Help as responsible for the constant problems of the institutions that they were supervising.[176] One of the young girls working in the Self-Help office described her work after the war as being "only to refuse, to postpone, or to provide insufficient aid."[177]

There is no doubt that despite the often incredible dedication and selflessness of individual activists, the sheer scale of the tragic situation in the ghetto meant that the help of either the Judenrat or the

Aleynhilf was in no way sufficient to meet the needs of the society. The situation was also made worse by the complete lack of coordination between these bodies.[178] The few successful undertakings in the ghetto seem to have succeeded due to the incredible energy of individual social activists—such as Korczak and his aide Stefania Wilczyńska; Dr. Anna Braude-Heller, the head of Bergson-Bauman hospital; and Róża Simchowicz, an organizer of children's corners—rather than any society-wide undertakings. Best documented of all these endeavors are undoubtedly that of Korczak, the head of an orphanage for 200 children at Sienna Street. Even though the institution was partially supported by Centos, the vast majority of funds were obtained by Korczak himself—from sources which ranged from the Judenrat, the AJDC, smugglers, and collaborators with the Order Service from which he took confiscated goods.[179] Korczak's plight showed to what extent true power over the social life of the ghetto was increasingly not in the hands of the *Aleynhilf* and the Judenrat, but rather of a third group—the new-rich smugglers and factory owners. Yet the successful attempt to fully incorporate these groups into the communal life of the ghetto did not happen until January 1942 when the *Dobra Wola* (pol. Good Will) Orphanage at 61 Dzielna Street was set up in the former refugee center and funded mainly by the brush makers association and their Polish and Jewish business partners. The better conditions in the orphanage placed it in stark contrast with the vast majority of other institutions.

Not much more could have been achieved, and a few months later, in the first days of August 1942, staff and children from *Dobra Wola*, alongside those from the Korczak Orphanage and the Council Orphanage at Dzika Street, were deported to Treblinka.

The Jewish Self-Help in Warsaw was dissolved on July 29, 1942. During the Aktion, surviving social welfare activists set up *Centralny Komitet Pomocy Pracy w Szopach* (CKPPwS, pol. Central Committee to Support Work in the Shops). The committee was officially overseen by the Judenrat, with the aim of coordinating self-help actions and organizing food allocations for those employed in the shops. Its statute was written by Emanuel Ringelblum. In the short time of its functioning, the Committee managed to undertake a number of valuable actions which included a collection of funds and clothes for those coming back from camps. Its work and subsequently all the social welfare undertakings in the Warsaw Ghetto were stopped by the 1943 Aktion.[180] From the end of 1942, the focus of Jewish social help was moved outside the ghetto walls, where the underground community of those who survived, the last Jews of Warsaw, was gradually being formed.

4

Polish-Language Cultural Life in the Warsaw Ghetto

An Overview of Cultural Life in the Ghetto

The enclosure of the ghetto also affected those who up until then seemed a world away from the crowds of Nalewki or Franciszkańska Streets—the heroes of popular imagination. Those who before the war could only be seen on the covers of popular magazines or in gossip columns, the most popular actors and musicians of interwar Poland, began their new life working as rickshaw drivers, street sellers, or soup kitchen employees. However, the closed quarter soon started organizing an artistic life of its own. With the curfew being a major factor influencing social and cultural life in the ghetto, the first hub of artistic activity was the house committees. *Oyneg Shabes* collaborator Stanisław Różycki explained: "At the latest by eight in the evening we are all back in our apartments. They close the gates at half eight and you are not allowed to leave after nine. The blackout starts already at five."[1] Strict adherence to the curfew meant that later afternoon or evening visits usually involved staying overnight. Not surprisingly, private apartments were sites of a thriving cultural life. On one evening, Stanisław Adler reported on a room full of "refined and intelligent people," who spent their time listening to popular pianists, both of them slightly tipsy, playing four hands compositions and later a medley of the best songs of singer Sonia Białostocka."[2]

Almost immediately after the enclosure of the ghetto, the back pages of *Gazeta Żydowska* started filling with adverts placed by famous and not-so-famous pre-war artists willing to perform at evenings organized in apartment blocks.[3] Describing the situation, social activist Rachela Auerbach wrote: "Whoever had some sort of solo repertoire started performing it. Those who did not have any, immediately started to look for it. Actors began to specialize in reciting poems. The most famous of them . . . were very much sought after and could make a rather good living out of it."[4] Especially prominent were artists who until then performed mainly in Polish theater and cabarets. Their appearance in the ghetto caused an uproar. According to theater director Jonas Turkow, who himself performed in apartment blocks: "any Jew from Franciszkańska or Nalewki street could feel like a member of the aristocracy when he could have in his house the most prominent pre-war performers." After the performance they might "recall their visit thousands of times, refer to them as close friends, who come round to his house . . . and who he is on first name basis with."[5]

Just as it happened on the other side of the wall, in the first months of the ghetto's existence every birthday, name day, or anniversary became a reason for celebration, and this usually involved listening to music.[6] Young people were in particular ready to go to great lengths to obtain the necessary equipment and records. A young woman, writing to a friend on the "Aryan" side, explained: "We managed with great difficulty to get some records. We already have Beethoven's Third, Fourth and Fifth symphonies and almost all of Chopin's; the most amazing recordings and various other gems."[7] Another teenager from an affluent family had a gramophone especially smuggled for her from the other side of the wall. She later recalled: "I passed a message to Auntie Maria begging her to send me my gramophone. I believe she had a hard time convincing her brother-in-law that such a thing was of vital importance to someone living behind the walls, but she managed and he brought me the gramophone."[8] Aside from providing entertainment, the main aim of events organized by the house committees was fundraising. Afternoon tea dances or all-night parties, to which tenants from neighboring houses and various friends were invited, were to become a major source of revenue and provided funds for helping the impoverished inhabitants of the blocks.[9]

Such performances and the rest of the unofficial cultural life were coordinated by *Centralna Komisja Imprezowa* (CKI, pol. Central Events Commission), an agency of the Jewish Self-Help created in September 1940. Within a year of its creation CKI organized 1,814 performances, including eight symphonic concerts.[10] It became an unofficial trade union of professional artists, providing them if necessary with material help. Events were also organized by the branch of *Aleynhilf* dealing with the coordination of Yiddish-language cultural life in the ghetto, Yikor. These initially took place in private apartments, and later in the former building of the Judaic Library at 5 Tłomackie Street, which quickly became the center of intellectual life in the ghetto. Events at the Library featured both well-known figures of the ghetto's artistic life and the established pre-war stars, such as actress Estera Goldinberg, who chose not to perform on the official ghetto stages.[11] These events were modestly priced at one złoty to allow as wide an audience as possible. The most successful artistic event in the Library was a November 1941 staging of Antoni Cwojdziński's comedy *Freud's Theory of Dreams* starring Diana Blumenfeld and Jonas Turkow. For the benefit of censorship the play was performed under the title *Comical Dialogues of a Jew, Sigmund Freud*. Aside from the Library and the house committees, social life was also organized in the soup kitchens. Rachela Auerbach, who oversaw the kitchen at 6 Orla Street, described it as "a sort of literary-artistic club, with a permanent buffet, art exhibitions, lectures, seminars, various literary and artistic events with singing and recitations of poems, and even showcases of children from Jewish schools."[12]

As with other areas of social life in the ghetto, the fields of culture and entertainment created acute competition between the Judenrat and the grass-root organizations. In this case the Judenrat finally got an upper hand and from the spring of 1942 all artistic events in the ghetto were to be organized by the Jewish Council's Entertainment Section. Yet, notwithstanding the new regulations, a large proportion of the cultural undertakings remained under the sole control of the powerful social organization.[13]

The content of the officially produced entertainment was considerably different depending on whether one was in the ghetto or on the "Aryan" side. On the "Aryan" side, where German policy was aimed at destroying high-level culture, the aim of the unofficial cultural life was to act as a counterpoint for heavily censored, restricted, and controlled official entertainment.[14] The only official plays performed in theaters were cheap comedies, often with quasi-pornographic content. According to the moral code that formed the backbone of civil resistance in occupied Warsaw, attending and performing in a licensed theater was inexcusable. In many venues the only members of the intelligentsia present in the auditorium were those who had to make a living as ushers.[15] The situation in the ghetto was different. A memorandum of the *Rassenpolitisches Amt* (ger. Office of Racial Policy) of the NSDAP on *The Treatment of the Population of the Former Polish Areas from the Racial-Political Point of View*, dated November 25, 1939, stated: "Jewish political groupings must be banned together with the Polish ones. On the other hand, Jewish cultural associations could be tolerated more freely than the Polish ones. Greater latitude should be given to the Jews in this respect than to the Poles, for politically they do not possess such real power as the Poles."[16] Jewish culture was clearly seen as harmless to the realization of German plans and if anything was considered to bring a degree of calm and a semblance of normality to ghetto life. The *Abteilung Volksaufklärung und Propaganda* (ger. Department for Public Enlightenment and Propaganda) in the Head of the District Office, which controlled the ghetto's cultural life, limited its censorship to ensuring that works of "Aryan" artists were not performed, and even in this case it was not particularly strict. The fact that the cultural section of *Gazeta Żydowska* regularly contained reviews of performances of works by non-Jewish authors did not meet with any reaction from the German authorities.[17]

A discussion of legal entertainment in the Warsaw Ghetto has to first examine its most developed branch: the theater. The first official theater in the ghetto opened in December 1940, causing a sensation on the streets of the closed quarter. Jonas Turkow recalled: "Whenever people had talked about any opening of Jewish theaters, they always added that Germans will never permit that. But it happened. Theaters were opened and crowds flowed in."[18] The licenses for the first venues were received by Regina Judt, rumored to have been a former lover of a prominent German officer, one of the most generally disliked and at the same time colorful personalities of the Warsaw Ghetto. Her "career" seems to have ended when Czerniaków, fed up with her constant harassment, issued an official statement forbidding Regina Judt from entering the building of the Jewish Council and from personally addressing members of the Judenrat or the Council's clerks.[19]

In the Warsaw Ghetto, the opening of a theater was highly dependent on money and contacts in the Judenrat, and probably in the Gestapo too. However, unlike in "Aryan" Warsaw, it was not considered a sign of outright collaboration. Aside from Judt, theater owners were mainly people connected with the Thirteen, but also included wealthy pre-war entrepreneurs, members of the Judenrat, and the Jewish Order Service. Despite theaters having dubious ownership, work in official entertainment venues was not seen as morally questionable and actors working in the ghetto theaters were exempted from the boycott of official stages introduced by the Polish Actors Union on the "Aryan" side.

This ruling meant that the ghetto audience gained access to some of the greatest personalities of the interwar theater, who found themselves trapped in the closed quarter. This diverse group of artists cooperated successfully despite differences that would have seemed insurmountable in pre-war life. The theater maker with the greatest artistic credibility was undoubtedly Andrzej Marek—one of the first well-known artists to use the Polish language to express Jewish cultural and national identity. Also in the ghetto was his great pre-war opponent, Jonas Turkow—a representative of the new wave of Yiddish artists who devoted their lives and careers to creating artistic, "European"-style Jewish theater. Together with his wife Diana Blumenfeld, Turkow was a former member of the critically acclaimed theater troupe led by Ester Rachel and Ida Kamińska—the *Varshever Yidisher Kunst-teater* (yid. Warsaw Yiddish Art Theater). Another important personality was Michał Weichert, creator of the *Yung Teater* (yid. Young Theater)—probably the most ambitious of the major Yiddish theater companies as well as the founder of the first institution in Poland devoted to the training of Yiddish actors. There was also Ajzyk Samberg—"the tzar of Yiddish theater"—the most famous actor on the Yiddish stage and the president of the Union of Yiddish Actors. At the other end of the artistic spectrum was Regina Cukier, a very popular singer of ballads and operettas, known as the queen of *shundt* (yid. rubbish)—sentimental plays with simple plots that dominated the repertoire of touring theater troupes. In the ghetto were also actors who acted in Polish-language theater and were usually completely assimilated and often baptized. The strongest group, which later formed the backbone of the café and literary cabaret *Sztuka* (pol. Art), was formed by past creators of Polish literary cabarets, such as Jerzy Jurandot, one of the best songwriters in interwar Poland and literary director of the famous *Qui Pro Quo* cabaret. There was also Wiera Gran—referred to in interwar Warsaw as "Greta Garbo née Grinberg"—probably the brightest young star of popular cabaret singing. The best known of all Polish-language actors was undoubtedly Michał Znicz—a star of countless interwar films. Andrzej Włast was an important figure, the champion of Polish low-brow entertainment and mass culture, "the king of kitsch," and an author of hundreds of songs sung in cabarets and revues both in Poland and in Europe. Among his greatest hits were: *Czy pani mieszka sama?* (pol. Do you live alone, madam?), *On nie powróci już, szkoda Twoich łez* (pol. He is not coming back, don't waste your tears), *Bo ja się boję sama spać* (pol. Because I am afraid to sleep alone), and, very popular in the ghetto, *Tango Milonga* (The tango of fantasies and dreams). These artists grouped themselves around five theaters functioning in the ghetto. Two of these theaters featured performances in Yiddish—*Nowy Azazel* (pol. New Azazel) and *Eldorado*; the other three—*Na Pięterku, Nowy Teatr Kameralny,* and Femina—in Polish.[20]

The first theater to start functioning in the ghetto was *Eldorado*, which opened in December 1940 with a similar aim as the official revue theaters on the "Aryan" side.[21] The theater specialized in the popular genre of "pseudo-folk" operetta and comedies. The author whose works were most often staged in *Eldorado* was Josef Lateiner, an extremely prolific Yiddish playwright, described as "synonymous with vulgar dramatic baked goods of uncertain freshness."[22] In keeping with the Yiddish theater tradition, *Eldorado* was very much a family business—the director of the venue was Karl Cymbalist, while his wife Regina Cukier was its biggest star. The second Yiddish-language theater in the ghetto, *Nowy Azazel*, which opened in May 1941 at 72 Nowolipie Street, had a much more ambitious character. Its name linked it to *Azazel*, a fashionable interwar Jewish literary cabaret. The quality of entertainment in *Nowy Azazel* was guaranteed by those involved in its creation. The director of the theater was Chaim Sandler, a prominent interwar theater personality. The company included his wife, actress Chana Lewin; their daughter Róża Sandlerowa; and her husband Yitzhak Salve. The brightest star of the theater was, however, undoubtedly Ajzyk Samberg, the most prominent actor in Jewish theater. The theater started ambitiously with Sholem Ash's *Got fun Nekome* (yid. The God of Vengeance) and later Ansky's *Der Dybbuk*. These were followed, however, by plays by Lateiner and others from a repertoire similar to that offered by *Eldorado*. Even classics, such as Moliere's *The Miser*, were reworked beyond recognition, usually turned into musicals, and had very little artistic value.

Similarly to the Yiddish theaters, Polish-language theaters had to find a balance between the ambitions of their creators and the demands of the wartime audience. The largest theater in the ghetto, the 800-seat Femina, directed by Jerzy Jurandot, was intended as a continuation of interwar literary cabarets and revues, showing sketch shows based on contemporary issues and pre-war comedies re-written to contain clear allusions to the current situation. The second venue, *Na Pięterku*, was a short-lived theater that showed revues built around its brightest star, Michał Znicz. Andrzej Marek's *Nowy Teatr Kameralny*, the only ambitious dramatic theater in the Warsaw Ghetto, was an extension of its author's mission to bring Yiddish classics to a Polish-speaking audience, and it showed mainly new versions of plays successfully staged by Marek before the war.

At first sight, it might seem that Polish-language theater would have a natural advantage over other types of ghetto entertainment, as it was created by well-known, experienced artists, and supported and frequented by the well-off assimilated community, including the most important personalities of the ghetto life. However, an interesting testimony to the contrary came from a review of social life in the ghetto complied for the *Oyneg Shabes* by Stanisław Różycki. According to Różycki:

> Jewish theaters have the same playbill, lodgings and actors; they are allowed to perform almost all past Jewish authors, censorship is more liberal in their case. Two Polish theaters face much greater difficulties. Aside from a few professional actors, they have only amateurs. Secondly, they have difficulties with repertoire, because they need to find plays written, or at least re-written by Jewish authors. Thirdly, the audience member in a Polish theater is much more difficult to satisfy, because he has his requirements both as a Jew and as a Pole. He has higher aspirations as usually he is a member of intelligentsia. Finally, censorship has much stricter control over Polish theater.[23]

In order to break even financially, the Polish-language theaters also performed plays aimed at the mass audience. The level of the vast majority of them did not differ much from those shown in the Yiddish venues. Even at their lowest, however, the comedies performed in the ghetto cannot be compared to the semi-pornographic, vulgar performances that ruled in the official German-licensed theater on the "Aryan" side of Warsaw.

Unlike Polish- and Yiddish-language artists and activists, those who performed in Hebrew never managed to gain a substantial following in the ghetto.[24] Despite successfully organizing various small-scale events, *Tkumah* (heb. Rebirth), an organization that coordinated Hebrew-language culture in the quarter, did not manage to achieve the goal of opening a permanent Hebrew-language theater. In June 1941 *Gazeta Żydowska*, which considered the introduction of such a theater, wrote about widespread support in the ghetto for "a Hebrew artistic institution which would promote a Palestinian atmosphere."[25]

However, this never came into being. Nonetheless, in 1942 *Tkumah* did succeed in setting up a dramatic studio, which was directed by poet Yitzhak Katzenelson.

As was the case with theater, the musical life of the ghetto began with a number of small musical performances and concerts organized by the house committees. In the early days of the ghetto, on November 25, 1940, the first performance of *Żydowska Orkiestra Symfoniczna* (ŻOS, pol. Jewish Symphonic Orchestra) took place in the hall of Femina Theater. ŻOS employed about seventy musicians, among them many former members of prestigious Polish and foreign orchestras, including three finalists of the famous *Chopin Piano Competition*—Leon Boruński, Róża Etkinowa, and Leopold Muzner. Describing the creation of the orchestra, Marcel Reich, music critic for *Gazeta Żydowska*, noted that the greatest problem was finding wind instrument players: "Suitable candidates were sought by means of advertisements in the only newspaper in the ghetto and on noticeboards. Trumpeters, trombonists, clarinetists and percussion players from jazz bands and dance orchestras responded. It soon turned out that, even though they had never played in a symphony orchestra, they could sight-read Schubert or Tchaikovsky perfectly."[26] The orchestra was conducted by Marian Neuteich, Adam Furmański, Israel Hamerman, and Szymon Pullman.

Similarly to theater, the functioning of the orchestra can be read as proof of a lack of interest on the part of the Nazi administration in the community affairs of the ghetto. The orchestra openly performed music by non-Jewish musicians and such concerts were thoroughly described in *Gazeta Żydowska*. It was only in April 1942 that German authorities suspended the orchestra for two months for playing "Aryan" composers.[27] According to Czerniaków, Heinz Auerswald, *Kommissar für den jüdischen Wohnbezirk* (ger. Commissioner for the Jewish Residential District), learned about the suspension from *Gazeta Żydowska*.[28] As already shown, however, information about the orchestra's repertoire appeared regularly in *Gazeta* from late 1940.

Aside from ŻOS there were countless other small groups performing in the ghetto. Chamber concerts, often arranged in thematic cycles, were organized in *Gospoda Artystów* (pol. Artists' Inn).[29] Numerous choirs, both for children and adults, were set up. The most famous of them, the *Shir* choir, consisted of eighty mainly working-class members who used to sing together before the war.[30] An interesting and artistically important undertaking in the ghetto was the *Orkiestra Służby Porządkowej* (pol. Order Service Orchestra) conducted by Szymon Kataszek. The orchestra was generally considered to perform at a very high level. Among its forty members, alongside genuine policemen, were over a dozen of the best jazz musicians who were attracted into it by an offer of work in the police on especially good conditions. The first concert that took place in Femina was attended by *Untersturmführer* Karl Brand and *Obersturmführer* Gerhard Mende from the Gestapo, and subsequent concerts that took place in café gardens proved extremely popular as tickets sold out a week in advance.[31]

Cafés played an important part in the entertainment life of the ghetto. In her excellent study of entertainment life in the ghetto, Barbara Engelking gathered over ninety addresses of cafés and nightclubs that existed at one point or another in the closed quarter.[32] Cafés were said to be functioning in "every second house" on Leszno Street,[33] as well as other exclusive streets of the ghetto: Chłodna, Nowolipki, and Sienna. Performances were organized in every usable space: offices, shops, or even private apartments, and many operated on a level that was not far from pre-war standards. Describing one such venue, café *Bajka* (pol. Fairy Tale), Mary Berg wrote: "The tables are outside and there is a little grass and two trees. The café covers the site of a completely bombed-out house. To one side stands a wall with burned window openings. This is an excellent backdrop." Nearby *Bajka* was a "beach"—a few deck chairs that could be rented for two złoty a day. Others wrote about cafés organized on roofs of apartment buildings or described a dusty ghetto courtyard transformed into a café "with grass, flowers, and even a small fountain."[34] Cafés in the ghetto were not uniform. The infamous hotel *Britania* and nightclub *Arizona* located at 18 Nowolipie Street were nothing more than thinly disguised brothels owned by members of the Thirteen. General opinion held that they served Jewish Gestapo collaborators, smugglers, and

Polish policemen.[35] *Café Hirszfeld* at Sienna was a well-known expensive restaurant and a meeting place of both new-rich smugglers as well as underground fighters. *Kawiarnia Literacka* (pol. Literary Café) at Rymarska on the other hand advertised itself as a "rendez-vous of Jewish intelligentsia" and among its regulars were many from the ghetto's intellectual elite.[36] The magnet that attracted audiences to the cafés was a performance by famous theater actors. Regina Cukier regularly appeared in *Bon Apetit*[37] and Ajzyk Samberg in *Odeon*.[38] The very popular singer Wiera Gran, who in March 1941 reached the Warsaw ghetto after spending the beginning of the occupation in Lvov, remembered being swamped by work offers from popular cafés and restaurants on her return.[39]

A clear void in the landscape of ghetto entertainment was the absence of cinemas, which on the "Aryan" side, despite constant calls for boycotts from the underground organizations, remained filled with people seeking entertainment in the form of cheap comedies, spy thrillers, or war movies.[40] Even though as late as February 1940, *Druga Młodość* (pol. Second Youth), a film starring Michał Znicz, was shown in official cinemas and was advertised as "entertainment for Jews and Poles,"[41] there were no cinemas operating in the ghetto at the moment of its enclosure. Adam Czerniaków noted filing for permission to open a cinema before the enclosure of the ghetto, on July 1, 1940. Even though in May 1941 *Gazeta Żydowska* published an enthusiastic note that the Judenrat had obtained permission to open two cinemas, and that the organization of this should not cause many problems,[42] they were never opened and the cinema halls were transformed into refugee hostels. Instead of the long-awaited cinema, a stereoscope was set up in the quarter in April 1941. Its owners advertised it in *Gazeta* as "the whole world in pictures," and during its brief existence it showed views from "Italy, Egypt, Japan and other places."[43] Plans for the opening of a cinema, a sign of the return of the semblance of normality to ghetto life, were revisited after the Aktion. One of the ghetto inhabitants wrote in December 1942: "The atmosphere in the ghetto improved. People said that those Jews who are left after the action will not be sent way. Apparently we were visited by some Swiss commission which said that what we lack is a cinema—so a cinema will be opened."[44] Once again, however, this hope never turned into reality.

Entertainment in the ghetto was undoubtedly a profitable business. The theaters offered altogether 4,000 seats, and were almost constantly filled to at least eighty percent capacity. The majority of cafés had 100–180 guests per evening, with the biggest (*L'Ours*, *Splendid*, *Fontanna*) attracting up to 200–250 an evening. Yet even the most popular actors were making no more than 600–700 złoty per month—a wage which allowed for only the lowest level of existence. Michał Znicz, by far the highest earning actor, whose appearance in a show guaranteed sold-out tickets, was paid 1,000 złoty per month.[45] The financial situation of musicians was even worse. In order to survive and support their families, artists had to take every possible manner of extra employment, including performing in cafés and private functions, usually in the houses of smugglers and collaborators. To secure their jobs they were prepared to work for next to nothing. According to a report from the Ringelblum Archive, artists were playing "merely for what customers and guests shove into their hands; otherwise, they go hungry, without a bit of bread."[46] Even Marysia Ajzensztadt, the so-called nightingale of the ghetto, had to accept all offers of employment, despite being the best-known and highest-paid star of the ghetto's musical world. According to *Gazeta*, Marysia could be heard "in smoky cafés, the large halls of Femina and Melody Palace, in courtyard gardens and private apartments."[47] She performed so often that in February 1942 *Gazeta* noted that "her voice is not as fresh as it used to be, which must be the result of its over-exploitation."[48]

The working conditions of performers were appalling. Due to constant electricity cuts all major venues other than *Nowy Azazel* and Melody Palace were never adequately heated or lit. Turkow described Femina as being "freezing cold," with "decollated actresses, the orchestra and the audience all trembling with cold."[49] Due to a lack of space, rehearsals were conducted in private apartments or in public kitchens. The repertoire of the orchestra was limited to certain pieces, the musical scores of which could be smuggled into the ghetto. These were hand copied at night by the musicians themselves and by the supporters of the orchestra. Yet, the bad light of carbide lamps meant that musicians often could not read the notes and sometimes performances had to be stopped halfway through. It should be underlined that those individuals described above were probably the luckiest of those artists who found themselves in the ghetto. Only those with the best-known names could think of being hired by a café or theater—the rest had to make a living by giving lessons or performing on the streets.

Cultural life in the Warsaw Ghetto was in no way confined to officially organized entertainment. For example, as most members of the assimilated intelligentsia who had to move into the ghetto were not able to take many books with them, the illegal exchange of books flourished. According to Ringelblum, libraries of Jewish and Polish books were to be found in dozens of courtyards.[50] In the spring of 1941 bookstores and lending libraries were again functioning legally. In March 1942 *Gazeta* proudly announced the opening of twenty-four libraries and eighteen bookstores "providing readers with books in Polish, Yiddish and Hebrew."[51] Yet, as the books in the libraries came mainly from private donations, the collections were at best haphazard. A young employee of a ghetto library commented: "We are completing Proust now. If someone has a spark for being a collector, he should open himself a library in the ghetto."[52]

Cultural undertakings organized for the benefit of children were a special branch of artistic life, on the border of entertainment, education, and social help. These were organized mainly by Centos and held in children's houses, children's corners, schools, and house committees. For example, the stage version of the Disney cartoon *Snow White* was performed in the infamously poverty-stricken refugee point at 19 Leszno Street, as well as in Café Sztuka and in a well-off house committee at Chłodna Street. Janina David, who performed at Chłodna wrote: "My memories of the Disney film came flooding back as I rehearsed the songs, and I was immensely happy. . . . We played only a few scenes, using the songs from the film. The rest of the performance, which went on for over two hours, was filled by a variety of numbers—songs, dances, comedy sketches. . . . The question of my dress occupied Mother and the young women for quite some time. I wanted it to be as similar to Disney's heroine as possible." The content of the performance at the refugee point or at Sztuka is not known. The possibility cannot be ruled out, however, that these performances were based on the standard fairy tale of *Snow White* and only referred to as "Disney's" in order to appease the censorship with regard to the ban on performing plays by non-Jewish writers.[53] A specific aspect of cultural work in the ghetto was the unprecedented involvement in children's work of the top practitioners from different fields of arts and culture. According to *Gazeta* the creation of Centos choirs involved the best-known Jewish conductors and composers.[54] Artist Gela Sekstein conducted art classes for children and created their costumes.[55] In *Nowy Teatr Kameralny*, children's entertainment was coordinated by a committee headed by Andrzej Marek. Ghetto artists involved in this work also utilized their colleagues from the "Aryan" side, as costumes and sets for the plays were smuggled into the ghetto from the National Theater in Warsaw.[56] Historian Frieda Aaron, who as a child was involved in such activities in the ghetto, underlined the impact that the presence of famous actors had on her and her peers:

> There were two Polish-Jewish actors, Irena Oberska and Michał Znicz (both ultimately killed), whose fame, I was told in the ghetto, had been well established on the Polish stage and screen before the war. I am not sure whether or not they were actually involved in directing any of the children's theaters, but I remember that they attended our performances, encouraging us all and assuring some, including me, that because of our talent they would, after the war, train us to become famous actors. Such assurances were a gift of hope, a promise not only of a future but also of normalcy . . . of happiness. These promises were a form of tentative redemption that sometimes managed to assuage the horror and the anguish.[57]

The showcases of children's work were also a significant method of fundraising. One such performance, *The Magic Flute,* was performed in Femina by an ensemble of sixty children. According to *Gazeta,* the performance was divided into three parts: *Awakening of Spring,*

Fantasy of the Midsummer Night, and *In the Light of the Sun*. These were followed by the "solo and ensemble dance divertissement—Tyrolean, Ukrainian, Russian and other dances."[58] To increase their fundraising potential, patronage over the shows was often assumed by important personalities in the ghetto—especially active were Felicja Czerniaków, wife of the chairman of the Judenrat, and Miriam Gancwajch, wife of the head of the Thirteen.

Teenagers also actively participated in the ghetto's cultural life. In November 1940 the Youth Entertainment Section was formed, the aim of which was to "introduce to the community high quality cultural materials through, for example, Peretz academies or classical music concerts."[59] The majority of youth performances were organized within house committees; larger events were often undertaken in cooperation with professional artists.[60]

Polish-Language Culture in the Ghetto

Despite the continuous effort of the Yiddish-speaking intelligentsia and political activists, Polish was undoubtedly the principal language of cultural life in the Warsaw Ghetto. Reading and exchange of the classics of Polish literature thrived in the ghetto, while performances of popular Polish musical pieces formed an important part of the musical evenings in the house committees. It seems clear that Polish literature and art provided a semblance of pre-war normality not only for the acculturated and assimilated community, but also for many others among the ghetto inhabitants, who were fully versed in Polish culture and saw it as their own, notwithstanding their ideological affiliation.

Simultaneously, a new Polish-language culture was being formed in the Warsaw Ghetto. It can be divided into two basic types, both of which were present in interwar Poland. The first, closely connected to the assimilated community, was based around artists of Jewish origin who before the war were completely integrated into the Polish artistic scene. They created what can be seen a distinctly Polish rather than Jewish culture.[61] The second type was a result of the acculturation of Polish Jewry and the growing phenomenon of expressing Jewish cultural, and indeed often national, identity, in Polish.

The most prominent members of the first group were the scions of the Polish interwar literary scene—Antoni Słonimski, Julian Tuwim, Józef Wittlin, Marian Hemar, and Bruno Schulz. Their mouthpiece was the most prestigious Polish literary periodical, *Wiadomości Literackie* (pol. Literary News), edited by Mieczysław Grydzewski. In articles such as Słonimski's *O drażliwości Żydow* (pol. On Jewish Oversensitivity), *Wiadomości* constantly criticized the lack of assimilation and cultural backwardness of the traditional Jewish community, causing outrage among the nationalistically oriented Jewish press and accusations of Jewish anti-Semitism. At the same time *Wiadomości* remained under constant attack from Polish anti-Semites, who accused them of "Jewifying" Polish culture. Discussing the group based around *Wiadomości*, Aleksander Hertz wrote: "They were of Jewish origin and constituted the contribution Polish Jewry made to Polish culture, but they neither considered themselves Jews nor could they be so considered. . . . If some of these people dealt with Jewish subjects, they viewed them from a Polish point of view, at best infusing them with greater warmth."[62] The issue of whether one could actually remain "a Pole of Jewish origin" within the often anti-Semitic atmosphere of the late 1930s is of course a matter of some debate. Yet, as Chone Shmeruk claimed, many of those writers were at that point not pushed into sporadic expressions of Jewish self-identification by their own free will, but rather "by hostile forces over which they had no control."[63] Notwithstanding the controversies over their stance on the issue of Jewish identity, by the power of their sheer talent alone this group of writers was considered across the ideological spectrum to be heroes of popular imagination, both in pre-war Warsaw and in the ghetto.

None of the great poets of Jewish origin found themselves in the ghetto, as the majority of them managed to leave Poland. Słonimski spent the war in England; Tuwim first went to Paris, then Rio de Janeiro and New York; Grydzewski went to London; Wittlin went to France and then later the United States. Their work did, however, find its way into the closed quarter. Such was the case of "Kwiaty Polskie" (pol. Polish Flowers), an epic poem written by Tuwim in New York, which was performed at countless unofficial events both in the ghetto and on the "Aryan" side. In a letter to a friend on the other side of the wall, Hala, a teenager from an assimilated family wrote: "Have you read a poem sent by Tuwim from America entitled *Polish Flowers*? It has been making rounds here for a few weeks already. If you don't know it I will send you a copy for your own use and to distribute around." She later added: "Yesterday we arranged a Tuwim evening. About 10 people took part and we brought back Tuwim's poems—from the earliest to the most recent ones. *Flowers* was the crowning of everything. It is an absolutely amazing poem."[64] The poems of another member of the *Wiadomości* group, Antoni Słonimski, also reached the ghetto. According to an assimilated ghetto inhabitant, his poems were "printed in underground newspapers, or scribbled on slips of paper" and they became "little flashes of light among the gloom of occupation."[65]

In the ghetto, the group with the closest connection to *Wiadomości Literackie* was theater makers, especially those connected to the milieu of interwar literary cabarets. One of the ghetto inhabitants wrote: "We knew them well from the pre-war times, read their poems in the best literary magazines, saw their names on playbills in the best theaters, hummed hit songs written by them. Never before did it cross our mind that we will be able to watch them, and so many of them. We didn't even know they were Jewish."[66] The group behind the interwar literary cabarets gathered mainly around the Femina Theater, which opened in June 1941 at 35 Leszno Street. The literary and artistic director of Femina was Jerzy Jurandot, a young and very talented songwriter, who before the war directed popular cabarets such as *Cyrulik Warszawski* (pol. The Barber of Warsaw) and *Małe Qui pro Quo* (pol. Small Qui pro Quo). The musical director and head of the orchestra was Iwo Wesby, a composer of many songs and the pre-war artistic director of the famous Syrena-Electro record company. Among the ensemble were singer Helena Ostrowska, theater and film actors Edmund Minowicz and Zygmunt Regro, and dancer Stefania Grodzieńska. Between June 20, 1941, and June 26, 1942, the theater showed fourteen different plays. Femina specialized in revues—among those performed were *Batalion Humour* (pol. Humor Battalion); *Szafa Gra* (pol. The Cupboard Plays); *Od Gminy do Feminy* (pol. From the Council to Femina); *Jarmark Śmiechu* (pol.

Market of the Laughter); and *Tylko Dla Dorosłych* (pol. Adults Only). It also put on comedies—Marian Hemar's *Jim i Jill* (pol. Jim and Jill); *Pan Hrabia to ja!* (pol. The Lord is I); and *Dziewczę do Wszystkiego* (pol. A Girl for Everything). Operettas which could be seen in Femina included Emerich Kalaman's *The Csardas Princess* and *The Bayadere*, and Leo Fall's *The Rose of Stamboul*. In March 1942 Jonas Turkow directed the first dramatic piece to be shown in Femina—Ladislaus Fodor's *Matura* (pol. Graduation), starring his wife Diana Blumenfeld. In June 1942 Edmund Minowicz put on a crime thriller *Sprawa przy drzwiach zamkniętych* (pol. Behind Closed Doors) by B. Weiler—the last play to be performed in Femina.

The revues produced by Femina consisted mainly of originally written or reworked texts that contained satire directed at social relations in the ghetto. In 1941 the theater put on a revue entitled *Od Gminy do Feminy* (pol. From the Council to Femina), the content of which was discussed in *Gazeta Żydowska*. According to *Gazeta*, the revue was a nice and pleasant combination, without unnecessary excess. It consisted of pre-war cabaret texts written by Tuwim as well more contemporary ones by Jerzy "Jerry" Ryba and Jurandot. The revue opened with Jurandot's *Yiddishe Kinder* (yid. Jewish Children)—a satirical opera about a love triangle between beautiful Rachel, a member of the Order Service, and a baker (a "magnate of recent times"). After that, on stage a ballet ensemble appeared with a piece entitled "Melody of the Street" and consisting of Argentinean, Spanish, and Jewish dances. This was followed by a musical piece "When You Dance Tango" as well as a comic duo "in the style of Laurel and Hardy, referring to contemporary issues." The show finished with a number entitled "Sweeten Up Your Life," at the end of which actors threw sweets into the audience.[67]

Undoubtedly, the biggest social event in Femina was the opening night of *Miłość szuka mieszkania* (pol. Love Seeks a Lodging), the first comedy written and publicly performed in the ghetto.[68] It opened on October 29, 1941, and was an instant success, especially with the assimilated audience.[69] The play was written by Jurandot and the cast included the best Polish-language actors from the quarter. It was an adaptation of the 1927 play *Kvadratura Kruga* (rus. Squaring the Circle), by Russian playwright Walentin Kataev, the background of which was the housing shortage of 1920s Moscow. *Miłość szuka mieszkania* tells a story of two couples, who due to lack of lodging in the ghetto are forced to move into one room. After a lot of comical complications the couples swap partners. The main attraction of the play was not so much the fairly simple and predictable plot but the number of in-jokes about the reality of ghetto life. The jokes in the play, as in other revues shown in the theater, were based on everyday experiences—illegal trade, smuggling, and bribery of the Jewish Council members. Its characters used popular ghetto sayings such as *Szafa Gra* (pol. the cupboard plays), *Ale Glaych* (yid. all equal), or *Gib di bone* (yid. give the ration card). They were members of the assimilated intelligentsia, people whom the audience of Femina could identify with, and the play gives a good insight into the living condition of fairly well-off middle classes in the ghetto. They may live in a cramped room, yet their living circumstances cannot be compared to the majority of the ghetto. Poverty in *Miłość szuka mieszkania* becomes a source of humor. The characters eat "stuffed trout made of horse meat" and "apple sauce from real beetroot." Though the only honeymoon trip that they can have is on the ghetto tram and they suffer the confiscation of their fur coats, they still go from time to time to a café at Leszno. The butt of many jokes is an overzealous house committee activist, who unsuccessfully tries to teach the main characters Yiddish. Many of the jokes were clearly targeted at the regular consumers of the ghetto's cultural life. The couples' neighbor was Iwo Wesby, the musical director of Femina. Stefcia, played by Stefania Grodzieńska, sings hits from *The Rose of Stamboul*, a play in which Grodzieńska starred at Femina a few months earlier.

Another group of assimilated Jews, gathered around the film star Michał Znicz, created the theater *Na Pięterku*, which functioned between April 1941 and July 1941 at 29 Nowolipki Street. On the day of its opening *Gazeta Żydowska* described it as "created by a group of Jewish actors of former Polish stages. The program is mixed, performed in Polish and Yiddish, interlinked with humor, singing and dancing."[70] During its brief existence, the theater managed to present three revues, opening consequently in April, May, and June 1941. The first one was entitled *Wiosna idzie* (pol. Spring Is Coming), with *Znicz na pięterku* (pol. Znicz on the Upper Floor) and *Szaleństwo na pięterku* (pol. Craziness on the Upper Floor) following. The first revue was performed both in Polish and Yiddish and the last two in Polish.

The second and much more numerous group of those involved in Polish-language culture in the ghetto was based around artists who linked the Polish language to Jewish national identity.[71] Through their work, Polish became a language of Jewish culture and literature, no longer serving only the interests of integration or emancipation. The reaction of the assimilated community to this artistic circle was often as harsh and disapproving as the anti-Semitic attacks of the nationalistic Poles. The group was also attacked by the Jewish national activists. Jonas Turkow accused them, for example, of "pulling Jewish audiences away from the 'unclean' Yiddish language," of "strengthening assimilation," and of actions leading to the collapse of Yiddish theater.[72] Even though the Polish-Jewish artists mainly expressed themselves through the medium of poetry, and to a lesser extent through prose, their most famous representative in the ghetto was a theater maker—Andrzej Marek. Between 1925 and 1929 Marek produced a number of Yiddish plays in Polish, directing them at Poles and Polish-speaking Jews. Among his most famous productions were *Der Dybbuk*, Sholem Ash's *Got fun nekome* (yid. The God of Revenge), and Jacob Gordin's *Mirele Efros*. The plays were critically acclaimed, yet their meaning went far beyond artistic success. As Michael Steinlauf noted, "In the highly charged national atmosphere of interwar Poland, to produce Jewish plays on the Polish stage was much more than an artistic event; it was to stride unavoidably into the political arena."[73] It was Marek's productions that in 1929 led to the first widespread and highly publicized discussions within the Jewish intelligentsia on the relations between Polish and Jewish culture and the role of the Polish language in expressing Jewish national identity. After entering the ghetto, Marek not only continued his mission of bringing Yiddish culture to Polish-speaking audiences but also managed to obtain his first permanent theater. *Nowy Teatr Kameralny* (NKT, pol. New Chamber Theater), which opened in July 1941, with Marek as the manager and artistic director, was located in the building of the closed-down church of St. Augustine at 52 Nowolipki Street. The brightest star of NTK was Michał Znicz, who moved there together with the rest of the ensemble after the closure of *Na Pięterku*. The first play shown in *Nowy Teatr Kameralny* was *Mirele Efros*—a great classic of Yiddish theater that Marek very successfully and famously produced in 1929, with Wanda Siemaszkowa, a star of Polish theater, taking the lead role. Later on NTK retained its high level, even though for financial reasons high quality drama had to be interwoven with lighter comedies, a genre for which Michał Znicz was particularly renowned and therefore bound to attract crowds. The theater performed *Moje żony mnie zdradzają, przygody rogacza w trzech aktach* (pol. My Wives Are Cheating on Me, the Adventures of a Cuckold in Three Acts); Marian Hemar's *Skarb pod latarnią* (pol. The Treasure under the Lamppost); James Montgomery's *Ready Money*; and Stefan Pollatschek's *Dr. Berghof Receives from Two until Four*. On March 17, 1942, NTK showed *Pieśniarze getta* (pol. Singers of the Ghetto), which became one of the main events in the cultural calendar of the ghetto. The play was written by Marek himself in 1902 and became a great success, having been performed in theaters in Europe and America. Later on, NTK returned to plays directed at a more general audience by showing *End of the Marriage*, again by Stefan Pollatschek, and later *The Kiss Before the Mirror*, directed by Turkow. The last play rehearsed at NTK was Leo Blum's *Road to Happiness*. The play was scheduled to open on July 22, 1942, was directed by Turkow, and had a starring role for Diana Blumenfeld.

Aside from Andrzej Marek, most of the Polish-Jewish writers did not achieve fame before the war. In the ghetto, they were unable to make a living purely from their trade and shared the fate of the rest of the working intelligentsia.[74] This, however, does not mean that they gave up writing. Janusz Korczak, as we already know, continued writing his diary when employed as the head of the ghetto orphanage. Another pre-war writer, Henryka Łazowert, who found employment in the propaganda department of the Jewish Self-Help, encapsulated her wartime experience in *Ballada o paczce* (pol. Ballad of the Parcel), sung in the ghetto cafés by Diana Blumenfeld. The ballad told the story of a starving family from Krochmalna Street writing letters begging their relatives for help. In the finale of the song, the postman carrying a food parcel reaches Krochmalna just as the body of the grandmother who initiated the writing of letters is being taken out of the house.[75] *Ballada o paczce*, performed in Polish-language shows, provided the assimilated audience with a picture of ghetto life that was very different from that shown in *Miłość szuka mieszkania* and Femina's satires. Its aim was not to provide escapism but to remind them what was taking place just one step outside the walls of the theater or café.

Café Sztuka

At first sight, Café Sztuka was no different than over a hundred other cafés that operated in the Warsaw Ghetto. Like most entertainment establishments it was located at Leszno, the thoroughfare of the ghetto, known as the "Broadway of the Jewish Quarter." It took over the site of Café Gertner—a few rather cramped rooms on the ground floor level of an apartment block at 12 Leszno Street. Sztuka also had a "garden"—a few fenced-off square meters of pavement adorned by some flowerpots. Like many others, the café offered a daily entertainment program, performed by well-known pre-war artists and widely advertised in *Gazeta Żydowska*. And just like other cafés in the ghetto, Sztuka had a rather unclear and murky system of ownership, with a number of co-owners, most of them with links to the Gestapo or the Judenrat. According to Turkow, among the owners were "Gurewicz from the movie business, Mrs Waintroub who had links with Germans, and the convert Czarnecki who was in charge of the transport bureau in the Jewish council."[76] Czarnecki's wife was one of the closest friends of the ghetto's "first lady," Felicja Czerniaków,[77] and Beniamin Zabłudowski, a member of the Judenrat, was a sleeping partner whose name was meant to protect the café from the Gestapo.[78]

Of all the cafés in the ghetto, it was Sztuka which was the most passionately discussed. It represented for some a symbol of the evils of assimilation, of the wealth and alienation of the Polish-Jewish intelligentsia, yet others saw it as the center of spiritual resistance. It is not difficult to see why. "The café was my home, not only my home but our home," Zbigniew Jankowski, one of its co-owners, testified after the war.[79] His testimony and that of others paint a picture of an establishment run by a close circle of friends, for a similarly exclusive close circle of friends, who before the war were involved in creating Warsaw's blossoming Polish-language light entertainment scene. One of the biggest stars of the ghetto, Wiera Gran, claimed in her memoirs that out of all jobs offered to her when she moved into the closed quarter, she chose the one in Sztuka because she wanted above all to work with her pre-war acquaintances.[80] And, indeed, according to witnesses, she was on first-name terms with most of the owners of the café and just like them she would spend all day in Sztuka, and later on even live in rooms attached to the café. The picture of an exclusive and perhaps slightly snobbish group was completed by the waitresses, who were heroines of the popular imagination. "Not everyone could be lucky enough to be a waitress in Sztuka," wrote one of the diarists, and others mirrored his words.[81] Waitresses in Sztuka were "former owners of large apartments, spoiled only daughters whose parents were finding times hard and money short, and career women without a career."[82] According to others, they were daughters of the highest-ranking Judenrat officials and were on a first-name basis with the customers.[83] In this aspect, Sztuka was similar to fashionable cafés on the "Aryan" side of Warsaw, where establishments such as *U Aktorek* (pol. At the Actresses) employed society ladies and famous stage artists as waitresses. Their presence was meant to attract attention to the cafés as well as bring in their friends and admirers.

So what sort of audience was attracted by Sztuka? Stanisław Różycki, in his report on the ghetto's entertainment life, gives a scathing description of the café's regulars:

> Sztuka. This is where *mekhes* rule, educated bourgeoisie, the "high life" of the ghetto. You can see that also before the war they were rich and they look with disdain at newly rich smugglers. The atmosphere

> of snobbery, aristocratic posing, vanity and fake elegance is swamping the room. . . . They remain fashionable, detach themselves from the "masses," they gather around Sztuka, which they cultivate with a passion similar to that from Ziemiańska. They are rather well-read, they used to read *Wiadomości Literackie*, they went to *Qui-Pro-Quo* or *Cyrulik*, they knew Tuwim, Słonimski, Hemar. There is no Jewish language or Jewish song here. . . . They have no links with the masses of the ghetto, they don't want to know the Jewry, they do after all go to church every Sunday, they hate the street, they despise the fact that they have to share a common fate with "the dirty Jews" . . . after all, aristocracy in France and Russia also went through difficult times. So their martyrdom is sacred too.[84]

The key word in Różycki's report is undoubtedly *Ziemiańska*—a name constantly brought up when referring to Sztuka, both by its critics and regular customers. Ziemiańska (also known as *Mała Ziemiańska*, due to its small size) was set up in 1918 at Mazowiecka Street and was the social nucleus for the interwar Warsaw intelligentsia. It was the favorite and most fashionable meeting place of writers, artists, and professors of the nearby Warsaw University. Among the regulars were the biggest stars of Warsaw's artistic life, including Tuwim and Słonimski. According to a popular saying, being invited to a table of the regulars in the café signified artistic success.

For regulars of Sztuka the association with the fashionable interwar scene undoubtedly enforced a degree of distance between themselves and the reality of the ghetto street. It did not necessarily matter whether they had actually belonged to the "scene" before the war, or rather only aspired to. A regular commented: "Obviously, coffee served here is not real, but if you really don't want to pay attention to such imperfections, you can feel like you used to at Ziemiańska."[85] Even if Tuwim, Hemar, and Słonimski were indeed gone, Sztuka could still provide its guests with the highest level of entertainment. Its stage hosted the likes of Diana Blumenfeld, Marysia Ajzensztadt, Władysław Szpilman, and Artur Goldfeder—the best talent in the ghetto. Undoubtedly, in the initial stages of the café's operation, its greatest attraction was Wiera Gran. Gran performed at Sztuka the greatest pre-war hits of literary cabarets, cafés, and theater revues—*The Three Letters*, *A Collection of Waltzes*, and *Madame Bovary*. According to one witness of her performances, "She sang them in her low husky voice with a sentimental yearning look on her face." The same person later wrote: "Her songs were about unrequited love, about trees murmuring in the wind to the rhythm of the waltz, about heroic sailors from the Albatross. The people who came there wanted to hear such songs; they wanted to close their eyes and to dream they were in pre-war *Adria* or in *Paradise*, and that the greatest problems facing them now were these frustrated, unhappy loves."[86] The most popular of Gran's songs in the ghetto was *Jej pierwszy bal* (pol. Her First Ball)—a song with lyrics by Władysław Szlengel and music written by Szpilman, based on a popular 1937 movie *Un carnet de bal*. The musical composition of "Her First Ball," the lyrics of which evolved around memories of past suitors, was very elaborate and included rumba, Viennese waltz, and Tahitian melodies, ending in a Chopin Mazurka. The sentimental songs sung by Gran brought crowds to Sztuka, including, in the first months after the closure of the ghetto, many guests from the other side of the wall. It seems clear that in the case of Sztuka, the escapism potential, based both on class and national identity factors, was especially strong. However, how long could one sit in the garden of a café located just a few paces from the ghetto wall, and pretend that "there is no ghetto"? According to one of the regulars: "After the show finished, we did not want to leave Sztuka because we knew that on the street we would enter a different world, the world of reality."[87] There is no doubt, however, that as time passed this world of reality gradually permeated Sztuka.

The first visible sign was the changing clientele of the café. Even though, as Różycki claims, the intelligentsia guests may have looked with disdain at smugglers and Gestapo collaborators seated at tables next to them, it was these "shady individuals," as they were known by Sztuka's owners, who really paid for the running of the café.[88] Among the café regulars was the *Kommissar für den jüdischen Wohnbezirk* himself,[89] and so many smugglers that the Gestapo was thought to be particularly interested in getting artists from Sztuka to collaborate and provide them with information extorted from guests.[90] It was also in Sztuka that, as a general rule, drinking sessions of the Jewish Council took place.[91] The clientele had a growing impact on the repertoire of the café. According to Wiera Gran, in the spring of 1942 the morning performances of Marysia Ajzensztadt had to be given up, as the guests were more interested in doing business than listening to music.[92]

Despite the fact that Różycki saw Sztuka as a completely "dejudified" establishment, it is clear that the artists performing and writing for Sztuka did not constitute a uniform group and instead represented the whole spectrum of Polish-Jewish culture. This included the completely assimilated Wiera Gran, who never considered herself to be part of the Jewish community;[93] pianist Goldfeder, "beautiful like a prince in exile" and with a Christian wife on the "Aryan" side; and also Henryka Łazowert and Władysław Szlengel, who promoted Jewish national and cultural identity in their work. Together, these artists created the weekly satirical program *Żywy Dziennik* (pol. Live Journal), which became a trademark of Sztuka and was copied in numerous other cafés in the ghetto. *Żywy Dziennik* was first performed in the spring of 1942 and was immediately very successful. The show consisted of sketches written by, among others, singer Pola Braun; satirist Leonid Fokszański; and songwriters Andrzej Włast and Józef Lipski. The master of ceremonies and author of most texts was Władysław Szlengel. According to *Gazeta Żydowska*, the second edition of *Dziennik* began with a sketch *From Office to Office*, described as "a very entertaining journey through various offices of the quarter." This was followed by songs: "Everyone Will Fit in," "Hey You, Open the Courtyard Gate," and a sentimental hit from 1939, "The Three Letters." The program concluded with a sketch about a chairwoman of a house committee, and finally "Her First Ball" sung by Gran.[94] *Gazeta*, for obvious reasons, does not describe the content of sketches and songs hiding behind the innocent-sounding titles. A song *Wszyscy się zmieszczą* (pol. Everyone Will Fit In), judged by some as "much too risky,"[95] masquerading under the thin guise of a story of the many lovers of one woman bumping into each other in her bedroom, was in fact a clear allusion to the crowded narrow passage between Karmelicka and Żelazna Street where Gestapo men often attacked the passersby on their way to *Pawiak* prison. In the crowded streets, the panic caused by approaching German cars only multiplied the number of victims. Not all pieces forming part of *Żywy Dziennik* dealt with such tragic subjects, even though, as Mary Berg noted, "in Sztuka even the typhus epidemic itself is a subject of jokes."[96] The majority of sketches seemed to poke fun at the corruption and bureaucracy of the Judenrat, and the bribery among the policemen or the new rich. Another ghetto inhabitant, who as a teenager attended a performance of *Dziennik* on July 16, 1942, just six days before the liquidation of the ghetto, commented: "Bitter and sharp, the sketches and couplets mercilessly lashed corruption and indifference, hinted at the hollowness of our 'cozy stability,' brought laughter to the audience as well as tears."[97]

Despite the exclusiveness and snobbishness of Sztuka, the café can undoubtedly be seen as an example of how some of the pre-war social and cultural boundaries were demolished in the ghetto. For those who saw Sztuka as a nest of assimilation, it can be argued that it was here that many members of the assimilated community first empathized with the Jewish national and cultural identity and began to feel part of the wider ghetto community. As one of the members of the assimilated community noted in her memoirs, *Żywy Dziennik* "was performed in the clearest and most correct Polish—but the humor was truly Jewish."[98] From that point of view Sztuka can be therefore seen as a great example of heterogeneous Jewish culture, even if it was profoundly influenced by and identified itself with Polish cultural values.

The Attitude toward Polish-language Culture

The attitude toward Polish-language cultural life in the Warsaw Ghetto was determined by two factors. The first involved a moral judgment of the appropriateness of entertainment in the environment of the ghetto. The second was a consequence of what Chone Shmeruk describes as "the over ideological character of cultural realms in the Jewish languages—a direct continuation of interwar competition, often accompanied by a fanatical claim to exclusivity between different linguistic systems within the Polish Jewry."[99]

As has been shown, ghetto inhabitants developed a hierarchy of appropriateness of cultural events in the ghetto, although this was nowhere as clear-cut as that which existed on the "Aryan" side. There is no doubt that attendance of house committee events was generally accepted and approved of, mainly due to their charitable character. Similarly, classical musical concerts as well as events organized in the Judaic Library were not morally questionable.[100] In the case of theater, the rules were much more blurred, dependent on the venue and the content of the performances. In general, dramatic plays in Polish-language theater were viewed as being of a high cultural level and thus were more acceptable. At the lower end of the hierarchy were revues and shows in the cafés, which became a symbol of hedonism in times of starvation and were perceived to be enjoyed by the worst part of the community—the new rich, smugglers, collaborators, and their lovers. The picture of children starving in front of cafés and restaurants became one of the most ingrained images of the ghetto. Describing the most infamous of all ghetto nightspots, Marek Edelman recalled:

> Every evening after the curfew cars were coming to Britania hotel. Germans entertained themselves there every night. They had their women there and nobody knew if it was an entertainment spot or a brothel. The streets were empty. You could hear music. The Germans were probably dancing. Next to the garden children were standing, waiting for someone to throw a cigarette butt out of the window. Every morning a trolley picked up a few children's bodies from there.[101]

Those who did not approve of entertainment in the ghetto often described it in the same breath as the Judenrat and the Jewish Police, as a sign of the moral decline of the Warsaw Ghetto. One of the religious ghetto inhabitants, representative of the majority of the ghetto community, wrote: "One could see in restaurants the elite entertaining themselves. Their poor brothers were at the same time dying in front of the doors of these restaurants. True Sodom and Gomorah."[102]

Other critics, like Ringelblum, underlined the negative image that the extensive entertainment life of the ghetto created on the "Aryan" side of Warsaw. He complained that: "On the other side they say that Jews are having a good time in the ghetto—with dancing, and new night clubs being opened all the time."[103] A few months later the diarist repeated his concerns by quoting a saying apparently circulating on the "Aryan" side: "If you want to have a good time—go to the ghetto."[104]

An important factor in judging cultural activities in the ghetto was the link between entertainment and the underworld of the ghetto—the Thirteen, smugglers, and Gestapo collaborators, who, as Ringelblum wrote, were trying to save their soul through literature and art.[105] These people not only filled the venues but the most prominent among them—the likes of Gancwajch, Kohn, and Heller—were also known for organizing "receptions" for Jewish writers and artists. These receptions were attended by basically all of the biggest stars of the ghetto's cultural life, including not only performers but also writers such as Shaul Stupnicki or Yitzhak Katzenelson. The testimonies of people involved in the cultural arena clearly state that contacts with the Thirteen were an unavoidable part of artistic success and as such were not condemned in the ghetto.[106]

The connection between entertainment and collaboration must have been strengthened by the fact that in the generally despised *Gazeta Żydowska*, cultural life was used as the main propaganda tool for creating a vision of fake stability in the ghetto.[107] In its pages *Gazeta* was determined to prove that life in the ghetto did not differ significantly from life before the war. Culture was an important part of creating a new reality of the "self-governing Jewish quarter," and was described in a serious, often almost quasi-religious, manner. All its aspects, from musical revues to symphony concerts, were analyzed in depth and judged on their social rather than cultural value. Following its "politics of exaggeration," *Gazeta* meticulously mentioned every concert, benefit, and charity performance, which contributed to the feeling that there were significantly more cultural activities in the ghetto than actually took place.[108] *Gazeta* also tried to actively participate in creating the cultural life of the ghetto. In 1942 the newspaper organized a literary contest for a piece of writing that would "speak to the soul of the nation like the spirit of the times requires." None of the pieces sent in were deemed fit to be printed. One of the authors was informed that "the subject is for our times too depressing and burdening. We want to publish poetry full of hope and belief in one's strength." Another was told openly: "the topics brought up by you are not fit for public discussion at the current time."[109] Very similar reasons were given to children whose pieces were rejected for publication. "We were all very touched by your piece but we don't know if it can be printed because not everything can be talked about," explained *Gazeta* to one of the young writers.[110]

Yet it must be emphasized that smugglers and collaborators constituted only the most extreme aspects of the ghetto community. Stefan Ernest, describing the social stratification of the ghetto, wrote of a 250,000-strong mass of beggars, 20–30,000 members of the social elite, and in between them "a group of about two hundred thousand 'ordinary people' who more or less manage to retain some sort of human face."[111] Barbara Engelking estimates the number of those participating actively in the cultural life of the Warsaw Ghetto at up to 40,000 people.[112] On the basis of diaries and memoirs we can conclude that among those 40,000 were not only smugglers and collaborators but also a large number of members of the impoverished intelligentsia. As has already been shown in the case of Sztuka, there is no doubt that culture and entertainment played a major part in lending "a little stability" to life in the ghetto. Commenting on this situation, Stanisław Adler wrote: "The majority sought escape from the consequence of logical thought. The easiest way was to drown oneself in everyday worries and in work. The remaining free time, if any, one kills by playing cards (bridge games flourished), or by intense reading, this being an antidote inferior to cards, and finally in meaningless merriment, mostly under the influence of alcohol."[113] This way of passing the time seems to have intensified in the latter part of the ghetto's existence, especially after the April 1942 massacres, when the first rumors of impending deportations circulated around the quarter. Describing that period Samuel Puterman noted:

> Cafés are overflowing, Femina has an operetta, *Maska* [Nowy Teatr Kameralny]—*Mirla Efros*, *Skala* [Eldorado]. . . . In the *Ogród Artystów* the orchestra of the Order Service is to perform *Rhapsody in Blue.* At Leszno 28 authorities allow for the opening of a beach with showers. The Judenrat opens an enormous garden for children. . . . Colorful posters keep informing about new events, all agreed by the authorities. In the shop windows one can see cakes, apples, grapes and luxurious conserves.[114]

At the same time, some saw behavior according to pre-war standards not as a form of escapism but as a sign of spiritual defiance against the occupier. Kaplan refers in his diary to dancing in the ghetto as a *mitzvah* (heb. commandment), "a sign of belief in the eternity of Israel and a protest against our oppressors."[115] It can be claimed that Kaplan was probably referring to Yiddish and Hebrew entertainment, as these could be seen as part of *kiddush ha-hayim*—the sanctification of life through preserving its Jewish quality in the face of persecution. Mary Berg, coming from an entirely different cultural background from Kaplan, and a regular at Polish-language performances in the ghetto cafés, also saw laughter at the revues as "our only weapon in the ghetto" and the only thing that the Nazis could not understand.[116]

When considering the reception of Polish-language culture additional factors feature. For those in the ghetto community who saw assimilation as a "ticket necessary for entry into an open, liberal society" and "an intellectual duty of every cultured and civilized man,"[117] participation in Polish arts was not only escapism and a continuation of pre-war life but also formed an important part of their identity. Interestingly, a similar phenomenon can be seen among ghetto inhabitants who were brought up in other cultures. The best example of such ingrained cultural attitudes is Marcel Reich, brought up in Germany, who throughout his time in the ghetto retained his devotion to German literature.[118]

As already mentioned, the subject of Polish-language culture, or, as Różewicz wrote, "the question of Polish or Jewish culture," became a topic of the utmost importance for the nationalistic part of the community.[119] Ringelblum, for example, wrote with disdain about Marek's theater being created by converts (Marek was indeed baptized, and so was his greatest star Michał Znicz), and for converts.[120] He also saw it as an unprecedented sign of the progress of assimilation that it was only in the ghetto that Marek managed to finally obtain his first permanent theater venue.[121] The success of Polish-language theater was hence seen as a success for the campaign of the Judenrat, which represented the most assimilated part of the community.[122] Such cultural life could never meet the real needs of the regular ghetto inhabitants where "seventy percent of the audience were people brought up with Yiddish culture and speaking Yiddish in everyday life, and despite that, seventy percent of theatrical performances are taking place in the Polish language."[123] A similar claim was made by Mrs. B., a librarian in the ghetto, who in a survey performed for the Ringelblum Archive stated that the prevalence of Polish books in the ghetto had a very bad effect on the readership of young lower-middle and working-class women. Such women, says B., who before the war were "swallowing books," stopped doing so in the ghetto as "books in a foreign language and about a foreign environment could not become their friends, as it would have happened, had they been written in the Jewish language and about issues known to them from their environment."[124]

While nationalists thought of language choice in pre-war terms of political implications, for many actors and directors from the Yiddish artistic theater its failure in the ghetto was undoubtedly a much more personal issue. Describing their situation before the war, Michael Steinlauf wrote:

> Rather than involving themselves in purely "theatrical" problems, they conceived of the theater as a force in the struggle for the survival of Yiddish culture and of Polish Jewish society itself. For the new Yiddish directors, who could have made a career for themselves on the prestigious Polish stage, commitment to the "poor" Yiddish theater was the product of a conscious choice made for "moral" and "national" reasons.[125]

It was therefore of a special significance that Miriam Orelska, the co-founder of the *Vilner Trupe*, and Jonas Turkow and Diana Blumenfeld from the *Varshever Yidisher Kunst-teater*, spent 1942 acting in the Femina Theater and later *Nowy Teatr Kameralny*. This switch between theaters performing in different languages, which in the interwar period would have been nothing out of the ordinary, in the ghetto took on a special meaning.[126] This phenomenon was not, however, a one-way process. At the same time a number of professional Polish theater actors, with no previous links to the Jewish community, started performing in Yiddish. According to one ghetto inhabitant, singer Helena Ostrowska, when participating in charity events, sang Jewish folk songs "which she performed very successfully despite not knowing the language."[127]

At the same time, the intensification of the sense of Jewish identity which was experienced by Polish-speaking ghetto inhabitants led to the need for new forms of expression. A reflection of this problem can be found in the diary of Mary Berg, who discusses the reception of Julian Tuwim's *Kwiaty Polskie* among her peers. As already stated, in interwar Poland Tuwim was the icon of cultural assimilation and remained extremely popular within the assimilated Jewish community after the enclosure of the ghetto. In the early days of the ghetto, the role played by Tuwim's poetry among polonized youth could be compared to that played by Chaim Bialik among young Zionists. Yet, as Berg notes: "The poem was full of love for Poland, the masterful verses contained profound symbols, but there was not a word of encouragement which all of us thirsted for."[128] Nostalgia for the Jewish past evidenced in *Kwiaty Polskie* no longer satisfied the reader behind the ghetto walls.[129] Assimilated artists in the ghetto, such as those gathered around Femina, replied to this need by writing and performing texts that referred directly to the Jewish experience in the ghetto. According to Frieda Aaron, satirical texts that proliferated in the ghettos "handled the initial period of occupation and its brutality with incredulity, believing that the war would soon end or the outside world or God would intervene on their behalf. This strategy helped them to achieve a semblance of distance from the increasingly intolerable reality."[130]

At the same time, many members of the assimilated community were searching for art that would express their newly found identity. Works in Polish on themes linked to Jewish identity, which before the war were seen as of inferior quality to those of the assimilated writers, began being read "at homes, at work, in shops and workshops, their handwritten copies were passed from hand to hand, transferred orally."[131] It is impossible to establish to what extent Polish-Jewish texts performed at Sztuka and other venues affected the self-perception of assimilated Jewry. Judging by the number of references to them by ghetto diarists, especially teenagers, who grew up in completely assimilated homes and whose national identity was only being forged in the ghetto, the influence was undoubtedly significant. A key factor that cannot be ignored is the age of Polish-Jewish artists. Szlengel, born in 1914, or Łazowert, born in 1910, were a few years younger than the assimilated group gathered around *Wiadomości*. They were the ones who found it easiest to reach the youth through their writings. Their role was especially important after the 1942 *Gross Aktion*, when for those left in the ghetto, mainly young people, culture became the "only consolation" after the harrowing experiences of deportations.[132] One of the few artists still actively working on cultural contributions in the ghetto after the Aktion was Władysław Szlengel. He kept writing and performing new installments of *Żywy Dziennik*, while also being employed in a brush-makers shop.[133] Later on, Szlengel, a Polish-language writer, became a hero-poet for the young Zionists fighting in the Warsaw Ghetto Uprising. By combining Polish and Jewish cultural inheritance he found the voice of the polonized Jewish community in the Warsaw Ghetto.

5

Assimilated Inhabitants of the Warsaw Ghetto after the *Gross Aktion*

Deportations

The *Gross Aktion*, the deportation of the Warsaw Ghetto inhabitants to Treblinka, caught the ghetto unaware and unprepared. Despite the growing persecution and increasingly threatening news reaching the quarter from other Jewish communities, very few seemed to believe that the largest ghetto in occupied Poland was also doomed. Yet, on July 22, 1942, SS-Sturmbannführer Hermann Höfle, Deportation Coordinator for Section "Operation Reinhardt" (Annihilation of the Jews of the Generalgouvernement) in the Office of the SS and Police Leader in Lublin District, informed Adam Czerniaków that the "resettlement to the East" was about to begin. From then on, until mid-September 1942 altogether between 265,000 and 280,000 people were deported from the ghetto, with approximately 20,000 to 35,000 killed in their homes, on the ghetto streets, or on the Umschlagsplatz. The Aktion ended with the so-called "cauldron," a roundup and selection of remaining ghetto inmates, lasting from September 6–12, 1942, after which the territory of the ghetto was shrunk to form the "Restghetto," divided into a small "central" ghetto and the "wild" ghetto, within which a number of apartment blocks were taken over by various German enterprises—the "shops." Approximately 70,000 Jews were left in the ghetto after the deportations ended in September.

As the first to go were the poorest from among the ghetto inhabitants, the assimilated community seemed initially immune from deportations. Policeman Stanisław Gombiński noted: "They're not touching the core; they're only hitting the back streets, driving out the beggars, the paupers, the refugees. . . . These people wouldn't survive anyway; they were dying by the day, by the hour, from hunger, typhus, tuberculosis."[1] Assimilated Jews, with high-level positions in the official ghetto institutions or the German shops, felt assured of their safety. It soon turned out that this was purely illusory. As the Aktion progressed, exemption documents and passes were proving invalid. Life and death became dependent on haphazard factors, and in a poem written at the time by Władysław Szlengel, even God himself was not able to bribe the guards "with the sun-like glitter of a hundred dollar coin."[2] Almost all of those described in this book, irrespective of their pre-war positions, money, or contacts in the ghetto, lost members of their immediate families in the Aktion. They themselves usually managed to leave the ghetto at some point between the summer of 1942 and January 1943. The majority achieved it through extensive bribes, most often, like Ludwik Hirszfeld or Henryk Makower, leaving together with workers going to *placówkas*. Stefan Ernest, who also left the ghetto this way, wrote:

> On 29 January 1943, at 5.15 AM, I leave that cursed city of insult and humiliation, of misery, pestilence, hunger, blood and death, that hellish home to every conceivable torture and suffering that can be devised by human beings: *the beast*. At about 7.30 AM I arrive at the worksite Ostbahn-Praga. At 5 PM, in the twilight, I break away from the returning column. For three years I've been wearing an armband; I now remove this badge of shame and slip away, alone, into the evening darkness and the traffic of the city. I am free.[3]

Yet, even for those with the best contacts, reaching the "Aryan" side was just the beginning of their ordeal. After the Hans Frank decree of October 15, 1941, which imposed the death penalty on those discovered outside the ghetto and also on those helping them, Jews caught on the "Aryan" side were in the vast majority of cases driven to the ghetto and then shot on the spot. Those with better-quality forged papers were imprisoned in the Jewish section of the infamous *Pawiak* Gestapo prison. There they waited for up to six weeks, often tortured, while the data from their "Aryan" papers were being meticulously checked. One of the Pawiak inmates described this group as "several long standing Warsaw residents, with names well-known to Jews and non-Jews alike, a substantial number of intellectuals, doctors, lawyers and engineers. Some of them had been converted to Christianity before the war, others merely possessed false certificates of baptism."[4] The painfully high cost of remaining in hiding and constant fear of denunciation meant that, as young underground activist Vladka Meed wrote, "The assimilated Jewish intelligentsia, the erstwhile merchants and social figures, were transformed into distressed, bewildered paupers."[5] Fear seems to be the one factor that united all of those in hiding, irrespective of their pre-war status, background, or financial situation. Stefan Ernest, summing up the experience of thousands of mainly assimilated Jews living on the "Aryan" side of Warsaw, noted that "the only thing they share is a fear of informers, an anxious anticipation of the end—and the fact that they are Jewish."[6]

For many, the pressure of life in hiding proved to be unbearable. In 1943, 2,500 Jews bought from Gestapo agents foreign passports, mainly South American, which were to allow them to emigrate. All those people, among them prominent social activists, artists, and even ghetto underground fighters, preferred to put their fate into the hands of the Germans rather than sustain the nightmare of a life on the "Aryan" side. The so-called "Hotel Polski affair," named after the hotel in which the would-be emigrants were ordered to gather, turned out to be a trap.[7] Yet some of those who were not murdered on the spot, but instead deported to Bergen Belsen or Vittel camps, managed to survive the war.

Assimilation, Youth, and Armed Resistance in the Warsaw Ghetto

Not all could, or sometimes wanted to, escape the ghetto during or after the summer deportations. The closed quarter, now de facto turned into a labor camp, succumbed in the autumn and winter of 1942 to the "little stabilization," one last attempt to rebuild lives ravaged by the Aktion. At the same time, with the power of the Judenrat exposed as being purely illusionary, authority in the quarter was taken over by what was known by the ghetto inhabitants as the "party"—the Jewish underground, led mainly by young people and increasingly aimed at armed resistance against the Nazis.

As already noted, in September 1939 many of the most prominent leaders of Jewish political and social life left Poland. This exodus left the core of the Jewish political parties badly shaken, but their youth divisions very quickly reorganized and recommenced their activities. Immediately after the enclosure of the ghetto, the cultural and social organization of community life, especially the network of self-help institutions, remained in the hands of older activists, but youth movements were gradually gaining independence from the collapsing political parties. By late 1942, they had risen to prominence as the de facto leadership of the Warsaw Ghetto underground life.

There is no information on any organization being comprised exclusively of assimilated youth. It seems that for the majority of young people from assimilated families, participation in a youth movement was replaced by friendship groups based on similar social and cultural backgrounds. There were, however, individual assimilationist activists who remained active in the ghetto and cooperated with the Polish underground and Jews who remained on the "Aryan" side.[8] The only trace of their activities that can be found today are three surviving issues of an underground publication, *Żagiew* (pol. The Torch), which they can be safely assumed to have published. *Żagiew* seems to have been a continuation of a periodical of the same title that was published in the 1920s by the *Związek Młodzieży Polskiej Pochodzenia Żydowskiego* (pol. Association of Polish Youth of Jewish Origin), and which promoted very strong assimilationism, sometimes accused of verging on anti-Semitism. Issues of *Żagiew* published in the ghetto seem to have continued along this ideological line. Its first issue, dated February 1942, begins with a foreword stating that "Jews are and will be members of the Great Commonwealth of Poland. They are the citizens of the country and the nation of Poland. They are Poles. This is why Free, Independent and Mighty Poland is our highest ideal and our most important task." The periodical portrays Jews as primarily Polish citizens, and their persecution as "nothing more than a part of the Nazi program."[9] Since only three issues of the publication survived, not much more than these ideological statements is known about the assimilationists in the Warsaw Ghetto. However, it can be assumed that, in relation to the ghetto's political underground, they were a group of only marginal importance.

The majority of politically active young people who found themselves in the ghetto joined one of many Zionist pioneering youth groups. These were represented by movements belonging to the *Hechalutz* Center: left-wing, pro-Soviet *Hashomer Hatzair* (heb. the Young Guard); socialist, working class *Dror Hechalutz* (heb. Freedom—the Pioneer), which was affiliated with *Left Poalei Zion*; social democratic *Gordonia*; and non-socialist, religious *Akiva*, which was affiliated with a moderate faction of general Zionists. Two other pioneering organizations were *Hanoar Hatzioni* (heb. Zionist Youth), affiliated with a radical faction of general Zionists; and *Hechalutz Hamizrachi* (heb. the Eastern Pioneer) which was affiliated with the religious Zionist *Hamizrachi*. The cultural and ideological work of Zionist groups in the ghetto was aimed primarily at counterbalancing assimilationism and at strengthening national identity in the Jewish youth. While Adam Czerniaków displayed over his desk a picture of Józef Piłsudski and Ber Mayzels, the hero of the 1863 Uprising,[10] young Polish Zionists saw their future in Palestine, not in Poland. Even though among their members were young people coming from assimilated and acculturated backgrounds, many of them with no knowledge of Hebrew or Yiddish and their concept of Jewish identity shaped by Polish Romanticism, assimilationist tendencies were very strongly fought against. Zionist publications devoted many pages to propaganda aimed against the ghetto's "golden youth"—young people from privileged assimilated backgrounds, associated in the underground press with "a complete rejection of morality, high-stake card playing, smoking, inappropriate dancing evenings and sexual excesses."[11] One of the underground periodicals stated strongly: "Against us is the street—whirling in a crazy carpe diem—live while there is still time and use life while you still can. . . . On our side is only the conviction that our road is the right one—and this has to be enough."[12]

Another major political force in the ghetto was formed by the Bund and its youth movement *Tzukunft*. Since the Bund established itself in interwar Poland as the party of the Jewish street, in the ghetto its main focus remained on practical work among the wider society. This was conducted mainly through setting up and running a network of Yiddish secular schools (*Tzisho*). Ideologically, the party continued a program of establishing national-cultural autonomy for the Jews within a Polish multinational state and hence saw itself as part of the Polish underground. It also remained in close contact with the Polish socialist underground—namely the left wing of the *Polska Partia Socjalistyczna Wolność-Równość-Niepodległość* (PPS-WRN, pol. Polish Socialist Party Freedom Equality Independence)—which from September 1941 established the independent underground group *Polscy Socjaliści* (PS, pol. Polish Socialists). This cooperation, though reduced on the Polish side mainly to help with circulating the Bund's clandestine press, was of great psychological importance to people behind the walls. This is clearly reflected in the Bund's underground publications, which often focused on the links between the fate of Jewish masses in the ghetto and that of the Polish working class. The two communities, as the Bundist underground press stated, were to prepare to "fight together for independence, freedom and socialism."[13]

Communist groups had an important influence on the youth. Before *Polska Partia Robotnicza* (PPR, pol. Polish Workers' Party) was recreated by the Communist International in January 1942, groups such as *Stowarzyszenie Przyjaciół ZSRR* (pol. Society of Friends of the USSR), *Sierp i Młot* (pol. Hammer and Sickle), *Robotniczo-Chłopska Organizacja Bojowa* (pol. Workers' and Peasants' Fighting Squad), and others were active in the ghetto. At the beginning of March 1942 all of these were incorporated into the local district committee of the PPR. Only a few months later, the party had 500 members in the ghetto, compared with only 400 members in the rest of Warsaw.[14] Following the political line of the PPR, its units in the ghetto called for immediate armed self-defense and conducted an extensive propaganda effort. Like other groups, PPR also held underground seminars. Even though the Communist underground was usually associated with the strongly acculturated youth, it seems that the majority of its assimilated members remained on the "Aryan" side. A teacher of PPR seminars in the ghetto recalled after the war: "I taught not only the 'religion' of Marxism-Leninism, but general knowledge as well. It was mainly youth from small towns, who barely spoke Polish. We believed at that point that they will all leave the ghetto and join the partisans so they should be prepared for life on the other side."[15]

One group which was absent from the ghetto's communal life until mid-1942 were the Revisionists, representatives of *Nowa Organizacja Syjonistyczna* (pol. New Zionist Organization)—a right-wing branch of Zionism created in the early 1920s by Vladimir Jabotinsky. The organization combined Jewish nationalism with the tradition of European independence movements and Polish Romanticism. After the death of Piłsudski, Revisionists started receiving unofficial support, mainly financial but also through help with military training, from the Polish government.[16] In the interwar period the Revisionists included among their supporters many middle-class members of the acculturated strata. Similarly, in the ghetto, the political and military leaders of the group came from acculturated circles.[17] The youth group affiliated with the Revisionists, *Betar* (a Hebrew acronym for the "League of Joseph Trumpeldor"[18]), was a quasi-military organization, dedicated to education and physical training, with an emphasis on discipline and hierarchy and the aim of preparing an army for the independent Palestine. For unknown reasons, unlike other major parties, after the enclosure of the ghetto *Betar* had limited its activities to only small-scale publishing. The largest religious Zionist party—*Mizrachi*—though very popular in interwar Warsaw, also had very little influence on ghetto life.[19]

As already shown, for many young people like Mary Berg, Antoni Marianowicz, or Marcel Reich, severing contact with the Polish environment was a traumatic experience. After the enclosure of the ghetto, these young people restricted their contacts to those who were from a similar background and, as Marianowicz wrote, "walked through the Warsaw Ghetto looking with horror at what was going on there, and yet always maintained a certain distance."[20] At the same time, however, for their peers of a moderately assimilated and acculturated background, time spent in the ghetto often resulted with them coming to terms with their Jewish identity. For those who found a resonance in the following words of a young diarist: "I want to be a Pole, you have not let me; I want to be a Jew, but I don't know how,"[21] the underground organizations offered an answer. One of the survivors wrote about her first year in the ghetto as "the most beautiful time in her life." Describing the work she had done with a group of girlfriends, ranging from "orthodox to coming from half-Zionist and half-assimilated families," she wrote: "It was a time when I was living fully, I knew why I am living and what for. I was thinking more about other people than about myself, every day had its meaning and value. Every group meeting, conversation, discussion, and good deed were a beautiful, happy event. Our aim was to become Jewish women."[22] According to a Zionist youth leader Zivia Lubetkin, the Dror Kibbutz at Dzielna Street became a home not only for Dror members from around the country but also for people very far from the ideology or even those who had never heard of it.[23] Her partner, Yitzhak Zuckerman, noted in his memoirs that within this group many different people could find a place, from former Communists to the former assimilationists.[24]

There is no doubt that the financial situation of young people from at least moderately assimilated or acculturated backgrounds was a major factor in their involvement in the activities of youth groups. As Israel Gutman admits, even before the war and much more so in the ghetto, youth groups recruited their members mainly from the middle class.[25] Unlike them, the vast majority of young people in the ghetto were too preoccupied with daily concerns to actively participate in the underground life. Already in the winter of 1941 a publication of Hashomer Hatzair stated that "in the current situation we cannot dream of taking on and educating children living in poverty. This youth needs in the first place bread, warm clothing and a place to live . . . out of necessity our youth recruits mainly from lower middle-class families, who though impoverished, thanks to either old savings or random jobs, do not live in complete poverty."[26] It has to be assumed that later on this problem escalated. As a result, underground organizations conducted outreach activities aimed at the middle-class acculturated group that can be seen as an effort to counteract their polonization. For example, the Bund ran courses in Yiddish for "those who had gotten along without it all their lives but found it indispensable under the ghetto conditions."[27] There were also underground secondary-level classes for those who after the war planned to join a Polish university.[28] Similarly, Dror conducted Yiddish and Hebrew classes for the Polish-speaking youth.[29] The publication of Polish-language clandestine periodicals can be seen as another means of reaching the acculturated groups. As already noted, the underground publications assumed the task of guiding the youth through any moral questions that may have arisen during everyday life in the ghetto, and they were, according to their own rhetoric, "the moral weapon" of the underground groups.[30] It should be noted here that according to those with a Zionist background, the Polish-language press published by the youth groups cannot be seen as a sign of progressing acculturation. Israel Gutman, for example, saw the choice of language as "not integration and certainly not assimilation." He writes: "The young people in question lived almost exclusively in a Jewish milieu, among Jews. The Polish language served as an instrument of thought, a medium of learning, reading and argument. The national identity of these youth movement members was clear-cut, there is no doubt about it."[31]

As the situation in the ghetto deteriorated, the objectives of the youth organizations changed from large-scale recruitment and mobilization to the formation of "small, unified group[s], aware of the aim and closely tied with the organization, which can face the difficulties of today's situation."[32] When military training supplanted the cultural activities of the majority of youth movements, the groups became naturally much more exclusive and this basically ruled out any involvement of young people from assimilated circles. One of the assimilated youth claimed: "I heard that there was resistance and I was trying to get in touch but there was just no way that I could get in touch with anybody. No way of making contact."[33] Marek Edelman, one of the leaders of Bundist *Tzukunft*, remembered that "you would not introduce into the organization anyone who you had not known since childhood. We were a group of boys and girls who had known each other for years, friends from schools, courtyards and youth groups."[34] As a result, the groups formed very tight links, to an extent similar to family relations.[35] According to Simhah "Kazik" Rotem from Akiva, those young activists took the name of their movement as part of their own, as "if it were another last name."[36]

The majority of underground *Żydowska Organizacja Bojowa* fighters came from working-class families and had only an elementary education. Having mainly attended state-founded Polish schools, and often growing up in mixed Polish-Jewish working-class quarters, they were undoubtedly acculturated, but at the same time were possessed of a strong Jewish national identity. Of those with a middle-class background, the majority were graduates of private Jewish educational institutions.[37] The few assimilated boys and girls who cooperated with the armed underground worked mainly as messengers—a task that required flawless Polish and "good" looks. A female messenger from an assimilated family, Marysia Warman, recalled that she never belonged to any organization but happened to be working in a hospital alongside Marek Edelman and he introduced her into the underground.[38] A similar image is evoked by Simhah Rotem, who, describing another female messenger, Bronka "Marysia" Feinmesser, wrote: "Marysia was from an assimilated family, wasn't a Zionist and didn't know a thing about Judaism. How she came to us, I don't know. She looked like a typical Pole, spoke perfect Polish and had big, somewhat sad blue eyes."[39] However, it seems that both girls were exceptions to the fact that there was not any mass involvement of the assimilated youth in the underground, as by the time of the first armed revolt in January 1943 barely any of the initial group of assimilated Jews were left in the ghetto. Some of them managed to escape; the rest perished in the Aktion.

An important factor shaping the ghetto underground's perception of Poles and assimilation was its cooperation with Polish clandestine authorities. ŻOB's contacts on the "Aryan" side were two-fold. On one hand, it cooperated with the underground affiliated with the Polish government-in-exile in London—including both its civilian authority, *Delegatura Rządu na Kraj* (pol. Government Delegation for Poland), and its military wing, *Armia Krajowa* (AK, pol. The Home Army). On the other hand, it remained close to the Communist underground, which received its instructions from Moscow and its armed force *Gwardia Ludowa* (GL, pol. People's Guard), renamed in 1944 as *Armia Ludowa* (AL, pol. People's Army). There is no doubt that for ardent leftist ghetto underground groups, contacts with PPR were easier on not only an ideological but also on a purely personal level. Both Edelman and Zuckerman claimed later that the PPR was much more sympathetic and had a better attitude toward the Jews.[40] Another important factor in these relations was that while Armia Krajowa rejected the idea of an uprising, PPR demanded immediate warfare whenever and wherever possible. However, the fact remained that at that time only the AK was capable of providing ghetto fighters with sufficient arms. In order to maximize the chances for support during the armed revolt, the ghetto underground leaders, irrespective of their personal preferences, had to remain on good terms with both sides of the underground political spectrum.

When it came to clandestine political parties on the "Aryan" side, the most active in supporting the Jewish underground were PPS-WRN, which traditionally had among its members many assimilated Jews, *Stronnictwo Demokratyczne* (SD, pol. Democratic Party), and the Catholic *Front Odrodzenia Polski* (FOP, pol. Front for the Rebirth of Poland), as well as various Communist groups. Yet a formal realization of this support did not take a concrete form until late September 1942, by which time the vast majority of Warsaw Jews had already been murdered.[41] The *Tymczasowy Komiet Pomocy Żydom* (pol. Provisional Committee to Aid Jews), affiliated with the Delegatura, was only set up on September 27, 1942, under the leadership of Zofia Kossak-Szucka, the president of FOP, and Wanda Krahelska-Filipowiczowa, from the SD. On December 4, 1942, it was replaced by the *Rada Pomocy Żydom* (pol. Council for Aid of Jews), code-named *Żegota*, a fundamental organization in providing material help to

Jews in hiding, irrespective of their political affiliations. Its presidium consisted of representatives of PPS WRN, SD, SL, and FOP, with Adolf Berman as the secretary.

Similarly to ŻOB, the fighting wing of the Revisionists, *Żydowski Związek Wojskowy* (ŻZW, pol. Jewish Fighting Union), was created primarily by the youth and set up after the members of the Betar youth movement returned to Warsaw from a training farm in Hrubieszów in the autumn of 1942.[42] Despite attempts to join forces, the conflicts between ŻOB and ŻZW did not allow for the creation of a unified fighting group. The main reason quoted by both groups was divided opinion over who would assume leadership of the group. Revisionists felt that due to their military training, it was only they who should command the fighting units.[43]

Despite the assimilatory backgrounds of some of its leaders and the history of cooperation with the Polish Army, the Revisionists cooperated extensively with only two relatively unknown Polish underground organizations—*Korpus Bezpieczeństwa* (KB, pol. Security Cadres), and, to a greater degree, *Polska Ludowa Akcja Niepodległościowa* (PLAN, pol. Polish Popular Independence Action).[44] Both of these organizations, affiliated with the AK, supplied them with arms and helped with training. Even though, to underline its cooperation with the "Aryan" side, the official stamp of the ŻZW showed two hands clasped together through a hole in a ghetto wall, its contacts with the Polish underground cannot be compared to those of ŻOB. It is difficult to establish why it was ŻOB and not ŻZW that was legitimized by the AK and Delegatura, despite Revisionists' interwar collaboration with the government.[45]

The turning point in the life of the ghetto came in January 1943. Between January 18–21, 1943, ŻOB fighters, at that point armed with only a few pistols, prevented Germans from conducting the second Aktion—what was planned to be a transfer of 8,000 workshop workers to labor camps near Lublin. On April 19, 1943, the Germans began the final liquidation of the Warsaw Ghetto. The ghetto youth groups replied with armed revolt, yet ŻOB's plan of a battle joined by Poles in both *Armia Ludowa* and *Armia Krajowa*[46] outside the ghetto never materialized. AL lacked the capability to help the ghetto. AK was at that time strongly opposed to a nationwide uprising, and aside from a few, mainly symbolic actions at the ghetto walls[47] and the supply of a limited number of arms, they did not help the fighters.[48] Even though some Polish fighters did fight alongside ŻOB in the January revolt,[49] there is no indication that Poles fought on the side of either ŻOB or ŻZW in the April Uprising. Even the socialists who were the closest to the Bund and sympathetic toward the ghetto underground completely rejected the idea of a general uprising. Trying to explain (though not excuse) the attitude of the AK, Marek Edelman wrote: "How were they to trust us? We were not a trained army, we had no officers, generals, plans, training. . . . That's the truth. We did not look serious in the eyes of professional soldiers."[50]

In order to understand both the attitude of the AK toward ghetto fighters and the concept of the Ghetto Uprising as an act of defense of the honor of the nation, it is crucial to examine the anti-Semitic stereotype of Jews as being deprived of any military talents and indeed interest in military training. Even in the twentieth century, the Polish Army authorities constantly rejected the notion of Jews as worthy of being Polish soldiers. Most notoriously, in 1920 over 10,000 Jewish soldiers and officers who volunteered for the Polish Army were interned in the military detention camp and prevented from participating in the decisive moment of the Polish-Soviet War. Even during the Ghetto Uprising, the stereotype of Jews not being able to fight was still being brought up on the "Aryan" side. It was widely believed that if someone was fighting in the ghetto, it must have been the Poles. Polish underground publications of all ideological backgrounds spread rumors of Polish armed groups participating in, and sometimes even leading, the revolt in the ghetto. Interestingly, the stereotype of Jewish passivity was also shared by many Jews in hiding. Even the meticulous and very well-informed Ludwik Landau wrote in his diary about a group of 1,500 Polish ghetto fighters that he described as "most probably really existing." He also mentions but does not comment on rumors that the Polish underground was sending fighting groups to the ghetto to practice fighting the Germans.[51]

Even those who agreed that the Jews were actually fighting stated that they were purely copying the Poles. Newspapers reported on groups of captured Jews who, while being marched away by the Germans, sang the nineteenth-century patriotic anthem *Nie Rzucim Ziemi* (pol. We Shall not Forsake the Land) and shouted "Long live Poland," while above their heads Polish and Jewish flags were flown.[52] The influential *Biuletyn AK* wrote that "Polish citizens fighting in the ghetto have become closer to the Warsaw inhabitants than those passively going to their death,"[53] while *Wiadomości* noted that "the fighting has much more than just Jewish character and that by reaching for arms the fighters fulfill the honor duty of Polish citizens."[54] Thus, the Polish underground press saw the uprising as part of the Polish national movement, and through participation the ghetto inhabitants had in a way gained the rights of "true Poles."

The belief that it was necessary for Jews to fight in order to prove their worth to the Poles was also discussed in the ghetto. The topic was brought up very early on after the ghetto's enclosure[55] and became especially prominent after the Aktion. Tellingly, in the period immediately before the uprising it formed one of the principal motifs of ghetto poetry. Interpretations differed according to the affiliations of the writers. At one end of the spectrum, Władysław Szlengel, a poet who exemplified Polish-Jewish culture, showed the conflict between Jewish identity and the myth of Polish romantic struggle, and called for a meaningful death "so that we too can have our Westerplatte,"[56] referring to the site of a heroic Polish defense in the September 1939 campaign. At the other end of the spectrum, Zionist Yitzhak Katzenelson in the "Song of the Murdered Jewish People," written in the camp in Vittel, argued that Jews do not have to copy anyone and do not have to fight "like Poles" in order to retain their national honor.[57]

For Poles and many assimilated Jews the symbol of the Polish-Jewish brotherhood of arms in April 1943 were the Polish and Zionist flags placed alongside each other on a tall building at Muranowski Square by ŻZW fighters. In the eyes of Stefan Ernest and many others who watched the uprising from the "Aryan" side, the two flags were to be a foundation for the future unity of the Jewish and Polish communities:

"a banner they raised in their last battle, in honor of the shared tragedy of enslavement and persecution and in the hope of better coexistence in the future."[58] Similarly, in the report to Delegatura Rządu na Kraj, Żegota described a "fidelity and manifestation of feelings for the country and nation of Poland, expressed in the face of death in a romantic form of hanging on the barricades the flag of the republic of Poland, which puts on the Polish nation and the Polish government the duty of taking up an appropriate stance towards the remnant of Jews dying with honor—Citizens of Poland."[59] The tradition of brotherhood in arms was not strong enough, however, to counterbalance the old stereotypes, both on the Jewish and Polish side. This attitude was not only limited to anti-Semitic right-wing Polish publications, which saw the use of a Polish flag by the ghetto fighters as a "cynical gesture of a nation whose hope and plans are more linked to the red flag rather than the white eagle."[60] Poignantly, as historian Paweł Szapiro noted, the Polish word *powstanie* (pol. uprising) in 1943 was never used in reference to the Jewish Uprising, either by the Polish or Jewish press or diarists. This clearly shows that the Jewish Uprising was not necessarily seen as a continuation of Polish traditions. Fighting in the ghetto was not deemed worthy of the "sacred" word. Powstanie was reserved for the general uprising of the Polish people, which in April 1943 was already anticipated.[61]

Understandably, not all Jews on the "Aryan" side focused in those days on the glory of the uprising or the brotherhood of arms. The thoughts of most were with friends and family members who remained in the burning ghetto. Numerous diarists recalled leaving their hideouts and standing near the ghetto walls, looking at the smoke covering the Jewish Quarter.[62] However, this was not the only feeling of those on the other side of the wall. A former ghetto inhabitant from an assimilated, well-off family admitted in his memoirs: "Aside from horror at the tragedy of perished people, I felt, which I have to admit with shame, relief and maybe even contentment that neither me nor my parents are there and that in the right moment I undertook the decision to escape from the ghetto."[63] There is no doubt that many others shared his feelings. A Pole who was helping Jews noted in May 1943 that some of the completely assimilated Jews held negative attitudes toward the uprising and saw it as endangering those in hiding on the "Aryan" side.[64]

Jewish Participation in the 1944 Warsaw Uprising

The failure of the Warsaw Ghetto Uprising did not signify the end of the Jewish armed struggle in occupied Warsaw. Over a year later, on August 1, 1944, the Warsaw Uprising began, a mass military effort to liberate Warsaw from the German occupation, initiated by the armed underground with the expectation that the Soviet Army would join in the fight. On reaching Warsaw, the Soviets did indeed liberate a small part of the city on the left side of the Vistula River but then stopped their advance and watched the uprising continue in central Warsaw for sixty-three more days. It is estimated that about 150,000 to 200,000 inhabitants of Warsaw were killed during the uprising, approximately fifty percent of those living in the parts of the city where combat was most intense.

Jews who actively fought in the Warsaw Uprising can be divided into two groups. The first, smaller but more visible, consisted of fighters who openly participated in the uprising as Jews. The most famous of these was the platoon of about twenty ŻOB fighters who fought as part of the AL in the Old Town. Their commander was Yitzhak "Antek" Zuckerman, who assumed leadership of Żydowska Organizacja Bojowa after the death of Mordechai Anielewicz. Members of this group were recruited from about eighty fighters who after the fall of the Ghetto Uprising were evacuated through canals to the "Aryan" side. Though it was small, its very existence undoubtedly had an important emotional significance for Jews participating in the uprising, both under their own or Christian names.[65] Aside from ŻOB's group there were a number of Jewish soldiers fighting in smaller units, including a Hashomer Hatzair group that was fighting under the ŻOB insignia in the Okęcie district. There were also individual survivors from ŻZW fighting in various AK units.[66] An unknown number of Jews participated in the uprising by working as couriers or, especially often, as doctors in the underground hospital. An important group among them was formed by Polish, Hungarian, Greek, and Romanian Jews freed by the AK on the first day of the uprising from the prison on Niska Street (a hundred Hungarian Jews) and four days later from "Gęsiówka" work camp (348 Jews, including eighty-nine of Polish nationality). The vast majority of them joined the uprising, mainly within the AK groups that freed them, though they principally worked in support units. A Jewish girl who was working as a nurse in the battalion that freed Greek Jews from Gęsiówka remembered that "they were given food but not arms, even though they kept asking for them."[67]

The second, much larger group consisted of those who chose to fight in the uprising without giving away their Jewish identity, in many cases retaining the Polish names under which they had survived the occupation. These included both those who joined the ranks of underground organizations long before the uprising and those who joined after August 1. Those who were active in the underground throughout the occupation were mainly assimilated Jews who never entered the ghetto or left it very early on.[68] Some from this group were already at that point involved in helping Jews in the ghetto or organizing cooperation between the Polish and Jewish underground. Many assimilated Jews or Poles of Jewish origin were, for example, among the activists of Żegota as well as *Biuro Informacji i Propagandy Komendy Głównej AK* (pol. Bureau of Information and Propaganda of the General Headquarters of the AK), which dealt with relations with the Jewish underground.[69] Though in the majority of sources revenge against the Germans is seen as the principal reason for Jews to participate in the uprising, it seems that among many of the strongly assimilated fighters, it was also a natural consequence of their upbringing. One of them, Stanisław Aronson, describing his family background, wrote:

> I went to a Polish school and was brought up entirely in Polish culture. In my year at school, over half of the students were Jewish, the majority of them thinking the way I did . . . In the days of my youth I thought that the time will come when my civil duty will be to fight in the Polish army, in defense of the country, just like many Polish Jews before me.[70]

During the uprising Jews were to become once again equal Polish citizens. Yet because the Polish community was perceived as predominantly hostile, many of those who participated in the uprising did not own up to being Jewish. Simhah "Kazik" Rotem wrote about his "good intuition" in not admitting to the AK soldiers that he was Jewish.[71] Another fighter wrote that by then he had been already for a long time "out of the habit of talking about things like that."[72] Many of the Jewish participants were advised by friendly Poles or by the leaders of their fighting groups not to own up to being Jewish. Others were warned against it by fellow Jews who participated in the uprising under their Catholic names.[73] As a result, many of them did not know who else in their own battalion was Jewish. According to one of the participants: "We felt that others were Jewish, but we never talked about it either to them or with others."[74] One diarist remembered that fighters in the Warsaw Ghetto Uprising would have pieces of paper with their names on them when going into the fight, so that their bodies could be identified should they ever be found.[75] The Jewish soldiers in the Warsaw Uprising had even that taken away from them. One of those participating in the fight under an assumed name wrote after the war: "How difficult it was to go and fight under a foreign name, when death was a daily occurrence. 'Who will know that we fought and died in the Warsaw Uprising' asked the Jewish boys."[76]

Those joining the uprising could choose between different fighting organizations. Aside from AK, there was the right-wing NSZ (pol. *Narodowe Siły Zbrojne*); SOB (pol. *Socjalistyczna Organizacja Bojowa*), the armed wing of PPS-WRN; AL (pol. *Armia Ludowa*, People's Army); and PAL (pol. *Polska Armia Ludowa*, Polish People's Army).[77] When Zuckerman wrote in the first days of August a proclamation encouraging Jews to fight in the uprising for a "free, independent, strong and just Poland"[78] he did not specify which formation they should join. Even though AK was the larger, better equipped, and more prestigious group, still the majority of those who fought openly joined the ranks of the AL, including Zuckerman's unit. While for some this was a decision based purely on ideological grounds, an expression of their pro-Soviet views, others saw AL as the only formation where Jews could fight on an equal footing with Poles, and as an alternative to AK, which was perceived to be dominated by a right-wing worldview. Explaining his decision to join the AL, Zuckerman wrote: "I had to be careful not only of the Germans, the blackmailers, and Poles in general, but also of our allies in the AK. I am sure the AK was quite capable of arming a small Jewish unit of a few dozen fighters; but they didn't. They didn't want us. They didn't want to see armed Jews."[79] As a result, among those fighting in the AL were even those whose personal ideological views were distinctly anti-Soviet, such as Bundist Marek Edelman. According to the general perception, the AL was simply a safer group for Jews than the AK, which from March 1942 incorporated the nationalistic forces of the NSZ. At the same time, in the turmoil of the first day of the uprising, many Jews joined fighting groups by pure chance, especially those who were not ideologically involved on either side. As one Jewish fighter remembered: "Nobody was at that point thinking if it is PAL, or AK or AL. We are beating Germans up and what does it matter who is called what."[80]

There was no consistent way in which the fighting units, even within one organization, treated Jews who chose to join their ranks. According to most testimonies, in the first days of the uprising Jews were welcomed on the barricades if not with enthusiasm, then at least with curiosity and sympathy.[81] At the same time, there is no doubt that the ranks of insurgent units included many who held distinctively anti-Semitic views of Jewish soldiers. Particularly serious cases were those associated with lynch law. Many of the fighters remembered being imprisoned by the insurgents on the grounds of collaboration.[82] Some of the survivors also wrote about cases of Jewish fighters being killed by fellow AK soldiers. Even though there were only isolated cases of violence against Jews participating in the uprising, and they were condemned by the military authorities, for its victims the brutality toward the Jews was one which shaped their experience of the uprising. One of the Jewish fighters wrote in an emotional passage of his memoir: "If I had believed in God, I would have said that He had punished Warsaw because of all those Polish cut-throats for whom the murder of millions of Jews was still not enough and who took the lives of those few who had escaped, those few for whom it might have been possible to see the end of the war and rejoice in liberation."[83]

Not all Jews hiding in Warsaw chose to or indeed could join the uprising. The vast majority of them, just like the majority of Warsaw's population, did not take up arms. "We were not heroes suitable for fighting," explained one of the survivors when asked if she had joined the uprising, "we were just frightened people trying to survive."[84] The greater part of Jews in Warsaw left their hiding places and shared the fate of the civilian population of the city—the initial euphoria and later growing disillusionment, hunger, and apathy.[85] Even though some of the AK authorities might have harbored negative attitudes toward the Jews, nonetheless the insurgent authorities provided Jewish civilians with food and shelter just like they did for the Polish population. The attitude of civilians toward the Jews varied. Many survivors remembered the unity of the civilian population linked by shared suffering.[86] Yet there were also instances of Jews who were not allowed into air-raid shelters. As a result, even in liberal intelligentsia neighborhoods such as Żoliborz, the vast majority of Jews in hiding there chose not to disclose their identity.[87] There is also no doubt that with the worsening military situation, the attitude of the Polish population toward Jews was deteriorating. According to one diarist: "the most vulgar and despicable elements of the population were again vociferous in their hatred of Jews, as if the failure of the Uprising could be blamed on them, almost non-existent as they were."[88] There were also cases of violence toward Jewish civilians. It is estimated that altogether about fifty Jews were murdered during the uprising, their deaths being immediately widely known in Warsaw's insurgent units and among the civilian population.[89]

Not all Jews hiding in Warsaw were caught up in the area taken over by the insurgents. A large group of Jews remained in hiding on the right side of the river, mainly in the Praga district, where the uprising lasted only for a few days. Many of them testified to the feeling of helplessness caused by not being able to join the battle in Warsaw. On August 7 one of them wrote: "The trial for patience is getting more and more difficult. My life has never been so idle and difficult at the same time."[90] The situation was made worse by a lack of reliable information as to what actually was happening on the other side of the river. For those on the right bank, the uprising ended with the Soviet offensive on September 15. On that day Marek Szapiro, an escapee from the Warsaw Ghetto, wrote in his diary: "And now the long-anticipated word, for which I had been waiting from the first page: THE END."[91] Those on the other side of the river still had four months of horror ahead of them. After the fall of the uprising on October 2, 1944, Jewish AK fighters could either surrender alongside the AK as prisoners of war or, together with the civilian population, be evacuated to transit camps. Due to the fear of repercussions some of the Jewish fighters, instead of joining the Warsaw inhabitants who were evacuated from Warsaw, decided to remain in hiding. One of them later defended his decision by saying: "In those camps, for a piece of bread people would turn in other Poles, not to even speak of the Jews."[92] As a result, he and others like him were to stay behind in Warsaw, hiding in the rubble until the arrival of the Red Army. One of them testified later:

> I stayed because I did not have the so-called "Aryan papers" or "good looks" and I was scared of Germans like the plague. I would rather die—even of hunger, than ever again set my eyes on a German. We prepared enough food and water for two weeks, because we calculated that in that time Germans should be out of Warsaw and the Soviets already in Praga.[93]

Instead of two weeks, their ordeal lasted for four long months of the cold Polish autumn and winter. The majority of Jews spent that time living solely on the remains of food and water that could be found in the ruined city, under constant danger from both the German army and looting bands. When on January 17, 1945, the Soviet Army entered the left bank of Warsaw, out of the pre-war population of 350,000 there were about 200 Jews left in the ruined city.[94]

6

Holocaust Survivors in Post-War Poland

Conclusion

Assimilated Jews in the Immediate Post-War Period

In the last words of his wartime testimony, painter and Warsaw Ghetto survivor Samuel Puterman wrote: "In the living hell of the concentration camp I wondered what it would be like to be free again—a stupid, naïve daydream—and yet it came true. I was freed; I went back. I was free but you weren't there."[1] This image reappears in countless memoirs and diaries of Polish-Jewish survivors, those whose pre-war communities were now wiped out, and who were met with hostility and sometimes violence upon their return to their hometowns and cities. Their houses were ruined or taken over. There was no doubt that anti-Semitism did not disappear during the course of the war. If anything, it only seemed to have been magnified.

Yet, until mid-1946, a large part of the Jewish community in Poland, including members of the Bund and *Polska Partia Robotnicza* (PPR, pol. Polish Workers' Party), still envisaged a rebuilt future in Poland. Jewish citizens of Poland were given equal rights and full rehabilitation by the July 1944 manifesto of the Polish Committee of National Liberation, and Communist Poland seemed to offer them what the interwar country did not—full cultural autonomy and equality. A great wave of people who had fled German-occupied Poland to the east at last returned, which meant that by the summer of 1946 the number of registered Holocaust survivors in Poland had risen to

216,000. Between 50,000 and 80,000 of them survived the Holocaust on the Polish soil.[2] The majority settled in Łódź, and in Silesia—regions which, with funding from abroad, quickly developed into centers of cultural and social life. Pre-war parties and organizations of all types were rebuilt. Though the newly created *Centralny Komitet Żydów w Polsce* (CKŻP, pol. Central Committee of Jews in Poland) renounced the religious duties of their pre-war counterpart, religious life was gradually re-established through the Orthodox parties Agudah and Mizrachi. Over seventy Jewish press titles in Polish, Yiddish, and Hebrew were established between 1944 and 1950. Schools teaching in all three languages were set up. The ORT returned with extensive vocational training, and the first post-war *kibbutzim* were set up by the Zionists, including a Haganah preparatory camp in Lower Silesia where, with the tacit support of the government, the youth prepared to fight British imperialism.

At the same time, Poland was becoming an increasingly threatening place, and as Jan T. Gross wrote, the predominant experience of Polish Jews in the immediate post-war period was increasingly that of fear.[3] From the end of the war, Holocaust survivors were the target of continuous physical violence, whether for anti-Semitic, political, or material reasons. The impact of the "rail" action, in which Jews returning to Poland were murdered, the expropriation of Jewish apartments, and attacks on Jewish orphanages and old people's homes, meant that many of those who hid Jews during the war chose to remain anonymous out of fear for their safety. The turning point was the Kielce Pogrom of July 1946 when forty-two Jews were killed by a mob accusing them of ritual murder. For many the Kielce Pogrom was a clear sign that Jews had no future in Poland. These occurrences were aligned with the policy shifts of the ruling Communist party. As mentioned, until 1947 the Communists did not pursue openly anti-Semitic policies, yet indicative of their attitude is the fact that they did not take any extensive preventive measures against anti-Semitic attacks aimed at Holocaust survivors.

From late 1948 this policy started to shift. The CKŻP was being gradually taken over by the Communists—either the Polish-Jewish

Communists who survived the war in the east or new members of the party. All Zionist Jewish organizations were dispelled after the consolidation of Communist power in Poland in 1949 and the Central Committee of Polish Jews itself was gradually becoming more hostile toward the "bourgeois-cosmopolitan institution" of Zionism. During the 1949 Ghetto Uprising anniversary celebrations the Zionists were already being compared to collaborationists, and the legacy of the Warsaw Ghetto was appropriated by the Communists.

The first mass exodus of Jews from Poland took place in 1946, after the Kielce Pogrom. Fear of anti-Semitic violence seemed to be stronger than the difficulty and risk involved in such a journey and it is estimated that around 92,000 people left from July 1946 until February 1947.[4] The second wave of emigration took place when, following the wave of repressions against Zionist organizations, the Central Committee decided in 1949 to grant certain members of the Jewish community in Poland, mainly Zionists, rabbis, members of the intelligentsia, and bourgeoisie, the chance to give up their Polish citizenship in return for a "document of travel" enabling them to cross the border. Those leaving were only entitled to take with them a minimal number of personal belongings. It is estimated that 30,000 Jews left this way, with the Jewish population in Poland stabilizing in 1951 at 60,000 to 80,000 people.[5]

Very little is known about the post-war choices of those who in the interwar period formed the assimilated community. We can assume that at one end of the spectrum were those who for various reasons chose not to disclose their Jewish identity after the war. The number of those who never registered as Holocaust survivors is impossible to establish, though individual Jewish committees estimated them in 1947 at about ten to twenty percent of Polish Jews. These numbers varied in different parts of Poland, and it can be assumed that they were higher in relatively assimilated Warsaw.[6] It seems that in the post-war situation many simply felt safer remaining "in hiding." Others, already distant from Jewish life before the war, simply never felt the need to reach out to its post-war structures. Aside from those who never registered, many others registered only to receive information about the fate of their families or for financial reasons. About twenty percent of those who registered as survivors cut their ties completely with the Jewish community immediately after the war.[7]

On the other side are those who after the war dissimilated[8] and established a strong Jewish identity, either due to their experience during the Holocaust or as the result of post-war anti-Semitic violence. It can be assumed that Zionism took hold most strongly among those groups who could not be accommodated in the new socialist system, such as former merchants, industrialists, and professionals such as lawyers or medical doctors, who felt alienated by the new Communist regime. We can assume that many of them chose to leave Poland for ideological reasons. At the same time, considering the progressive sovietization of the country and growing repression, such an option must have been very attractive to many, irrespective of their degree of Jewish national identity. For example, the editor of *Wiadomości Literackie*, Mieczysław Grydzewski, remained outside Poland due to his strong anti-Communist views. Similarly, assimilated Stanisław Aronson, fleeing from persecution as a member of the underground army, left Poland and settled in Palestine. At the same time, even those who left for ideological reasons often retained strong links with Polish culture. One such individual was social activist Barbara Berman. In the ghetto she set up Yiddish libraries in her role as a Yikor activist; in Israel, with equal determination she devoted herself to the creation of a Polish library and cultural center.

Taking into consideration the scale of emigration, those who stayed after all the mass exoduses must have had very strong motivation to do so. The most common reasons were marriages with non-Jewish Poles. A Holocaust survivor explained: "I was thinking about leaving, but I got married, got sucked in by this life—children, house, moving home, illnesses. You know, people get stuck in everyday life. And above all, I am linked to this country with everything: language, literature, culture, my past. . . ."[9] Another very strong reason to stay was one's career, in many cases linked to the army or the Communist party. Even though, as research shows, the support for the Communist party among the wider Jewish community was not high, there was nonetheless a definite overrepresentation of Jews in the top leadership positions of the new government.[10] The national identification of those joining the party differed. Joanna Michlic underlines differences of national identification between those who chose to join the Jewish section of the PPR, thereby emphasizing their Jewish roots, and those who joined the main party.[11] The attachment of the latter group to Jewishness seems to have been mainly sentimental; they did not hide it nor draw attention to it. Jews chose this path for various reasons, perhaps because of gratitude for liberation, the possibility of upward social mobility, or a genuine belief in equality and social justice. However, soon after most of them usually fell victim to one of the anti-Semitic campaigns and left Poland in the 1956 or 1968 mass emigrations.

While in the immediate post-war years those with a stronger Jewish identity tended to settle in the larger Jewish communities of Łódź and Silesia, Warsaw was the city of choice for assimilated Jews. While the official Jewish registered community numbered 23,407 people,[12] it can be assumed that many more never got in touch with the Central Jewish Community. Due to its assimilated character Warsaw was also much less affected than other regions of Poland by the subsequent waves of mass emigration.[13]

These ensuing waves of emigration led to a growing percentage of people with no links to social and religious Jewish life in Poland. Yet, in 1957, still as many as seventy-five percent of Polish Jews retained a Jewish national identity.[14] Irena Hurwic-Nowakowska, a scholar who between 1947 and 1950 conducted a survey among the Polish-Jewish community, concluded it by saying: "The racial criterion of a Jew is still current—even Jews who have undergone baptism are still categorized as Jews. Jewish parentage determines Jewishness, regardless of the self-identity of the individual."[15] And indeed though few of them might have participated in Jewish social or religious life, they were still regarded by those around them, including both regular Poles and, as consequent policies demonstrated, by the Communist authorities, as Jews. It seems that during the first few post-war years the social circles of even the most assimilated remained predominantly Jewish. For some, full social integration within the wider non-Jewish community, of which the majority was opposed to the new government, was disabled by their engagement with the Communist party.[16] Even among the assimilated circles in post-war Warsaw full social integration took place only in the generation of the children of Holocaust survivors, and was caused mainly by intermarriage and participation in the communal life of non-Jewish Poles. However, as the "anti-Zionist" campaign of 1968 showed, even twenty years after the end of the war Jews were still treated in Poland as the "Other." Paradoxically it was those events that in many cases reshaped the identity of the second generation of Holocaust survivors from assimilated and acculturated families. Often it was this generation, of the children of Jewish polonized intelligentsia who decided to remain in Poland, that from the 1960s played a key role in cultivating the memory of the Holocaust. While some of their parents attempted to forfeit their Jewish identity, others, usually from a secular, Yiddish-speaking background, created some semblance of Jewish communal life within the Communist framework, while their children could link their Jewish identity with participation in the democratic, anti-Communist opposition. It was also members of this generation that with faith and extreme persistence led to the rebuilding of Jewish communal structures, both secular and religious, in post-Communist Poland.

Assimilated Jews described in this book fully shared the fate of their community. Naturally, it was the youngest of those presented in my research who found it the easiest to rebuild their lives after the war. Antoni Marianowicz stayed in Poland. He became a successful writer and satirist and translated into Polish *Alice in Wonderland*. Marcel Reich left for Germany and became a literature critic. Janina David left Poland in 1946 and later became a writer and a translator. Those who already had established careers before the outbreak of the war often kept practicing their profession in Communist Poland. Jerzy Jurandot, the director of Femina, set up a musical theater employing the greatest stars of post-war Poland. He was denied directorship in the 1950s but continued to work as a very successful songwriter, playwright, and film script writer. Władysław Szlengel went on to gain fame as a pianist and composer of numerous hit songs. Ludwik

Hirszfeld also stayed in Poland and became the first head of the medical department of the newly established Polish university in Wrocław. He worked together with another ghetto survivor, Henryk Makower. Some wrote diaries and memoirs, but countless others, like Mary Berg, who together with her family left Poland for the United States, chose to never again speak of their ordeal.

Some of those recorded in this book were tried in various martial tribunals and honor courts by professional bodies. Civic courts were established by the Central Committee of Polish Jews to serve the specific needs of the Jewish community and judge the members of the German-appointed Jewish councils, including members of the Jewish Order Service and also German agents and collaborators.[17] Another body was the District Martial Courts, which in political trials sentenced mainly members of the non-Communist Polish fighting underground. Almost all of the Jewish policemen who featured in my work were tried by the post-war courts. Though all of them were acquitted, they usually fell victim to the "private" memory that developed alongside the public memory of events. Those tried often faced social ostracism, insinuations, and accusations. As David Engel noted in his discussion of collaboration in 1940s, there was no middle ground.[18] One of the best known of the ghetto personalities who spent their lives haunted by the shadow of accusations was singer Wiera Gran. Accused by some of the ghetto survivors of collaboration, she was acquitted by the Jewish Civic Court. Even though she left Poland for France, Wiera Gran devoted the rest of her life to reclaiming her good name. Others fought their battles in private. One of them, Stanisław Adler, assimilated attorney and member of the Jewish Order Service, committed suicide after the Kielce Pogrom.

Conclusion

For those who spent their lives fighting against anti-Semitism and proving their Polishness, being forced back into the ghetto could be a denial of their whole identity. In one moment they realized how illusionary their integration into Polish society was. They were put on the same level as people they felt either completely disassociated with, or sometimes ashamed to be associated with. Probably as a result, in order to reinforce their identity, the assimilated and acculturated strata started organizing a very successful communal life of their own, including Polish-language schools and cultural activities. As should be underlined, these were made possible largely through the help of Poles, mainly friends and former work colleagues. At the same time, even though the majority of the assimilated community had emotional links with an often idealized pre-war Warsaw, this did not extend to the physical space on the other side of the wall, which they associated with the danger of denunciation. As a result very few of them escaped the ghetto before the July 1942 Aktion.

When it comes to their involvement in the life of the ghetto, the group of assimilated and acculturated ghetto inhabitants can be divided into two groups: those who merged with the community around them and those who remained apart from it. Those whose Jewish identity was strengthened or even re-established in the ghetto came mainly from families where such affiliations were still at least partially alive. We can therefore assume that such people might have reinforced their Jewish identity through contact with Zionist intelligentsia, the Polish-language underground press, or social work. Władysław Szlengel is demonstrative of this, as are a few of the young people from assimilated families who collaborated with ŻOB. The identity of those already born into families that were fully assimilated into Polish culture and national identity usually did not undergo significant changes. Even in the ghetto they remained within a closed circle comprised of those of a similar background. The most extreme case was the baptized community. Testimonies from ghetto inhabitants of all walks of life underline this group's separateness, the symbols of which were the two Catholic churches functioning in the quarter. For the converts themselves, participation in Sunday masses went beyond religious practice and was also an important reinforcement of their identity. The controversies around the person of Ludwik Hirszfeld reflect on the emotions that this group awoke both in the ghetto and after the war.

At the same time, despite the fears of Zionist community leaders, there are no grounds for believing that the inhabitants of the ghetto underwent any process of assimilation or acculturation. It seems clear that both the prevalence of Polish in the ghetto and the wave of baptisms were happening primarily for utilitarian reasons and not due to profound changes in the identity of ghetto inhabitants.

It should also be noted that both assimilated and nationalistic individuals formed but a marginal part of the whole of the ghetto society, which was dominated by traditional, religious Jews. As a result, they were naturally forced to form personal and professional alliances. The main field in which they cooperated were the house committees, which grouped together the socially active inhabitants of the same block, irrespective of their political, cultural, or national affiliations. The conflict in worldviews was not extended to personal relations. It seems that the shock of being in the ghetto and lack of cohesive social links drew members of the intelligentsia closer together despite their ideological differences. Yet those personal contacts and acquaintances did not necessarily lead to changes in reciprocal opinion between those two groups. The negative view of assimilation was still omnipresent in the nationalists' discourse. Why was it so crucial in a situation when the progressing assimilation, if indeed it was even happening, was the least of the problems in the closed quarter? One can delineate a number of reasons. The first is the disappointment of the activists with social developments in the ghetto. For some it might have seemed that after years of fighting for some sort of Jewish autonomy or rights in Poland the ghetto would be, at least to an extent, a self-governing Jewish quarter. Soon, however, the dire poverty, restrictive German policies, and the progressive degeneration of the society proved to be too overwhelming for even the most experienced activists. It was the ghetto's authorities, the assimilated group, that in the absence of Germans and Poles were blamed, even if partly justifiably, for the situation in the quarter.

For some, the ideological fight must have also provided an outlet for escapism. This is reflected in the content of the *Oyneg Shabes* Archive, which contains an astonishingly high number of documents dealing with the post-war future. There was no doubt in the mind of assimilated and non-assimilated ghetto inhabitants alike that there was a future to look forward to and that there was to be a Poland after the war. The fight for the shape of post-war Poland was already happening in the ghetto. The conflict was also undoubtedly fueled by the presence of the elite of the assimilated Jewish community in the ghetto, those who until then remained almost exclusively within their own circles. Converts, including people with well-known, established names who normally lived in "Polish" quarters, were particularly visible against the extreme poverty of the ghetto street.

The living situation of this group cannot be compared with that of Gestapo collaborators, new rich, or smugglers. Yet, in the social reality of the ghetto, the very fact that their lives were not directly threatened until the Aktion was alone a sign of privilege. In a world where the norm was physical degradation and material ruin, anything beyond what was absolutely necessary for pure physical survival was seen as a luxury. In the ghetto environment, leading a relatively "normal" or even very modest life could become morally unforgivable. As a result, in the eyes of many of the ghetto inhabitants, the vast majority of the assimilated community remained in the "gray zone" of moral responsibility. It seems that the assimilated strata did not become closer but rather grew apart from the rest of the ghetto inhabitants, mainly through their higher chance of survival. What should be remembered today, when viewing from a safe distance the situation in the ghetto, is that, as Raul Hilberg wrote, "even the nicest apartment in a ghetto was still a ghetto apartment, and the armband made of silk was still an emblem of subjugation."[19] Even for those more fortunately placed, the ghetto, or even a life in hiding on the "Aryan" side, was an all-encompassing struggle for survival. It seems that time for personal reflections came only after the war, especially as this was to be the first time that the Polish-Jewish community had a chance of either fully assimilating into the Polish society or emigrating to Palestine. The situation in which Polish Jews found themselves after the war presented clear choices, and non-ambiguous self-definition. There was no longer a place for ambivalence, which was the essence and maybe also a source of strength for the interwar community of assimilated Jews.

Abbreviations

Notes

Glossary

Bibliography

Index

Abbreviations

AAN	Archiwum Akt Nowych, Warsaw
AK	Armia Krajowa (pol. The Home Army)
AL	Armia Ludowa (pol. People's Army)
APW	Archiwum Państwowe m. st. Warszawy, Warsaw
AR	Ringelblum Archive (Underground Archive of the Warsaw Ghetto)
Centos	Centralne Towarzystwo Opieki nad Sierotami i Dziećmi Opuszczonymi (pol. Central Society for the Care of Orphans)
CKI	Centralna Komisja Imprezowa (pol. Central Events Commission)
CKŻP	Centralny Komitet Żydów w Polsce (pol. Central Committee of Jews in Poland)
FOP	Front Odrodzenia Polski (pol. Front for the Rebirth of Poland)
G.G.	Generalgouvernement für die Besetzten Polnischen Gebiete (ger. General Government for the Occupied Polish Territories)
GL	Gwardia Ludowa (pol. People's Guard)
JHIA	Jewish Historical Institute Archive, Warsaw
KB	Korpus Bezpieczeństwa (pol. Security Cadres)
KK	Komisja Koordynacyjna (pol. Coordinating Commission)
KPP	Komunistyczna Partia Polski (pol. The Communist Party of Poland)
NKT	Nowy Teatr Kameralny (pol. New Chamber Theater)
NRO	Naczelna Rada Opiekuńcza (pol. General Welfare Council)
NSZ	Narodowe Siły Zbrojne (pol. National Armed Forces)
ORT	Obshestvo Remeslenofo zemledelcheskofo Truda, (rus. The Society for Trades and Agricultural Labor)
PAL	Polska Armia Ludowa (pol. Polish People's Army)

PLAN	Polska Ludowa Akcja Niepodległościowa (pol. Polish Popular Independence Action)
PPR	Polska Partia Robotnicza (pol. Polish Workers' Party)
PPS	Polska Partia Socjalistyczna (pol. Polish Socialist Party)
PPS-WRN	Polska Partia Socjalistyczna—Wolność, Równość, Niepodległość (pol. Polish Socialist Party—Freedom, Equality, Independence)
PS	Polscy Socjaliści (pol. Polish Socialists)
RGO	Rada Główna Opiekuńcza (pol. Main Welfare Council)
SD	Stronnictwo Demokratyczne (pol. Democratic Party)
SEPOR	Sekcja Pomocy Rzeczowej (pol. Section of Material Aid)
SKSS	Stołeczny Komitet Samopomocy Społecznej (pol. Metropolitan Committee of Mutual Social Aid)
SOB	Socjalistyczna Organizacja Bojowa (pol. Socialist Combat Organization)
TOZ	Towarzystwo Opieki Zdrowotnej (pol. Society for the Preservation of Health)
VHA	The Shoah Foundation Visual History Archive
YVA	Yad Vashem Archive, Jerusalem
ŻOB	Żydowska Organizacja Bojowa (pol. Jewish Combat Organization)
ŻOS	Żydowska Orkiestra Symfoniczna (pol. Jewish Symphonic Orchestra)
ŻOS	Żydowska Opieka Społeczna (pol. Jewish Social Welfare)
ŻSS	Żydowska Samopomoc Społeczna (pol. Jewish Self-Help)
ŻSS-KK	Żydowska Samopomoc Społeczna – Komisja Koordynacyjna (pol. Jewish Self-Help – Coordinating Commission)
ŻTOS	Żydowskie Towarzystwo Opieki Społecznej (pol. Jewish Social Welfare Association)
ŻZW	Żydowski Związek Wojskowy (pol. Jewish Fighting Union)

Notes

1. Introduction

1. Arnold Szyfman, *Moja tułaczka wojenna* (Warszawa: MON, 1960), 61.

2. Ernest W. Burgess, Robert E. Park, *Introduction to the Science of Sociology* (Chicago: University of Chicago Press, 1921), 735.

3. Todd Endelman, "Assimilation," in *The YIVO Encyclopaedia of Jews in Eastern Europe*, vol. 1, ed. G. D. Hundert (New Haven: Yale University Press, 2008), 81.

4. Jonathan Frankel, "Assimilation and the Jews in Nineteenth-Century Europe," in *Assimilation and Community: The Jews in Nineteenth-century Europe*, ed. J. Frankel, S. J. Zipperstein (Cambridge: Cambridge University Press, 1992), 16.

5. On this term see Aleksander Hertz, *The Jews in Polish Culture*, trans. Richard Lourie (Evanston, IL: Northwestern University Press, 1988).

6. On these four groups see Anna Landau-Czajka, *Syn będzie Lech . . . Asymilacja Żydów w Polsce międzywojennej* (Warszawa: Neriton, 2006), 44–45.

7. Hertz, *The Jews in Polish Culture*, 87. For more on Jewish conversion in Poland see a collection of studies in Agnieszka Jagodzińska, ed., *W poszukiwaniu religii doskonałej? Konwersja a Żydzi* (Wrocław: Wydawnictwo Uniwersytetu Wrocławskiego, 2011).

8. Magdalena Teter, "Conversions to Catholicism in the Polish-Lithuanian Commonwealth of the Seventeenth and Eighteenth Centuries," *Jewish History* 17, no. 3 (2003): 257–83.

9. Marcin Wodziński, *Haskalah and Hasidism in the Kingdom of Poland: A History of Conflict*, trans. S. Cozens (Oxford: The Littman Library of Jewish Civilization, 2005), 155.

10. Ezra Mendelsohn, "Jewish Assimilation in the Polish Lands," in *Jewish Assimilation in Modern Times*, ed. Bela Vago (Boulder, CO: Westview Press, 1981), 143.

11. It should be noted that, as Theodore R. Weeks wrote, Polish-Jewish "brotherhood" concerned only the relatively educated, "enlightened" strata of the Jewish and Polish populations, and that to a great extent this "brotherhood"—and the myth it generated—appears to have been limited to Warsaw. See Theodore R. Weeks, "Poles,

Jews and Russians, 1863–1914: The Death of the Ideal of Assimilation in the Kingdom of Poland," *Polin* 12 (1993): 243. For more on the Jewish participation in the January Uprising, see Israel Bartal and Magdalena Opalski, *Poles and Jews: A Failed Brotherhood* (Hanover: Brandeis University Press, 1992).

12. Alina Cała, *Asymilacja Żydów w Królestwie Polskim (1864–1897)* (Warszawa: PIW, 1989), 82–83.

13. According to Todd Endelman, more than half of the converts in nineteenth-century Poland came from a lower-middle class background. See "Jewish Converts in Nineteenth-Century Warsaw: A Quantitative Analysis," *Jewish Social Studies* 4, no. 1 (1997): 28–59.

14. On the Rabbinic School in Warsaw see Antony Polonsky, "Warszawska Szkoła Rabinów: Orędowniczka narodowej integracji w Królestwie Polskim," in *Duchowość żydowska w Polsce. Materiały z konferencji*, ed. M. Galas, 287–307 (Kraków: UJ, 2000). The Rabbinic School and Warsaw as the center of the Reform Movement are discussed by François Guesnet in *Polnische Juden im 19. Jahrhundert: Lebensbedingungen, Rechtsnormen und Organisation im Wandel* (Köln: Böhlau, 1998), 285–95. For the process of assimilation in nineteenth-century Polish lands see among others: Theodore Weeks, *From Assimilation to Antisemitism: The "Jewish Question" in Poland, 1850–1914* (DeKalb: Northern Illinois University Press, 2006); Agnieszka Jagodzińska, *Pomiędzy: Akulturacja Żydów Warszawy w drugiej połowie XIX wieku* (Wrocław: Wydawnictwo Uniwersytetu Wrocławskiego, 2008); Helena Datner, *Ta i tamta strona: żydowska inteligencja Warszawy drugiej połowy XIX wieku* (Warszawa: ŻIH, 2007); Alina Cała, *Asymilacja Żydów w Królestwie Polskim*; and Artur Eisenbach, *Emancypacja Żydów na ziemiach polskich 1785–1870 na tle europejskim* (Warszawa: PIW, 1988).

15. Israel Gutman, *Resistance: The Warsaw Ghetto Uprising* (Boston: Houghton Mifflin, 1994), 26–32.

16. Datner, *Ta i tamta strona*, 228–51.

17. Lucy Dawidowicz, *The Jewish Presence: Essays on Identity and History* (New York: Holt, Rinehart and Winston, 1977), 7.

18. Marek Jabłonowski, "Związek Żydów Uczestników Walk o Niepodległość Polski," in *Żydzi w Obronie Rzeczypospolitej*, ed. J. Tomaszewski (Warszawa: Cyklady, 1996), 116.

19. Joseph Lichten, "Notes on the Assimilation and Acculturation of Jews in Poland," in *The Jews in Poland*, ed. C. Abramsky, M. Jachimczyk, A. Polonsky (Oxford: Basil Blackwell, 1986), 119.

20. Endelman, "Jewish Converts in Nineteenth-Century Warsaw," 50.

21. See Landau-Czajka, *Syn będzie Lech*, 24.

22. Chone Schmeruk, "Hebrew-Yiddish-Polish: A Trilingual Jewish Culture," in *The Jews of Poland Between Two World Wars*, ed. I. Gutman, 285–311 (London: University Press of New England, 1989).

23. For more see Sean Martin, "Jewish Youth Between Tradition and Assimilation: Exploring Jewish Identity in Interwar Kraków," *The Polish Review* 46, no. 4 (2001): 461–77.

24. Hertz, *The Jews in Polish Culture*, 210.

25. Monika Adamczyk-Garbowska, "Literatura jidysz w polskich przekładach dawniej i dziś," in *Jidyszland—polskie przestrzenie*, ed. E. Geller, M. Polit (Warszawa: Wydawnictwo UW, 2008), 160.

26. Eugenia Prokop-Janiec, *Polish-Jewish Literature in the Interwar Years*, trans. A. Shenitzer (Syracuse: Syracuse University Press, 2003), 26. For more on this group see also Antony Polonsky, "'Why Did They Hate Tuwim and Boy So Much': Jews and 'Artificial Jews' in the Literary Polemics of the Second Polish Republic," in *Antisemitism and its Opponents in Modern Poland*, ed. R. Blobaum, 189–209 (Ithaca: Cornell University Press, 2005); and Alina Molisak, Zuzanna Kołodziejska, ed., *Żydowski Polak, polski Żyd. Problem tożsamości w literaturze polsko-żydowskiej* (Warszawa: Elipsa, 2011).

27. Prokop-Janiec, *Polish-Jewish Literature*, 82. On the view of assimilation in *Nasz Przegląd* and its evolution through the 1930s see Anna Landau-Czajka, "Polacy w oczach 'Naszego Przeglądu,'" *Kwartalnik Historii Żydów* 240, no. 4 (2011): 491–506.

28. Shimon Frost, *Schooling as a Socio-political Expression: Jewish Education in Interwar Poland* (Jerusalem: The Magnes Press, The Hebrew University, 1998), 25–26.

29. Gershon Bacon, "National Revival, Ongoing Acculturation—Jewish Education in Interwar Poland," *Simon Dubnow Institut Yearbook*, no. 1 (2002): 83.

30. Celia Heller, *On the Edge of Destruction: Jews of Poland between the Two World Wars* (New York: Columbia University Press, 1977), 220.

31. Bacon, "National Revival, Ongoing Acculturation," 89.

32. Visual History Archive (VHA) 12827 (Interview with Jerzy Lando).

33. Joanna Rostropowicz Clark, "Adam Mickiewicz's 'Forty and Four' or the Dangers of Playing with Kabbalah," *Polin* 7 (1992): 57–62.

34. For more, see for example Laura Quercioli Mincer, "The Controversy over Mickiewicz's Jewish Origin," *Polin* 19 (2007): 447–57.

35. Magdalena Opalski, "Polish-Jewish Relations and the January Uprising: the Polish Perspective," *Polin* 1 (1988), 71.

36. The text of the proclamation can be found in E. Luninski, *Berek Joselewicz i jego syn. Zarys Historyczny* (Warszawa, 1909), 116–17. Quoted after Maria Janion, *Bohater, spisek, śmierć. Wykłady żydowskie* (Warszawa: WAB, 2009), 26.

37. Maria Janion, *Pułkownik żydowski: życiorys romantyczny i nieromantyczny* (Kraków: Judaica, 2008), 90–91.

38. Katrin Steffen, *Jüdische Polonität. Ethnizität und Nation im Spiegel der polnischsprachigen jüdischen Presse 1918–1939* (Göttingen: Vandenhoeck & Ruprecht, 2004), 143.

39. A selection of diaries translated into English can be found in Jeffrey Shandler, ed., *Awakening Lives: Autobiographies of Jewish Youth in Poland before the Holocaust* (London: Yale University Press, 2002).

40. See Lichten, "Notes on the Assimilation," 117–21.

41. Jerzy Holzer, "Relations between Polish and Jewish left wing groups in interwar Poland," in *The Jews in Poland*, 145.

42. Jaff Schatz, *The Generation: The Rise and Fall of the Jewish Communists of Poland* (Berkeley: University of California Press, 1991), 53.

43. Gertrud Pickhan, "Yiddishkayt and Class Consciousness: The Bund and its Minority Concept," *East European Jewish Affairs* 39, no. 2 (2009), 259.

44. Ezra Mendelsohn, *Zionism in Poland: The Formative Years, 1915–1926* (New Haven: Yale University Press, 1981), 346.

45. Steffen, *Jüdische Polonität*, 12.

46. *Zjednoczenie* Jan. 15, 1932. Quoted in Lichten, "Notes on the Assimilation," 123.

47. VHA 31709 (Interview with Alina Prądzyńska).

48. VHA 45905 (Interview with Alina Brodzka-Wald).

49. On the use of diaries and memoirs in Holocaust research, see among others James E. Young, *Writing and Re-writing the Holocaust* (Bloomington: Indiana University Press, 1988); Lawrence E. Langer, *Holocaust Testimonies: The Ruins of Memory* (New Haven: Yale University Press, 1991); Zoë Waxman, *Writing the Holocaust: Identity, Testimony, Representation* (Oxford: Oxford University Press, 2006). On the use of Holocaust sources in general see Raul Hilberg, *Sources of Holocaust Research: An Analysis* (Chicago: Ivan R. Dee, 2001). Two very thorough guides to the sources for the Holocaust in Poland are Alina Skibińska, *Źródła do badań nad zagładą Żydów na okupowanych ziemiach polskich. Przewodnik archiwalno-bibliograficzny* (Warszawa: Cyklady, 2007) and Bolesław Woszczyński and Violetta Urbaniak, ed., *Źródła archiwalne do dziejów Żydów w Polsce* (Warszawa: Naczelna Dyrekcja Archiwów Państwowych, 2001).

50. Janusz Korczak, *The Ghetto Years 1939–1942*, trans. J. Bachrach (Tel Aviv: The Ghetto Fighters House, 1980), 174.

51. Waxman, *Writing the Holocaust*, 158. See also Susan L. Pentlin, "Holocaust Victims of Privilege," in *Problems Unique to the Holocaust*, ed. H. J. Cargas, 25–42 (Lexington: The University Press of Kentucky, 1999). On how Holocaust experience influenced survivors' perception of pre-war Poland see Shandler, *Awakening Lives*, xvi–xvii.

52. For the English translation of a selection of documents from the archive see Joseph Kermish, ed., *To Live With Honor and Die with Honor: Selected Documents from the Warsaw Ghetto Underground Archives "O.S." ["Oneg Shabbath"]* (Jerusalem: Yad Vashem, 1986), Marta Markowska, ed., *The Ringelblum Archive: Annihilation—Day by Day* (Warszawa: KARTA, 2008).

53. Samuel D. Kassow, *Who Will Write Our History? Emanuel Ringelblum, the Warsaw Ghetto, and the Oyneg Shabes Archive* (Bloomington: Indiana University Press, 2007), 8.

54. On this see David Roskies, "Landkentenish: Yiddish Belles Lettres in the Warsaw Ghetto," in *Holocaust Chronicles: Individualizing the Holocaust through Diaries and Other Contemporaneous Personal Accounts*, ed. R. M. Shapiro (Hoboken, NJ: KTAV, 1999), 21.

55. Moshe Rosman, *How Jewish Is Jewish History?* (Oxford: The Littman Library of Jewish Civilization, 2007), 53.

56. On the Nazi ghettoization policy in occupied Poland see Dan Michman, *The Emergence of Jewish Ghettos during the Holocaust*, trans. L. J. Schramm (Cambridge: Cambridge University Press, 2011) and "The Polish Ghettos," in Christopher R. Browning, *The Origins of the Final Solution: The Evolution of Nazi Jewish Policy, September 1939 – March 1942*, 111–68 (London: William Heinemann, 2004). The authoritative work on the Warsaw ghetto is Barbara Engelking and Jacek Leociak, *The Warsaw Ghetto: A Guide to the Perished City*, trans. E. Harris (New Haven: Yale University Press, 2009).

57. Antoni Marianowicz, *Life Strictly Forbidden*, trans. A. Nitecki (London: Vallentine Mitchell, 2004), 4.

2. In the Warsaw Ghetto

1. Chaim A. Kaplan, *Scroll of Agony: The Warsaw Diary of Chaim A. Kaplan*, trans. and ed. A. I. Katsh (Bloomington: Indiana University Press, 1999), 2.

2. Quoted in Joseph Lichten, "Notes on the Assimilation," 124.

3. JHIA, Ringelblum Archive (AR) II/129 ("Wspomnienia z pierwszych miesięcy okupacji w Warszawie (09.1939–01.1940)"), 1.

4. See for example Adam Starkopf, *There Is Always Time to Die*, ed. G. Hirschler (New York: Holocaust Library, 1981), 10; and Adina Blady Szwajger, *I Remember Nothing More: The Warsaw Children's Hospital and the Jewish Resistance*, trans. T. Darowska and D. Stok (London: Collins Harvill, 1990), 6.

5. Emanuel Ringelblum, *Polish-Jewish Relations during the Second World War*, ed. J. Kermish, S. Krakowski (Jerusalem: Yad Vashem, 1974), 32.

6. See also Benjamin Meritchak, *Jews-Officers in the Polish Armed Forces 1939–1945* (Tel Aviv: Association of Jewish War Veterans of Polish Armies in Israel, 2001), 39–196. Among 2,261 names of Jewish officers taking part in the September campaign, there are 470 names of officers from Warsaw. A vast majority of them are medical doctors.

7. Ringelblum, *Polish-Jewish Relations*, 24.

8. Ibid., 34.

9. According to *Gazeta Żydowska*, just before the establishment of the ghetto seventy-five percent of pre-war Jewish businesses had been liquidated and Jewish

employment was only twelve percent of the pre-war total in industry and sixteen percent in commerce. See Kassow, *Who Will Write Our History?*, 423.

10. *Nowy Kurier Warszawski* 24 Nov. 1939. Quoted in Jan Grabowski, *Ja tego Żyda znam!' Szantażowanie Żydów w Warszawie 1939–1943* (Warszawa: IFiS PAN, 2004), 61.

11. Ludwik Landau, *Kronika lat wojny i okupacji*, vol. 1, ed. Z. Landau, J. Tomaszewski (Warszawa: PWN, 1962), 122.

12. Ibid., 185.

13. Ibid., 191. According to historian Tomasz Szarota, a proof of "Arian background" for the *mischlinge* (people coming from mixed, Polish-Jewish marriages) cost 1,200 złoty while foreign passports for Jews were valued at 20 to 1,000 dollars. Tomasz Szarota, *Okupowanej Warszawy dzień powszedni: Studium historyczne* (Warszawa: Czytelnik, 1982), 479.

14. Landau, *Kronika*, 239.

15. Ibid., 230.

16. Kaplan, *Scroll of Agony*, 78.

17. Yad Vashem Archive (YVA) O.33/438 (Pola Rotszyld).

18. Landau, *Kronika*, 606.

19. Starkopf, *There is Always Time to Die*, 6.

20. Landau, *Kronika*, 176.

21. Ibid., 290. See also Witold Kula, *Dziennik czasu okupacji*, ed. M. Kula (Warszawa: PIW, 1994), 57.

22. Yitzhak Arad, ed., *Documents on the Holocaust: Selected Sources on the Destruction of the Jews of Germany and Austria, Poland and the Soviet Union* (Jerusalem: Yad Vashem, 1981), 220–21.

23. Henryk Makower, *Pamiętnik z getta warszawskiego. Październik 1940–Styczeń 1943*, ed. N. Makower (Wrocław: Zakład Narodowy im. Ossolińskich, 1987), 25. Stanisław Różycki attributes a similar way of thinking to those who decided to come back to Warsaw and move into the ghetto after spending the first part of the occupation in the East: "After all, ghetto is not the worst that can happen. I will be among my own, surrounded by family, friends, people who wish each other well, people of the same faith and brothers in unhappiness. It will be easier to deal with difficult moments. There are two sides to every story." JHIA AR I/428 (Stanisław Różycki, To jest getto! (reportaż z inferna XX Wieku) [7.12.1941], 1. For detailed information on anti-Semitic incidents in occupied Warsaw prior to the establishment of the ghetto see Tomasz Szarota, *U progu zagłady. Zajścia antyżydowskie i pogromy w okupowanej Europie: Warszawa, Paryż, Amsterdam, Antwerpia, Kowno* (Warszawa: Sic!, 2000), 19–83.

24. Landau, *Kronika*, 57.

25. Barbara Engelking, *Holocaust and Memory: The Experience of Holocaust and Its Consequences: An Investigation Based on Personal Narratives*, ed. G. Paulsson, trans. E. Harris (London: Leicester University Press, 2001), 87.

26. Landau, *Kronika*, 556.

27. VHA 25555 (Interview with Helena Balicka).

28. Ibid.

29. Ringelblum, *Polish-Jewish Relations*, 53.

30. Landau, *Kronika*, 771.

31. Foreign citizens were initially allowed to stay on the "Aryan" side. Later they had to move into the ghetto, but did not have to wear armbands and were not subjected to forced labor. They also received extra food rations. On that see Agnieszka Haska, *"Jestem Żydem, chcę wejść": Hotel Polski w Warszawie, 1943* (Warszawa: IFiS PAN, 2006), 27–28.

32. Janina Kruszewska, "Roman," in Renata Piątkowska, *Roman Kramsztyk: Miedzy "Ziemiańską" a Montparnassem* (Warszawa: Neriton, 2004), 162.

33. Emanuel Ringelblum, *Ksovim fun geto*, vol. 1 (Varshe: Yidish Bukh: 1961), 316 (not in the English edition). Whenever possible I will quote from the English edition of Ringelblum's chronicle. As, however, it is an abridged version, based on the 1952 Polish edition rather than on the original text, in some instances I will refer to the Yiddish edition. See also Katarzyna Person, "The Initial Reception and First Publications from the Ringelblum Archive in Poland, 1946–1952," *Gal-Ed* 23 (2012): 59–76.

34. Ringelblum, *Ksovim fun geto*: 1, 232.

35. Stanisław Adler, *In the Warsaw Ghetto: 1940–1943; An Account of a Witness*, trans. S. Chmielewska-Philip (Jerusalem: Yad Vashem, 1982), 8. Similarly, on the "Aryan" side of Warsaw, the Warsaw City Council employed as clerks the elite of Warsaw's intellectual life, including the former Dean of the Warsaw University. Szarota, *Okupowanej Warszawy*, 115.

36. Stefan Ernest, *O wojnie wielkich Niemiec z Żydami Europy 1939–1943*, ed. M. Młodkowska (Warszawa: Czytelnik, ŻIH, 2003), 28.

37. According to Reich: "One of the greatest problems of work in the Judenrat was that one had to employ many people who had no qualifications. For example there were no schools in the ghetto so the teachers were unemployed and had to be given jobs. Judenrat had therefore scores of employees with lack of qualifications and not fit for office work." YVA 03/2996 (Marceli Reich).

38. JHIA, 301/4492 (Judyta Truskier), 1. Peretz Opoczyński described the ghetto post office as "run by a small clique of Polish-speaking Jews who grabbed all the lucrative jobs for themselves." Quoted in Kassow, *Who Will Write our History?*, 187.

39. Anka Grupińska, *Ciągle po kole: Rozmowy z żołnierzami getta warszawskiego* (Warszawa: Twój Styl, 2001), 150.

40. Testimony of Szlomo Szapira, quoted in Engelking and Leociak, *The Warsaw Ghetto*, 368.

41. Michael Mazor, *The Vanished City: Everyday Life in the Warsaw Ghetto*, trans. D. Jacobson (New York: Marsilio Publishers, 1993), 37.

42. JHIA 302/38 (Stanisław Gombiński), 19.

43. Makower, *Pamiętnik*, 22.

44. Ibid., 20. See also a report in JHIA AR I/81 ("Opracowanie dotyczące statystyki ludności żydowskiej w Warszawie 1939–1941") for a comparison between earnings of various professional groups. According to the report clerks employed in the Jewish Self-Help and the Judenrat earned in August 1941 250 złoty a month as opposed to 320 złoty for a manual worker in a German "shop" and 260 złoty for a manual worker in a private enterprise. A worker at *placówka* would make only 93,37 złoty, but his earnings were multiplied by smuggling opportunities.

45. Daniel Blatman and Israel Gutman, "Youth and Resistance Movements in Historical Perspectives," *Yad Vashem Studies* 23 (1993), 20.

46. Helena Szereszewska, *Memoirs from Occupied Warsaw 1940–1945*, trans. A. Mariańska (London: Vallentine Mitchell, 1997), 24.

47. Marianowicz, *Life Strictly Forbidden*, 232.

48. Korczak, *The Ghetto Years*, 48.

49. Marek Edelman, quoted in Władysław Bartoszewski, *The Warsaw Ghetto: A Christian's Testimony*, trans. S.G. Cappellari (London: Lamp Press, 1987), 16.

50. AAN, 202/II-28 (Delegatura Rządu na Kraj, "Meldunki o sytuacji w getcie warszawskim"), quoted in Engelking, Leociak, *The Warsaw Ghetto*, 396.

51. JHIA AR I/428 (Stanisław Różycki, "To jest getto!"), 24.

52. AR I/65 ("Boy branzhe"), trans. *To Live with Honor*, 345.

53. Emanuel Ringelblum, *Notes from the Warsaw Ghetto: The Journal of Emanuel Ringelblum*, trans. J. Sloan (New York: Schocken Books, 1988), 282.

54. Rachela Auerbach, "Lament Rzeczy Martwych," *Przełom* no. 2 (1946), 7.

55. AR I/36 ("Asymilatorzy i neofici w okresie działań wojennych i zamkniętej dzielnicy żydowskiej"), 1.

56. Ryszad, Interview 34 in Engelking, *Holocaust and Memory*, 41.

57. Ludwik Hirszfeld, *Historia jednego życia* (Warszawa: Czytelnik, 2000), 320.

58. AR I/38 (Marian Małowist, "Referat o zainteresowaniach i postawach młodzieży polskiej i żydowskiej przed wojna i w czasie okupacji"), 11.

59. For example, Michael Zylberberg, an observant Jew and a secretary of the House Committee at 33 Chłodna Street, recounts the following members of the Committee: "Isidor Krongold-Kronski, an active member of the Polish Socialist Party, was one. There was also Joseph Kilbert, a Talmudic scholar and former pupil of the famous Lublin Yeshiva; Mieczyslaw Ferster, a baptised Jew, the Warsaw representative of a Scandinavian engineering firm (S.K.F); Dr. Korman, a pediatrician; Michael Schenker, an engineer; Herman, an industrialist, a relative of the historian Emanuel Ringelblum; and, most important of all, Korczak himself." Michael Zylberberg, *A Warsaw Diary, 1939–1945* (London, Vallentine Mitchell, 1969), 25.

60. AR I/36 ("Asymilatorzy i neofici w okresie działań wojennych i zamkniętej dzielnicy żydowskiej"), trans. *To Live with Honor*, 634.

61. Abraham Lewin, *A Cup of Tears: A Diary of the Warsaw Ghetto*, ed. A. Polonsky, trans. C. Hutton (London: Fontana 1990), 86.

62. Jerzy, Interview 35 in Engelking, *Holocaust and Memory*, 195.

63. Ringelblum, *Ksovim fun geto*: 1, 90.

64. This is the term that, according to Nathan Eck, workers in the Alexander Landau shop used when revolting against members of the *Oyneg Shabes* seeking refuge in the shop. Quoted by Antony Polonsky in Lewin, *A Cup of Tears*, 179n245. See also Blatman, Gutman, "Youth and Resistance Movements in Historical Perspectives," 41.

65. Adam Czerniaków, *The Warsaw Diary of Adam Czerniakow: Prelude to Doom*, ed. R. Hilberg, S. Staron, J. Kermisz (Chicago: Ivan R. Dee, 1999), 105.

66. For religious life in the Warsaw Ghetto see Shimon Huberband, *Kiddush Hashem: Jewish Religious and Cultural Life in Poland during the Holocaust*, ed. J. Gurock and R. Hirt (New York: Yeshiva University Press, 1987). More information on religious life after the 1942 Aktion can be found in Hillel Seidman, *Togbukh fun varshaver geto* (Buenos Ayres: Tsentral-farband fun Poylishe Yidn in Argentine, 1947).

67. Probably the most famous rabbi who found refuge in the Warsaw ghetto was Kalonymus Kalmish Shapira, a tzaddik from Piaseczno. On that see Nehemia Polen, *The Holy Fire: The Teachings of Rabbi Kalonymus Kalman Shapira, the Rebbe of the Warsaw Ghetto* (Northvale, NJ: Jason Aronson, 1994). On how the religious department coexisted with the rest of the Self-Help and especially with its ardent atheist members see Ruta Sakowska, *Ludzie z dzielnicy zamkniętej: Z dziejów Żydów w Warszawie w latach okupacji hitlerowskiej październik 1939–marzec 1943* (Warszawa: PWN, 1993), 137.

68. Archiwum Państwowe m. st. Warszawy [APW], ObJ, syg. 5, Wydział Ewidencji Ludności Żydowskiej, Stan ilości mieszkańców i nieruchomości w dzielnicy żydowskiej na dzień 1 stycznia 1941 r.

69. See Peter F. Dembowski, *Christians in the Warsaw Ghetto: An Epitaph for the Unremembered* (Notre Dame, IN: University of Notre Dame Press, 2005), 66. See also Havi Ben-Sasson, "Christians in the Ghetto: All Saint's Church, Birth of the Holy Virgin Mary Church and the Jews of the Warsaw Ghetto," *Yad Vashem Studies* 31 (2003): 153–73.

70. On the other hand, Rudolf Hermelin notes in his testimony that only about 100 people at a time gathered for Sunday masses (see JHIA 301/4151 Rudolf Hermelin).

71. See Dembowski, *Christians*, 65–67. See also Philip Friedman, "For Your Freedom as Well as Ours," in *Their Brothers' Keepers* (New York: Crown Publishers, 1957), 125.

72. Kaplan, *Scroll of Agony*, 309.

73. Antoni Czarnecki, "Parafia Wszystkich Świętych," in *Za co groziła śmierć: Polacy z pomocą Żydom w czasie okupacji*, ed. A. Smólski (Warsaw: PAX, 1981), 208.

74. Alexander Donat, *The Holocaust Kingdom: A Memoir* (New York: Holocaust Library, 1978), 29. Antoni Szydłowski quoted in Bartoszewski, *Warsaw Ghetto*, 34.

75. Ringelblum, *Notes from the Warsaw Ghetto*, 101–2 and 327.

76. Hirszfeld, *Historia*, 364.

77. JHIA AR/I/100 (Zygmunt Millet, "Wspomnienie o pracy w Służbie Porządkowej"), 3.

78. ARG II/129 ("Wspomnienia z pierwszych miesięcy okupacji w Warszawie (09.1939–01.1940)"), 15. Witold Kula, whose wife was of Jewish origin, noted at that point in his diary that the only choice was "between going East or to the ghetto." Kula, *Dziennik*, 35.

79. Letter from the Superintendent of the Protestant Church in Poland to Adam Roniker of November 25, 1940 (AAN RGO (Krakow) 5 ("Korespondencja w sprawach mniejszości narodowych").

80. Letter of Archbishop Adam Sapieha to Roniker, October 30, 1940 (AAN, RGO (Kraków) 5:19–20 (Korespondencja w sprawach mniejszości narodowych)).

81. See the protocol from the RGO meeting of November 21, 1940, (AAN, RGO (Kraków) 5 (Korespondencja w sprawach mniejszości narodowych)).

82. See Ringelblum, *Notes from the Warsaw Ghetto*, 129. Even though Hirszfeld claims that it was Roniker himself who handed the list to the Gestapo, this is not proved. Hirszfeld, *Historia*, 129. In a list of potential German collaborators active in the Warsaw Ghetto dated to 1941, an RGO employee of Jewish origin is accused of having handed the list to the Gestapo (AAN 202/II-26 "Meldunki o sytuacji w getcie").

83. Adler, *In the Warsaw Ghetto*, 169. According to the RGO archives, in December 1941 Germans suddenly proposed to free thirty to forty of those identified by Archbishop Adam Sapieha, the de facto head of the Polish Catholic Church, as "Catholics of non-'Aryan' origin" from the rigors of anti-Jewish legislation. This offer was turned down in all likelihood because of fears of possibly unmasking Jewish converts hiding on the "Aryan" side. Quoted in Dariusz Libionka, "Antisemitism, Anti-Judaism, and the Polish Catholic Clergy during the Second World War, 1939–1945," in *Antisemitism and its Opponents in Modern Poland*, ed. R. Blobaum (Ithaca: Cornell University Press 2005), 338.

84. Ringelblum, *Notes from the Warsaw Ghetto*, 236.

85. Kaplan, *Scroll of Agony*, 250.

86. Czarnecki, "Parafia Wszystkich Świętych," 207.

87. Adler, *In the Warsaw Ghetto*, 171. See also Hirszfeld, *Historia*, 324.

88. Ringelblum, *Notes from the Warsaw Ghetto*, 214.

89. Adler, *In the Warsaw Ghetto*, 62 and 181.

90. Ringelblum, *Notes from the Warsaw Ghetto*, 146. According to Michael Mazor, Czerniaków was to say: "We are no longer the Israelite community of pre-war

times, but the Jewish sector of the capital, where all inhabitants enjoy the same rights." Mazor, *The Vanished City*, 28.

91. Adler, *In the Warsaw Ghetto*, 170.

92. Czerniaków, *The Warsaw Diary*, 263.

93. Hirszfeld, *Historia*, 369.

94. Further on Godlewski, see Karol Madaj, Małgorzata Żuławik, *Proboszcz getta* (Warszawa: IPN, 2010).

95. The other Catholic priests in the ghetto were as follows. In the Nativity of the Blessed Virgin Mary: Seweryn Popławski and Henryk Komorowski. In All Saints: Antoni Czarnecki. Czarnecki was the only one to leave a very brief and factual testimony detailing his time in the ghetto. The third church in the ghetto, St. Augustine, at 48/50 NowolipkiSstreet, remained closed. Andrzej Marek ran in its cellars his theater—Teatr Nowy Kameralny (see chapter 4). The Reformed Evangelical Church was placed just outside the ghetto wall, and a corridor linking it to the ghetto was made through the house on Przejazd Street.

96. VHA 45905 (Interview with Alina Brodzka-Wald).

97. AR I/282 ([Natan Koniński?], "Relacja o pogrzebie Żyda–katolika w getcie warszawskim. (10.08.1941)").

98. On that see JHIA 301/4809 (A. Górska-Oppenheim, P. Landsbergowa). According to this testimony, seventy percent of children attending the school were not baptized.

99. Adler, *In the Warsaw Ghetto*, 171.

100. Hirszfield, *Historia*, 361.

101. Makower, *Pamiętnik*, 180.

102. JHIA 301/4151 (Rudolf Hermelin). The list includes twenty-two families, seventeen of which were baptized. Out of the five non-baptized ones, two were connected by family ties to baptized inhabitants of the building.

103. JHIA 301/4151 (Rudolf Hermelin) also Czarnecki, "Parafia Wszystkich Świętych," 208.

104. Ringelblum, *Notes from the Warsaw Ghetto*, 210 and 623. This is contradicted by Rev. Czarnecki who recalls problems with getting food supplies for the converts. Czarnecki, "Parafia Wszystkich Świętych," 210.

105. Donat, *The Holocaust Kingdom*, 28.

106. Czarnecki, "Parafia Wszystkich Świętych," 208.

107. For one such case, the baptism of attorney Tadeusz Edelman just before the first action, see Hirszfeld, *Historia*, 386.

108. AR I/86 ("Questionnaire on the situation in the Warsaw Ghetto"), trans. *To Live with Honor*, 746.

109. Kaplan, *Scroll of Agony*, 78–79 and 250.

110. Lewin, *A Cup of Tears*, 116.

111. Jerzy, Interview 35 in Engelking, *Holocaust and Memory*, 198.

112. Mieczysław Stawski, *Deszcz pada wszędzie* (Stockholm: Jednośćć, 1981), 78.

113. Blady-Szwajger, *I Remember Nothing More*, 49.

114. Adler, *In the Warsaw Ghetto*, 183; Mary Berg, *The Diary of Mary Berg: Growing up in the Warsaw Ghetto*, ed. S. L. Pentlin (Oxford: Oneworld, 2006), 118.

115. Itzhak Katzenelson, *Vittel Diary (22.5.43–16.9.43)*, trans. M. Coben (Ghetto Fighters House, 1964), 80.

116. YVA O.3/2358 (Dr. Stanisław Waller).

117. See Jonathan Webber, "Jewish Identities in the Holocaust: Martyrdom as a Representative Category," *Polin* 13 (2000): 128–46.

118. See YVA O.33/258 (Tadeusz Szymkiewicz), YVA M.49/5688 (Anonymous), YVA M.49.E/5624 (Helena Gadomska).

119. Hirszfeld, *Historia*, 364.

120. Ibid.

121. Quoted in Sakowska, *Ludzie z dzielnicy zamkniętej*, 140. "God Who for Centuries" is a Polish Catholic hymn, the unofficial anthem of Poland in the nineteenth century, and one probably most strongly associated with Catholic patriotism. From January 1941, singing "God Who for Centuries" was forbidden in churches on the "Aryan" side of Warsaw.

122. YVA O.3/2358 (Dr. Stanisław Waller).

123. According to an anonymous testimony Godlewski saved children from the ghetto by hiding them in a convent in the suburbs of Warsaw (JHIA 301/5688). In 2009 Godlewski posthumously received the title of the Righteous Among the Nations.

124. Ewa Geller, "The Jews of Warsaw as a Speech Community: Homage to Warsaw Yiddish," in *Żydzi Warszawy: Materiały konferencji w 100. rocznicę urodzin Emanuela Ringelbluma*, ed. E. Bergman (Warszawa: ŻIH, 2000), 115.

125. Ringelblum, *Notes from the Warsaw Ghetto*, 62. Similarly, Antoni Marianowicz notes that in the first days of the ghetto he was reproached by a passerby for speaking Polish. Marianowicz, *Life Strictly Forbidden*, 46.

126. Ringelblum, *Ksovim fun geto*: 1, 232.

127. Adler, *In the Warsaw Ghetto*, 11.

128. Blady-Szwajger, *I Remember Nothing More*, 36. On the same point see VHA 28478 (Interview with Marysia Warman).

129. JHIA AR I/74 ("Szkolnictwo").

130. JHIA AR I/38 (Marian Małowist, "Referat o zainteresowaniach i postawach młodzieży polskiej i żydowskiej przed wojną i w czasie okupacji"), 9.

131. Hersz Wasser, "Yiddish Culture Organization "YIKOR," Warsaw Ghetto, 1940–1942," trans. *To Live with Honor*, 442.

132. *Gazeta Żydowska* 20 (1940), 3.

133. JHIA 302/121 (Beniamin Horowitz), 176.

134. Wanda Lubelska, *Listy z getta* (Warszawa: Biblioteka Narodowa, 2000), 23.

135. Yitzhak Zuckerman, *A Surplus of Memory: Chronicle of the Warsaw Ghetto Uprising*, ed. and trans. B. Harshav (Oxford: University of California Press, 1986), 87. Similarly to Zionists described by Zuckerman, Marek Edelman from the Bund claims that he spoke Yiddish but he never learned to read it well. Joanna Szczęsna, "I już nic nie było tak jak przedtem: Rozmowa z Markiem Edelmanem," *Gazeta Wyborcza* April 22, 1999, http://wyborcza.pl/1,89798,5119367.html (accessed September 2012).

136. For underground publications from the Warsaw Ghetto see the Ringelblum Archive.

137. JHIA AR I/87 ("Protest-briv gegn di handlung fun der artist Diana Blumenfeld").

138. Ringelblum, *Notes from the Warsaw Ghetto*, 289.

139. AR I/86 ("Questionnaire on the situation in the Warsaw Ghetto"), trans. *To Live with Honor*, 756.

140. Ibid., 734–37.

141. Answering in Polish "nie rozumiem" (pol. I do not understand) to any questions in German was one of the guidelines of the Polish underground, which discouraged people from engaging in conversations with German soldiers. See Szarota, *Okupowanej Warszawy*, 563.

142. Ringleblum, *Notes from the Warsaw Ghetto*, 289.

143. AR I/86 ("Questionnaire on the situation in the Warsaw Ghetto"), trans. *To Live with Honor*, 753.

144. On this see Israel Gutman interviewed by Barbara Engelking in "O tym jak z wewnątrz getta patrzono na stronę aryjską z profesorem Israelem Gutmanem rozmawia Barbara Engelking," *Zagłada Żydow. Studia i Materiały* 1 (2005): 232.

145. Antonina Gurycka, *Nigdy nic nie wiadomo . . .* (Warszawa: WIP, 2001), 24. Quoted in Joanna Nalewajko-Kulikov, *Strategie przetrwania: Żydzi po aryjskiej stronie Warszawy* (Warszawa: Neriton, 2004).

146. Hirszfeld, *Historia*, 279.

147. Bożena Umińska, "Recenzja: Jacek Leociak, Tekst wobec zagłady (O relacjach getta warszawskiego)," *Biuletyn Żydowskiego Instytutu Historycznego* 190, no. 2 (1999): 172.

148. JIHA Kolekcja Bernarda Marka no. 546 (Listy Hali do Pani Stefanii).

149. Władysław Szlengel, "Paszport," trans. R. Gliniak, www.zchor.org/szlengel/poems2.htm (accessed September 2009).

150. See Barbara Temkin-Bermanowa, *Dziennik z Podziemia*, ed. A. Grupińska, P. Szapiro (Warszawa: Twój Styl 2000), 31.

151. Mazor, *The Vanished City*, 114. It is difficult to assess to what extent this was a realistic view of the situation on the "Aryan" side and to what extent it was oversimplification. See Gunnar Paulsson, *Secret City: The Hidden Jews of Warsaw,*

1940–1945 (London: Yale University Press, 2002), 246, and Ringelblum, *Polish-Jewish Relations*, 101.

152. Franciszka Grünberg in *Words To Outlive Us: Eyewitness Accounts from the Warsaw Ghetto*, ed. M. Grynberg, trans. P. Boehm (New York: Holt and Company, 2002), 317.

153. Temkin-Bermanowa, *Dziennik z Podziemia*, 35. This feeling that the ghetto was safer than the "Aryan" side was also commonly shared by those who nonetheless chose to stay outside it. See JHIA 301/4651 (Frajnd), 6. See also the memoirs of Maria Szelestowska who, starving while in hiding on the "Aryan" side, often visited her family in the ghetto to get fed. Maria Szelestowska, *Lubię żyć* (Warszawa: Czytelnik, 2000), 20.

154. Lubelska, *Listy*, 55.

155. Makower, *Pamiętnik*, 16.

156. Ludwig Fischer, *Raporty Ludwiga Fischera, gubernatora Dystryktu Warszawskiego 1939–1944*, ed. K. Dunin-Wąsowicz et al. (Warszawa, 1987), 260.

157. Donat, *The Holocaust Kingdom*, 29.

158. JHIA 301/6094 (Zdzisław Libera), 2.

159. See Israel Gutman, Shmuel Krakowski, *Unequal Victims: Poles and Jews during Word War Two* (New York: Holocaust Library, 1986), 148.

160. Gutman, "O tym jak z wewnątrz getta patrzono na stronę aryjską," 230.

161. JHIA AR I/323 Peretz Opoczyński ("Goyim in geto"), trans. Samuel Kassow, "Polish Jewish Relations in the Writings of Emanuel Ringelblum," in *Contested Memories*, 149n37. For the extent of smuggling and the variety of objects that could be smuggled into and from the ghetto see descriptions of legal cases against smugglers in the Stadthauptmannschaft Warschau collection (no. 485) in Archiwum Państwowe m.st. Warszawy.

162. See Kassow, *Who Will Write*, 374.

163. Huberband, *Kiddush Hashem*, 208.

164. Ibid., 350.

165. Gutman, "O tym jak z wewnątrz getta patrzono na stronę aryjską," 230. Among *placówki* workers were, however, also those who after bribing the guards would leave the groups and spend their time on the "Aryan" side meeting Polish friends. JHIA 301/5815 (Stanisław Chmielewski), 14.

166. Only a few Jewish diarists try to defend Poles, blaming the situation on Germans or the pre-war anti-Semitic authorities. See Landau, *Kronika*, 228 and 367.

167. Havi Ben Sasson, "'Chcemy wierzyć w inną Polskę' Stosunki Polsko-Żydowskie w prasie podziemnej getta warszawskiego," *Zagłada Żydów Studia i Materiały*, no. 1 (2005): 103.

168. Avraham Lewin, "Twilight Days: Missing Pages from Avraham Lewin's Warsaw Ghetto Diary, May–July 1942," ed. H. Ben-Sasson and L. Preiss, *Yad Vashem Studies* 33 (2005): 38.

169. Gutman, "O tym jak z wewnątrz getta patrzono na stronę aryjską," 232. For hearsay about conditions on the "Aryan" side circulating in the ghetto see also Szereszewska, *Memoirs*, 150.

170. JIHA Kolekcja Bernarda Marka no. 546 (Listy Hali do Pani Stefanii).

171. Szczęsna, "I już nic nie było jak przedtem."

172. Kassow, "Polish-Jewish Relations," 150.

3. The Judenrat, Self-Help, and the Fight for the Soul of the Ghetto

1. "Dziennik Urzędowy Szefa Okręgu Warszawskiego," Jan. 15, 1940. Quoted in Engelking, Leociak, *The Warsaw Ghetto*, 138.

2. Raul Hilberg, Stanislaw Staron, "Introduction," in Czerniaków, *The Warsaw Diary*, 43.

3. JHIA 302/38 (Stanisław Gombiński), 56.

4. Czerniaków, *The Warsaw Diary*, 172.

5. The so far unparalleled study of the subject is Tatiana Bernstein, "Żydzi warszawscy w hitlerowskich obozach pracy przymusowej," *Biuletyn Żydowskiego Instytutu Historycznego* 67, no. 3 (1968): 39–65. See also Marta Janczewska, "Obozy pracy przymusowej dla Żydow na terenie dystryktu warszawskiego," in *Prowincja noc: Życie i zagłada Żydów w dystrykcie warszawskim*, ed. Barbara Engelking, Jacek Leociak, Dariusz Libionka, 271–320 (Warszawa: IFiS PAN, 2007).

6. JHIA AR II/376 ("Serye: arbets-lagern. Band III. Der froyen arbets-lager in Lublin"), trans. *The Ringelblum Archive: Annihilation—Day by Day*, 54. Reportages from work camps were also published in the underground press. See for example JHIA AR I/705 *Dror* no. 7–8 (May–June 1941): 49–52 for an article by Yitzchak Zuckerman published under the name A. Wilcz.

7. Mazor, *The Vanished City*, 38. Henryk Makower, who as a medical doctor participated in recruitment for labor camps, claimed that the Judenrat did undertake some, though insufficient, steps toward helping those in camps, for example sending them food parcels. Makower, *Pamiętnik*, 44.

8. Ringelblum, *Notes from the Warsaw Ghetto*, 161.

9. Ibid., 162.

10. For example, in the spring of 1941 the consequences for not delivering the requested number of forced laborers were limited food allocations for the ghetto and sanctions against laborers who were already in the camps. See Sakowska, *Ludzie z dzielnicy zamkniętej*, 50.

11. Czerniaków, *The Warsaw Diary*, 202.

12. Ibid., 204.

13. Ibid., 159.

14. JHIA AR I/28 ("Sprawozdanie ogólne Batalionu Pracy za rok 1940"). Quoted in Bernstein, "Żydzi warszawscy w hitlerowskich obozach pracy," 64.

15. Hilberg, Staron, "Introduction," in Czerniaków, *The Warsaw Diary*, 36.

16. Ringelblum, *Notes from the Warsaw Ghetto*, 164.

17. Makower, *Pamiętnik*, 44.

18. Report of March 23, 1942. Quoted in *Martyrs and Fighters: The Epic of the Warsaw Ghetto*, ed. P. Friedman (London: Routledge and Kegan, 1952), 72–73.

19. JHIA 302/38 (Stanisław Gombiński), 57.

20. Isaiah Trunk, *Judenrat: The Jewish Councils in Eastern Europe under Nazi Occupation* (New York: Macmillan, 1972), 364.

21. Czerniaków, *The Warsaw Diary*, 126.

22. Ibid., 130.

23. YVA O.3/2996 (Marceli Reich).

24. Adler, *In the Warsaw Ghetto*, 166.

25. Even Stefan Ernest, who in his wartime memoirs left a very sympathetic picture of the Judenrat, describes Beniamin Zabłudowski as someone who was to see in his position mainly personal gain, fulfillment of the ambition of leadership, a chance for open nepotism, and a possibility of leading an extravagant lifestyle. Ernest, *O wojnie wielkich Niemiec z Żydami Europy*, 160.

26. Archiwum Akt Nowych (AAN) 202 II/28, 14–19 ("Sprawozdanie z przeglądu spraw zleconych w biurze kwaterunkowych").

27. Kaplan, *Scroll of Agony*, 273.

28. Mazor, *The Vanished City*, 27.

29. Czerniaków, *The Warsaw Diary*, 221.

30. JHIA AR I/773 (*Getto Podziemne* no. 2 [March 20, 1942]), 3.

31. Marcel Reich-Ranicki, *The Author of Himself: The Life of Marcel Reich-Ranicki*, trans. E. Osers (London: Weidenfeld and Nicolson, 2001), 173.

32. Szereszewska, *Memoirs*, 34.

33. See JHIA AR I/18 ("Memoriał przedstawicieli społeczeństwa żydowskiego dotyczący działalności Komisji przy RŻ w Warszawie (czerwiec 1941 r.)").

34. Ruta Sakowska, *Dwa etapy: hitlerowska polityka eksterminacji Żydów w oczach ofiar: szkic historyczny i dokumenty* (Wrocław: Zakład Narodowy im. Ossolińskich, 1986), 47.

35. Huberband, *Kiddush Hashem*, 136.

36. AR I/86 ("Questionnaire on the situation in the Warsaw Ghetto"), trans. *To Live with Honor*, 744.

37. Adler, *In the Warsaw Ghetto*, 130.

38. Ringelblum, *Notes from the Warsaw Ghetto*, 248. For more on Gancwajch and his reports to the Gestapo see Seidman, *Togbukh fun varshaver geto*, 215–21.

39. Ernest, *O wojnie wielkich Niemiec z Żydami Europy*, 117.

40. Czerniaków, *The Warsaw Diary*, 257.

41. Yitzhak Zuckerman in *Martyrs and Fighters*, 83. A different view is presented by Judenrat clerk Stefan Ernest, who claimed that confidantes were indeed present in the Judenrat structure but only on the lowest level of its structure. Ernest, *O wojnie wielkich Niemiec z Żydami Europy*, 115.

42. Ernest, *O wojnie wielkich Niemiec z Żydami Europy*, 115.

43. Adler, *In the Warsaw Ghetto*, 262. On the cooperation of Fritz Seifter, editor-in-chief of *Gazeta Żydowska* with the German authorities see Lars Jockheck, "Vom Agenten zum Kollaborateur? Die Zusammenarbeit des jüdischen Publizisten Fritz Seifter aus Bielitz mit deutschen Behörden in den 1930er und 1940er Jahren," in *"Kollaboration" in Nordosteuropa: Erscheinungsformen und Deutungen im 20. Jahrhundert*, ed. J. Tauber, 192–205 (Wiesbaden: Harrassowitz, 2006). Among *Gazeta*'s contributors were also Jewish Council employees, such as Marcel Reich or Hillel Seidman and a high-rank activist of the Jewish Self-Help, Edmund Stein.

44. Seidman, *Togbukh fun varshaver geto*, 47.

45. Israel Gutman, "Adam Czerniakow—The Man and His Diary," in *The Catastrophe of European Jewry*, ed. I. Gutman, L. Rothkirchen (Jerusalem: Yad Vashem, 1976), 459.

46. Hilberg, Staron, "Introduction," in Czerniaków, *The Warsaw Diary*, 27.

47. Marcin Urynowicz, "Adam Czerniaków a Muzeum im. Matthiasa Bersohna przy Gminie Żydowskiej w Warszawie 1908–1940," *Biuletyn Żydowskiego Instytutu Historycznego* 228, no. 4 (1998): 477n2.

48. Kaplan, *Scroll of Agony*, 215.

49. For a full picture see the memoirs of Judenrat members who decided to leave Poland in the first weeks of the war: Chaim Shaskes, *Bleter fun a Geto Togbukh* (New York: C.H. Glants, 1943); Apolinary Hartglas, *Na pograniczu dwóch światów*, ed. J. Żyndul (Warszawa: Rytm, 1996). See also Pnina Weiss, "The Memoirs of Pnina Weiss—Wife of a Member of the First Judenrat in Warsaw," ed. E. Farbstein *Yad Vashem Studies* 33 (2005): 61–100.

50. Czerniaków, *The Warsaw Diary*, 120.

51. Ibid., 148.

52. Ibid., 285.

53. Engelking, Leociak, *The Warsaw Ghetto*, 165.

54. Ibid., 166.

55. Joanna Wiszniewicz, *A jednak czasem miewam sny: historia pewnej samotności* (Warszawa: Agencja Wydawnicza "Tu," 1996), 86.

56. See Czerniaków, *The Warsaw Diary*, 199.

57. See the speech of Rachel Auerbach in JHIA 313/109 (Szapsl Rotholc). Also see VHA 14342 (Interview with Jacob Epstein) for the testimony of a former policeman who joined the Service after an acquaintance in the Judenrat gave him "all the instructions,

how to pass the doctors and everything." He described the length of the process of getting into the Service as three to four weeks.

58. Szereszewska, *Memoirs*, 28.

59. JHIA 302/129 (Anonymous), 18.

60. JHIA 302/38 (Stanisław Gombiński), 131.

61. Hersh Wasser, "Daily Entries of Hersh Wasser," ed. J. Kermish, *Yad Vashem Studies* 15 (1983): 247. See also JHIA 301/474 (Eugenia Truskier), 1, for the same observation.

62. See Berg, *The Diary of Mary Berg*, and Janina Bauman, *Winter in the Morning: A Young Girl's Life in the Warsaw Ghetto and Beyond, 1939–1945* (London: Virago, 1986). Both Berg and Bauman had numerous friends under the age of sixteen joining the Order Service.

63. JHIA AR I/502 (Tadeusz Witelson, "Opracowanie na temat SP w getcie warszawskim"), 8. According to a member of the Service, Jerzy Lewiński, there were about 200 attorneys in the Service. See JHIA S/366 "Kolekcja Jerzego Lewińskiego" ("Protokół Sądu Partyjnego PPS z 22.05.1948").

64. YVA 033/1161 (Leon Tyszka), 20. On the basis of Czerniaków's diary we can assume that he must have held Szeryński in esteem, even if only on a professional level. There is no clear information on whether the nomination of Szeryński was initiated by the Germans, by Czerniaków, or by one of the important personalities of ghetto life. See JHIA S/366 "Kolekcja Jerzego Lewińskiego" ("Główna Komisja Badania Zbrodni Hitlerowskich w Polsce. Protokół przesłuchania świadka KPP 12/72/MW").

65. Turkow in *Martyrs and Fighters*, 79. There are grounds to believe that Szeryński introduced converts to the Order Service authorities against the will of the Judenrat councilmen.

66. JHIA 302/129 (Anonymous), 45.

67. See among others: Adler, *In the Warsaw Ghetto*, 174; JHIA 302/129 (Anonymous), 45; and JHIA 313/92 (Karol Peczenik).

68. JHIA 313/92 (Karol Peczenik).

69. JHIA 302/38 (Stanisław Gombiński), 18.

70. JHIA 302/129 (Anonymous), 60.

71. Adler, *In the Warsaw Ghetto*, 174.

72. See Adam Hempel, *Pogrobowcy klęski: rzecz o policji "granatowej" w Generalnym Gubernatorstwie 1939–1945* (Warszawa: PWN, 1990), 345.

73. "Rozmowa z Michaliną Prokopczuk," in Barbara Engelking, *Na łące popiołów, Ocaleni z Holocaustu* (Warszawa: Cyklady, 1997), 97.

74. Kaplan, *Scroll of Agony*, 234. For the attitude in the ghetto toward "blue" police see Andrzej Żbikowski, "Posłowie," in Samuel Willenberg, *Bunt w Treblince* (Warszawa: Biblioteka "Więzi", 2004), 181.

75. JHIA *Gazeta Żydowska*, no. 6 (1941), 2.

76. Berg, *The Diary*, 34.

77. Witold Bereś, Marek Burnetko, *Marek Edelman: Życie Po prostu* (Warszawa: Świat Książki, 2008), 82.

78. JHIA 302/129 (Anonymous), 223.

79. Aharon Weiss, *Hamishtara hayehudit baGeneral-Gouvernement uvi-Shlezia Ha'ilit bitkufat ha-Shoa* (Jerusalem: The Hebrew University, 1973), ix.

80. See JHIA AR I/502 (Tadeusz Witelson, Opracowanie na temat SP w Getcie Warszawskim), 13.

81. Jan Grabowski, "Jewish Defendants in German and Polish Courts in the Warsaw District, 1939–1942," *Yad Vashem Studies* 35, no. 1 (2007), 67. See also the archival collections of the wartime Polish and German courts for the Warsaw District area in Archiwum Miasta Stołecznego Warszawy in Warsaw.

82. JHIA 302/129 (Anonymous), 9.

83. Władysław Szpilman, *The Pianist: The Extraordinary Story of One Man's Survival in Warsaw, 1939–45*, trans. A. Bell (London: Gollancz, 1999), 77.

84. "Money, oh Money (Moes, oy, moes)," trans. D. Chazen in *Martyrs and Fighters*, 75.

85. VHA 14342 (Interview with Jacob Epstein).

86. Huberband, *Kiddush Hashem*, 155. For more on the executions, see also 151–71.

87. Ringelblum, *Notes from the Warsaw Ghetto*, 229.

88. Ibid., 236.

89. AR II/237 (Yehiel Górny, "Daily Memoranda from the Warsaw Ghetto"), trans. *To Live with Honor*, 96.

90. JHIA 302/129 (Anonymous), 6.

91. For cooperation between the smugglers and the police see the JHIA 301/4235 (Szapsl Rotholc). Rotholc was a famous pre-war boxer and probably the most famous "player" (a policeman who could easily be bribed) among the Order Service members.

92. Adler, *In the Warsaw Ghetto*, 96. This information is confirmed by a publication of the Polish Socialists, *Getto Podziemne* no. 2 (3.02.1942) p. 3 (JHIA AR I/733), though the publication quotes an amount of 7,200 złoty.

93. Wasser, "Daily Entries," 241.

94. Ringelblum, *Notes from the Warsaw Ghetto*, 199.

95. Szymon Rogoziński, *My Fortunate Life* (Melbourne: Bookaburra, 2000), 109.

96. Wasser, "Daily Entries," 233.

97. Ibid., 238.

98. JHIA 302/38 (Stanisław Gombiński), 48.

99. "Report for January" (Polen 365e) Ludwigsburg, quoted in Hilberg, Staron "Introduction," in Czerniaków, *The Warsaw Diary*, 58.

100. Adler, *In the Warsaw Ghetto*, 193.

101. Ibid., 196.

102. Ibid., 204; JHIA 302/129 (Anonymous), 51.

103. See JHIA 313/35 (Stanisław Gombiński).

104. JHIA 313/35 (Stanisław Gombiński).

105. For example, one ghetto inhabitant remembered a friend, married to a Jewish policemen, who was in "an absolutely tragic living situation." YVA O.33/1158 (Roma Elster), 3. According to former policeman Jerzy Lewiński, at least a few hundred Jewish policemen could not financially support themselves at an adequate level. VHA 4903 (Interview with Jerzy Lewiński).

106. The involvement of PPS in the Order Service was discussed during the court proceedings against Jerzy Lewiński. See JHIA 366 S/366 "Kolekcja Jerzego Lewińskiego" ("Protokół Centralnego Sądu Partyjnego w Warszawie z 22.05.1948").

107. Bereś, Burnetko, *Marek Edelman*, 81.

108. Hela Rufeisen-Schupper, *Pożegnanie Miłej 18* (Kraków: Beseder, 1996), 33.

109. Ringelblum, *Notes from the Warsaw Ghetto*, 155.

110. See Wasser, "Daily Entries," 223, 225.

111. JHIA 302/172 (Jan Przedborski), 6. The ghetto in Otwock was liquidated on August 19, 1942. On that day the Germans also murdered the patients of the Zofiówka Jewish sanatorium in Otwock, up to then widely considered to be a safe haven.

112. JHIA 302/167 (Stefania Szochur), 29.

113. See for example JHIA 301/3072 (Sabina Kupercyn) and many others. One ghetto inhabitant remembered: "Blockade at Leszno street. A Jewish policeman comes up to me: 'ID please.' I proudly take out my card with 'Exempted from deportation.' The policeman looks at it: 'Are you a student? You should go home immediately. As from today we are not accepting these IDs'" (YVA M-49/P-77, 3).

114. JHIA 302/129 (Anonymous), 160.

115. AAN 202 II/28 ("Meldunki o sytuacji w getcie warszawskim").

116. See JHIA S/366 "Kolekcja Jerzego Lewińskiego" ("Protokół z posiedzenie Centralnego Sądu Partyjnego w dniu 12.06.1948").

117. JHIA 313/65 (Jerzy Lewiński).

118. This opinion was confirmed by the final ruling of the Centralny Sąd Partyjny Polskiej Partii Socjalistycznej, which acquitted Lewiński. According to the ruling, the very fact of wearing a police uniform during the Aktion did not mean participating in it. Many, especially high-level, policemen could and did refrain from it. See: JHIA S/366 "Kolekcja Jerzego Lewińskiego" ("Wyrok w imieniu Polskiej Partii Socjalistycznej, 19.10.1948").

119. JHIA AR II/197 (Gustawa Jarecka, "Ostatnim etapem przesiedlenia jest śmierć"), 10.

120. JHIA 313/65 (Jerzy Lewiński).

121. Lewin, *A Cup of Tears*, 184.

122. AR I/981 (Peretz Opoczyński, "Varshever geto-khronik" (10–25.05.1942 r.)), trans. *To Live with Honor*, 110.

123. JHIA 313/109 (Szapsl Rotholc).

124. Wiszniewicz, *A jednak czasem miewam sny*, 74.

125. Marian Berland, *Dni długie jak wieki* (Warszawa: Niezależna Oficyna Wydawnicza, 1992), 17. For a description of violence against the Jewish policeman in camps after deportations see Willenberg, *Bunt w Treblince*, 94.

126. Blatman, Gutman, "Youth and Resistance Movements in Historical Perspectives," 50.

127. Wiszniewicz, *A jednak czasem miewam sny*, 56.

128. AR II/199 (Yehoshua Perle, "Khurbn Varshe") quoted in Kassow, *Who Will Write Our History?*, 195.

129. Mazor, *The Vanished City*, 78.

130. Szpilman, *The Pianist*, 77.

131. VHA 4903 (Interview with Jerzy Lewiński).

132. According to Charles Roland, in the spring of 1940, TOZ employed almost 200 doctors, over 100 nurses, 65 pharmacists, 14 dentists, and 8 laboratory workers. It ran two surgical institutions, three maternity hospitals, and four establishments for orphans, as well as the Otwock hospitals (Medem tuberculosis sanatorium and Zofiowka mental health hospital) and several establishments for sanitary and disinfection duties. Charles Roland, *Courage Under Siege: Starvation, Disease, and Death in the Warsaw Ghetto* (New York: Oxford University Press, 1992), 56.

133. For more on ORT's activities in the Warsaw Ghetto see Sarah Kavanaugh, *ORT, the Second World War and the Rehabilitation of Holocaust Survivors* (London: Vallentine Mitchell, 2008), 36–43.

134. Emanuel Ringelblum, *Ksovim fun geto*, vol. 2 (Varshe: Yidish Bukh, 1963), 165.

135. Adolf Berman, "The Fate of Children in the Warsaw Ghetto," in *The Catastrophe of European Jewry: Antecedents, History, Reflections: Selected Papers*, ed. I. Gutman (Jerusalem: Yad Vashem, 1976), 406.

136. Czerniaków, *The Warsaw Diary*, 140.

137. AR I/86 ("Questionnaire on the situation in the Warsaw Ghetto"), trans. *To Live with Honor*, 750.

138. Ringelblum, *Ksovim fun geto*: 2, 109.

139. According to Samuel Kassow: "During all of 1940 the Joint spent a total of 14.735 million zlotys on its Polish operations; ominously this figure fell to about 8 million zlotys in 1941. After Germany declared war on the United States in December 1941, the main source of funds dried up, but Giterman and Guzik [leaders of Joint] continued to play a major role in Aleynhilf." Kassow, *Who Will Write Our History?*, 114.

140. Sakowska, *Ludzie z dzielnicy zamkniętej*, 78.

141. Kaplan, *Scroll of Agony*, 259.

142. JHIA 302/27 (Puterman), 15.

143. Ruta Sakowska, "Komitety Domowe w getcie warszawskim," *BŻIH* 61, no. 1 (1967): 72.

144. JHIA AR I/33 (Peretz Opoczyński, "Di geshikhte fun a hojz-komitet, a hoyz komitet oyf Volinska").

145. Quoted in Kassow, *Who Will Write Our History?*, 126.

146. Sakowska, "Komitety Domowe w getcie warszawskim," 69.

147. Ernest, *O wojnie wielkich Niemiec z Żydami Europy*, 136.

148. Trunk, *Judenrat*, 344.

149. Mazor, *The Vanished City*, 33.

150. Ringelblum, *Ksovim fun geto*: 2, 109.

151. AR I/86 ("Questionnaire on the situation in the Warsaw Ghetto"), trans. *To Live with Honor*, 751.

152. Ernest, *O wojnie wielkich Niemiec z Żydami Europy*, 66.

153. See Engelking, Leociak, *The Warsaw Ghetto*, 303.

154. AR I/425 ([A. Reinberg], "Uwagi [o obozach pracy?] przymusowej w Lubelszczyźnie i możliwości [poprawy?] warunków pracy w tych obozach"), trans. *The Ringelblum Archive*, 88–90.

155. Szpilman, *The Pianist*, 83.

156. Mina Tomkiewicz, *Of Bombs and Mice: A Novel of War-time Warsaw* (London: George Allen and Unwin, 1970), 60 and 112. Even though written in the convention of a novel, *Of Bombs and Mice* is an autobiographical text, and as such can be seen as a source for the history of the Warsaw Ghetto.

157. Sakowska, "Komitety Domowe w getcie warszawskim," 70.

158. See AR II/107 ("A bezukh bay di umgliklikhe kinder").

159. Adler, *In the Warsaw Ghetto*, 133.

160. JHIA 302/27 (Samuel Puterman), 12.

161. Ernest, *O wojnie wielkich Niemiec z Żydami Europy*, 121. There are a number of testimonies to prove this, especially from among refugees who, through Kohn and Heller, brought to Warsaw their families left behind in Łódź. See VHA 32695 (Interview with Irena Wittek), VHA 12827 (Interview with Jerzy Lando).

162. See for example YVA O.33/1984 ("Wspomnienia Arona Szwarcbarda z lat 1939–1945"), 6. This is also confirmed by Rachela Auerbach in "Z ludem pospołu: O losie pisarzy i artystów żydowskich w getcie warszawskim," *Nasze Słowo* no. 1 (1948), 9.

163. Adolf Berman, *Vos der goyrl hoṭ mir basherṭ: miṭ Yidn in Ṿarshe, 1939–1942* (Tel Aviv: Beit Lohamei Hagettaot, 1980), 11.

164. Makower, *Pamiętnik z getta warszawskiego*, 18.

165. "The Reports of the Jewish 'Informer' in the Warsaw Ghetto—Selected Documents," ed. Ch. R. Browning and I. Gutman, *Yad Vashem Studies* 17 (1986), 257.

166. Wiszniewicz, *A jednak czasem miewam sny*, 66–67.

167. JHIA 302/129 (Anonymous), 218–19.

168. On this see Rogoziński, *My Fortunate Life*, 102–6. According to Rogoziński, who worked as a secretary of the Section: "Such aid was essential, especially for some of the refugees from Lodz. The Jewish Mutual Assistance Society had established a special Intelligentsia Assistance Section for this purpose. However little attracted Nazi persecution more than the caption 'intelligentsia,' so the word was replaced by 'individual,'" 102.

169. Kassow, *Who Will Write Our History?*, 336.

170. JHIA 302/90 (Henryk Bryskier), 207–8.

171. Ibid., 208.

172. YVA O.3 V.T./1683 (Viera Sierpiński). Another former Self-Help administrative employee described his employment in its structures as "pretended work, boring and not giving me any satisfaction," underlining only that it saved him from forced labor. Stefan Chaskielewicz, *Ukrywałem się w Warszawie Styczeń 1943–Styczeń 1945* (Kraków: Znak, 1988), 12.

173. YVA O.33/1216 (Kopel Piżyc, "Tarbut"). A social worker from an assimilated family remembered that there was a "certain distance" between her and the nationalistically oriented activists. VHA 48865 (Zofia Lubińska).

174. Kaplan, *A Scroll of Agony*, 260.

175. JHIA 302/90 (Henryk Bryskier), 207; also JHIA 302/129 (Anonymous).

176. Proof that the ghetto street probably had little idea about the organization of social welfare in the quarter and the areas of responsibility can be found in the memoirs of Stefan Ernest. Ernest, a mid-level Judenrat clerk, in his memoirs written in 1943, is not familiar with the organization of Self-Help in the ghetto. See Ernest, *O wojnie wielkich Niemiec z Żydami Europy*, 78.

177. Tomkiewicz, *Of Bombs and Mice*, 59.

178. On how this lack of coordination affected the situation of refugees in the ghetto see Andrzej Żbikowski, "Żydowscy przesiedleńcy z dystryktu warszawskiego w getcie warszawskim, 1939–1942 (z pogranicza opisu i interpretacji)," in *Prowincja noc. Życie i zagłada Żydów w dystrykcie warszawskim*, ed. B. Engelking, J. Leociak, and D. Libionka (Warszawa: IFiS Pan, 2007), 244.

179. Janusz Korczak, "Pismo do Natana Jaszuńskiego, kierownika Żydowskiego Biura Przyjmowania Przesyłek Pocztowych," in *Janusz Korczak w getcie: nowe źródła*, ed. A. Lewin (Warszawa: Latona, 1992), 47.

180. See Ringelblum, *Ksovim fun geto*: 2, 138. In the spring of 1943 the German authorities attempted to reconstruct the headquarters of ŻSS in Kraków as Jüdische Unterstützungstelle (JUS, ger. Jewish Relief Office), still under the leadership of Michal Weichert. Weichert was later deemed to be a collaborator by the Jewish Social Court in Warsaw. On that see David Engel, "Who is a Collaborator? The Trials of Michal

Weichert," in *The Jews in Poland*, vol. 2, ed. S. Kapralski, 339–70 (Kraków: Judaica Foundation Center for Jewish Culture, 1999).

4. Polish-Language Cultural Life in the Warsaw Ghetto

1. JHIA, AR I/428 (Stanisław Różycki, "To jest getto!"), 20.

2. Adler, *In the Warsaw Ghetto*, 58–60.

3. *Gazeta Żydowska*, no. 29 (1941), 8.

4. Rachela Auerbach, "Z ludem pospołu: O losie pisarzy i artystów żydowskich w getcie warszawskim," *Nasze Słowo* no. 11 (1948), 11.

5. JHIA AR I/90 (Jonas Turkow, "Varshe vaylt zikh"), 4.

6. Tomasz Szarota, *Okupowanej Warszawy*, 384.

7. JHIA Kolekcja Bernarda Marka (KBM) no. 546 ("Listy Hali do Pani Stefanii").

8. Janina Bauman, *Winter in the Morning*, 98.

9. JHIA 302/27 (Samuel Puterman), 15.

10. Jonas Turkow, *Azoy iz es geven: Khurbn Varshe* (Buenos Aires: Tsentral-farband fun Poylishe Yidn in Argentine, 1948), 203.

11. Ringelblum, *Ksovim fun geto*: 2, 201.

12. Rachela Auerbach, "Z ludem pospołu. O losie pisarzy i artystów żydowskich w getcie warszawskim," *Nasze Słowo* no. 19 (1947), 10. Further information about the kitchen at 6 Orla Street can be found in AR I/641 (Rachela Auerbach, "Dziennik," 4.08.1941–26.07.1942 r.) See also the description in JHIA 302/27 (Samuel Puterman), 36.

13. Engelking, Leociak, *The Warsaw Ghetto*, 539.

14. For the content of theater plays in occupied Warsaw see Stanisław Marczak-Oborski, *Teatr czasu wojny. Polskie życie teatralne w latach II wojny światowej, 1939–1945* (Warszawa: PIW, 1967), 58–72.

15. Szarota, *Okupowanej Warszawy*, 374.

16. *Documenta Occupationis Theutonicae*, vol. 5 (Poznań, 1952), 35, quoted in Isaiah Trunk, "Religious, Educational and Cultural Problems in the Eastern European Ghettos under German Occupation," *YIVO Annual of Jewish Social Studies* 14 (1965), 179.

17. See also Michał Borwicz, ed., *Pieśń ginących: z dziejów twórczości Żydów pod hitlerowską okupacją* (Warszawa: Wyd. Centralnej Żydowskiej Komisji Historycznej, 1947), 28–29, for a case of an underground event in the Lvov ghetto reviewed in *Gazeta Żydowska*.

18. Turkow, *Azoy iz es geven*, 206.

19. Ringelblum, *Notes from the Warsaw Ghetto*, 282, and JHIA AR I/260 ("Biuletyn Tygodniowy. Przeznaczony dla wszystkich funkcjonariuszy i pracowników Wydziału Zdrowia nr 1/8.03.1942"), 1–2.

20. Among the ghetto theaters I have not included *Melody Palace*, which can be classified as a musical revue rather than a theater. It showed very light entertainment

in Polish and was run by an acting family: David Zajderman, his wife Chana Lerner, and son Harry Zajderman.

21. Ruta Sakowska-Pups, "O działalności teatralnej w getcie warszawskim," BŻIH 69, no. 1 (1969): 51.

22. Nahma Sandrow, *Vagabond Stars: A World History of Yiddish Theater* (New York: Harper and Row, 1977), 105.

23. JHIA AR I/428 (Stanisław Różycki, "To jest getto!"), 18–19.

24. While Hebrew literature originating in Poland never reached widespread popularity, that created in Palestine was received in Poland with much interest. Even though Hebrew theater as such did not exist in Poland, tours of *Habimah* Theater were very successful and well received also by non-Hebrew-speaking audiences, which must have given hope of establishing Hebrew theater in the ghetto.

25. *Gazeta Żydowska*, no. 48 (1941), 3.

26. Reich-Ranicki, *The Author of Himself*, 153–54.

27. See JHIA AR I/272 ("A letter of 8 April 1942 from Der Kommissar fur den Judischen Wohnbezirk in Warschau to the Chairman of Jewish Council in Warsaw"). The letter states that the program of all cultural events in the ghetto must be presented to German authorities for acceptance and that it is forbidden to play non-Jewish composers and to sell and lend German and other foreign books. The letter is signed by Dr. Franz Grassler.

28. Czerniaków, *The Warsaw Diary*, 342.

29. JHIA *Gazeta Żydowska*, no. 42 (1942), 2.

30. Among other choirs active in the ghetto, Turkow also enumerates, "Zak's choir, Jakub Goldstein's folk choir, his brother Israel Goldstein's folk choir, Anna Oser's female trio, A. Kaminska's and Z. Szklar's children's choirs." Turkow, *Azoy iz es geven*, 204.

31. JHIA 302/27 (Samuel Puterman), 55, and 302/129 (NN), 96–97.

32. Engelking, Leociak, *The Warsaw Ghetto*, 634–40.

33. Turkow, *Azoy iz es geven*, 130.

34. Mina Tomkiewicz, *Of Bombs and Mice*, 100; Mazor, *The Vanished City*, 43.

35. Prostitution in the ghetto is mentioned in many memoirs and diaries. Krystyna Żywulska, for example, writes that she quit working as a waitress in a ghetto restaurant after she was told that she was expected to have sexual relations with the clients. Krystyna Żywulska, *Pusta Woda* (Michałów-Grabina: Instytut Wydawniczy Latarnik, 2008), 31. On prostitution in Hotel Britania see JHIA 302/27 (Samuel Puterman), 70.

36. According to a report compiled for the Ringelblum Archive, even though the new rich were the most visible clients of the cafés, "you can also see owners of grocery stores, policemen, a few doctors, a lot of youth, bourgeoisie, not necessarily dealing with business but living off capital, the vast majority of them rich, well fed." JHIA AR I/50 ("Teatr w getcie"), 10.

37. JHIA *Gazeta Żydowska*, no. 24 (1940), 11.

38. JHIA *Gazeta Żydowska*, no. 48 (1941), 3.

39. Wiera Gran, *Sztafeta Oszczerców: autobiografia śpiewaczki* (Paris, 1980), 17.

40. Szarota, *Okupowanej Warszawy*, 360.

41. Ibid., 361.

42. *Gazeta Żydowska*, no. 43 (1941), 3. There is no mention of such permission in the diary of Adam Czerniaków. See however AR II/281 for a letter from Nazi collaborator Josef Ehrlich to Sicherheitspolizei in Warsaw of May 27, 1941, asking for help with getting permission to open a cinema in the ghetto. According to Engelking and Leociak, as a result of conflicts between German authorities or Ehrlich's loss of favor, the license was granted to the Judenrat. Engelking, Leociak, *The Warsaw Ghetto*, 580.

43. JHIA *Gazeta Żydowska*, no. 29 (1941), 8. For more on the stereoscope see Huberband, *Kiddush Hashem*, 132–35.

44. YVA E/438 (Pola Rotszyld).

45. JHIA AR I/50 ("Teatr w getcie"), 17.

46. AR I/341 ("Report on the cultural life in the ghetto"), trans. *To Live with Honor*, 516.

47. JHIA *Gazeta Żydowska*, no. 126 (1941), 2. The difficult living conditions of the actors were also reflected by the number of fundraising events and anniversaries organized in the ghetto. The main one was the "Month of the Artist" which took place between August and October 1941. The event was started by artists themselves in order to help poor artists in the community and comprised of money collections in theaters, cafés, and nightclubs, as well as collections of food in groceries and restaurants. As a sign of solidarity, all famous artists took part in the shows. See Turkow, *Azoy iz es geven*, 240.

48. JHIA *Gazeta Żydowska*, no. 24 (1942), 2.

49. Turkow, *Azoy iz es geven*, 215.

50. Ringelblum, *Notes from the Warsaw Ghetto*, 128.

51. JHIA *Gazeta Żydowska*, no. 57 (1941), 2.

52. JIHA KBM no. 546 ("Listy Hali do Pani Stefanii").

53. JHIA *Gazeta Żydowska*, no. 44 (1941), 2; and Janina David, *A Square of Sky: Memoirs of Wartime Childhood* (London: Eland, 1992), 96.

54. JHIA *Gazeta Żydowska*, no. 90 (1941), 5.

55. Gela Seksztajn, "Fragment Dziennika," *Nasze Słowo*, no. 6–7 (1948), 37.

56. YVA O.33/1158 (Roma Elster).

57. Frieda W. Aaron, *Bearing the Unbearable: Yiddish and Polish Poetry in the Ghettos and Concentration Camps* (Albany: SUNY Press, 1990), 201.

58. JHIA *Gazeta Żydowska*, no. 34 (1941), 3.

59. JHIA *Gazeta Żydowska*, no. 59 (1941), 3.

60. One such performance was *Szczęśliwe Dni* (pol. Happy Days) performed in NTK (JHIA *Gazeta Żydowska*, no. 20 (1942), 2).

61. See Shmeruk, "Hebrew-Yiddish-Polish," 286.

62. Hertz, *The Jews in Polish Culture*, 237.

63. Shmeruk, "Hebrew-Yiddish-Polish," 286.

64. Even though "Kwiaty Polskie" was first sent to the ghetto from the "Aryan" side, there is evidence that inhabitants of the ghetto copied it and sent it across the wall. For information about Warsaw University professors sending the poem to their former colleagues in ghetto, see the testimony of Zdzisław Libera (JHIA 301/6094), 2.

65. Marianowicz, *Life Strictly Forbidden*, 210. According to Marczak-Oborski, Tuwim's *Kwiaty Polskie* and Słonimski's *Alarm* were the other poems most commonly read on the underground evenings on the "Aryan" side of Warsaw. Marczak-Oborski, *Teatr czasu wojny*, 171.

66. Irena Śmigielska, *Skradzione lata* (Warszawa: ŻIH, 2001), 44. Many other diarists claim not to have known that some of the famous artists were Jewish. This statement was often repeated in reference to Wiera Gran (see JHIA 313/36).

67. JHIA *Gazeta Żydowska*, no. 76 (1941), 3.

68. There were of course other plays written in the ghetto but they were not performed in the official theater. For example, Yehoshua Perle wrote a comedy about relations in the ghetto, with very strong anti-Judenrat accents. See Jonas Turkow, *Farloshene shtern* (Buenos Aires: Tsentraln-Farband fun Poylishe Yidn in Argentine, 1953), 29, quoted in Sakowska-Pups, "O działalności teatralnej w getcie," 59.

69. For example, in a letter to a friend on the "Aryan" side, Hala, describing problems with finding private space to see her boyfriend, refers to *Miłość szuka mieszkania*. JHIA KBM no. 546 ("Listy Hali do Pani Stefanii"). The full text of *Miłość szuka mieszkania* can be found in the Ringelblum Archive (JHIA AR I/519).

70. JHIA *Gazeta Żydowska*, no. 30 (1941), 2.

71. For more on the various degrees of acculturation of Polish-Jewish writers see Prokop-Janiec, *Polish-Jewish Literature*, 109.

72. Jonas Turkow, "Yidish teater on yidish," *Literarishe Bleter*, August 16, 1929, no. 33, 641. Quoted in Steinlauf, "Mark Arnshteyn and Polish-Jewish Theater," 408.

73. Michael Steinlauf, "Mark Arnshteyn and Polish-Jewish Theater," in *The Jews of Poland Between Two World Wars*, ed. I. Gutman, 404.

74. JHIA AR I/92 ("Polish writers"), 3.

75. JHIA "Varia. Utwory literackie," no. 187 (Henryka Łazowert, "Ballada o Paczce").

76. Turkow, *Azoy iz es geven*, 199. Maciej Czarnecki, the main owner of *Sztuka*, before the war was the owner of a coal mine and a cement mixing plant and was the largest coal wholesaler in the country. He also owned a number of cinemas and was the

vice president of the Main Council of the Film Industry. In the ghetto he was the head of the Fuel Commission. Czarnecki claimed that he set up the café only with a few friends. As with other cafés, the structure of ownership must have been more complex than that, however—one of the owners, testifying just after the war, was not able to name all of those who had their shares in Sztuka (JHIA 313/36 (Wiera Gran)).

77. Ewa Koźmińska-Frejlak, "Świadectwo milczenia . . . Rozmowa z Jerzym Lewińskim, byłym funkcjonariuszem Służby Porządkowej getta warszawskiego," *Zagłada Żydów. Źródła i materiały* 2 (2006), 264.

78. AAN 202/ II- 28 ("Meldunki o sytuacji w getcie warszawskim—Notatka o Beniaminie Zabłudowskim").

79. JHIA 313/36 (Wiera Gran).

80. Gran, *Sztafeta oszczerców,* 17.

81. Tomkiewicz, *Of Bombs and Mice,* 116. This is confirmed by testimonies of girls from well-off families who worked in the ghetto as waitresses. See VHA 28419 (Interview with Maria Sikorska) and VHA 5218 (Interview with Maria Krych).

82. Tomkiewicz, *Of Bombs and Mice,* 116.

83. Marek Groński, *Proca Dawida: kabaret w przedsionku piekieł* (Warszawa: Muza, 2007), 73; Śmigielska, *Skradzione lata,* 43.

84. JHIA AR I/50 ("Teatr w getcie"), 18–19.

85. Śmigielska, *Skradzione lata,* 43. Describing the group of regulars at Ziemiańska (and later probably in Sztuka) Marci Shore wrote: "For this generation of Varsovian intellectuals born at the fin de siècle, life was unbearably heavy. They moved about in entangled circles with shifting boundaries, connected to one another by not more than one or two degrees of separation. They were quintessential cosmopolitans, polyglots who felt at home in Moscow, Paris and Berlin, yet who at once felt inextricably bound to Poland, who believed in their role as the 'conscience of the nation,' who very much felt that Warsaw belonged to them. They suffered (sometimes advantageously, sometimes painfully) from a certain pathological narcissism. They sat in their café called Ziemiańska and believed, with absolute sincerity, that the world turned on what they said there." Marci Shore, *Caviar and Ashes: A Warsaw Generation's Life and Death in Marxism, 1918–1968* (New Haven: Yale University Press, 2006), 4. For those in the ghetto, which is apparent in wartime diaries, the name Ziemiańska signified the best qualities of pre-war Warsaw.

86. Tomkiewicz, *Of Bombs and Mice,* 117.

87. Śmigielska, *Skradzione lata,* 45.

88. JHIA 313/36 (Wiera Gran).

89. Turkow, *Azoy iz es geven,* 199.

90. JHIA 313/36 (Wiera Gran).

91. AAN 202/ II- 28 ("Meldunki o sytuacji w getcie warszawskim—Notatka o Beniaminie Zabłudowskim").

92. Gran, *Sztafeta oszczerców*, 22.

93. See VHA 8086 (Interview with Wiera Gran).

94. JHIA *Gazeta Żydowska*, no. 31 (1942), 2.

95. Michał Borwicz, ed., *Pieśń ujdzie cało. Antologia wierszy o Żydach pod okupacją niemiecką* (Warszawa: Wyd. Centralnej Żydowskiej Komisji Historycznej, 1947), 23.

96. Berg, *The Diary*, 104.

97. Bauman, *Winter in the Morning*, 116.

98. Śmigielska, *Stracone lata*, 44.

99. Shmeruk, "Hebrew-Yiddish-Polish," 286.

100. Very positive remarks on classical concerts can be found, for example, in the memoir of Orthodox activist Hillel Seidman. See *Togbukh fun varshaver geto*, 185–88.

101. Marek Edelman, *I była miłość w getcie* (Warszawa: Świat Książki, 2009), 75.

102. YVA O.3/260 (Mordka Purman).

103. Ringelblum, *Notes from the Warsaw Ghetto*, 133.

104. Ibid., 249.

105. Ibid., 243.

106. See the records of the trial of Wiera Gran (JHIA 313/36). Gran was performing for the Gestapo collaborators, yet this fact was seen by the judge who acquitted her as a part of artists' life in the ghetto and not morally questionable. Ringelblum tries to explain those attending by blaming it on "the spell of Gancwajch's sweet talk—his energetic demonstration of the great services he is capable of performing for the Jews, the evil decrees he has already averted, and the things he could do if he had support of Jewish society." Ringelblum, *Notes from the Warsaw Ghetto*, 193.

107. According to Lucjan Doroszycki, despite the constant exaggeration, German-licensed newspapers (so-called *gadzinówki* [pol. reptile press]) gave rather reliable pictures of cultural life in occupied countries. According to Dobroszycki: "Without getting into an evaluation of the contents of these events produced by the German Propaganda Department, or judging the attitude of Polish artists, musicians and performers who cooperated in them, one must observe that the occupation press conveyed an accurate picture of public cultural life in the GG. In this area, the Polish language press can serve as a reliable, often even the only source for research on these issues." Lucjan Dobroszycki, *Reptile Journalism: The Official Polish-language Press under the Nazis, 1939–1945* (London: Yale University Press, 1994), 106.

108. The first note was usually published with the beginning of the rehearsals. A few weeks later readers could find information about the approaching opening night and the first ads. A longer note and a larger ad were published on the day of the opening night, followed by a full-length review and more ads. Considering that theaters in the ghetto would on average produce a new play every two weeks, information on theater productions constituted a sizable portion of every issue of the newspaper. To this should be added reviews from concerts and various others forms of entertainment.

109. JHIA *Gazeta Żydowska*, no. 18 (1940), 3.

110. JHIA *Gazeta Żydowska*, no. 39 (1940), 7.

111. Stefan Ernest, *O wojnie wielkich Niemiec z Żydami Europy*, 104.

112. Engelking, Leociak, *The Warsaw Ghetto*, 531.

113. Adler, *In the Warsaw Ghetto*, 263.

114. JHIA 302/27 (Samuel Puterman), 71.

115. Kaplan, *Scroll of Agony*, 244.

116. Berg, *The Diary*, 104.

117. Joanna Wiszniewicz, *Z Polski do Izraela. Rozmowy z pokoleniem '68* (Warszawa: Karta 1992), 6.

118. This was pointed out by Bożena Umińska in a lecture, "Podróż do Polski. Cudzoziemcy w poszukiwaniu własnych śladów," during the conference *Das Bild Polens in der jüdishen Kultur, Österreichisches Kulturforum Warschau*, Warsaw, February 2010.

119. JHIA AR I/50 ("Teatr w getcie"), 41.

120. Ringelblum, *Ksovim fun geto*: 1, 283. See also a report on the Jewish theater and entertainment in JHIA AR I/105 ("Tsvey un halbn yor milkhome"). The first point of the report is entitled: "Actors-converts and the performance of Polish scenes in general/ does Jewish theater have, thanks to these new forces—their interaction with the Jewish actor and the Jewish stage—a positive or negative influence?"

121. Ringelblum, *Ksovim fun geto*: 1, 195.

122. YVA O.3/2996 (Marceli Reich).

123. JHIA AR I/50 ("Teatr w getcie"), 20.

124. JHIA AR I/49 ("Kobieta żydowska w Warszawie od września 1939 do chwili bieżącej [1942]"), 67.

125. Michael C. Steinlauf, "Jewish Theater in Poland," *Polin* 16 (2003), 86.

126. On the contacts between Polish and Yiddish theaters in interwar Poland, see Mirosława M. Bułat, '"Cwiszn cwej teaters-na pograniczu dwóch teatrów. Źródła jidysz w badaniach nad kontaktami międzykulturowymi w polskim teatrze-kilka przypomnień, szereg uzupełnień," in *Jidyszland—polskie przestrzenie*, 121–41.

127. Grodzieńska, *Urodził go "Niebieski Ptak"* (Łódź: Akapit Press, 2002), 177.

128. Berg, *The Diary*, 127–28.

129. On nostalgia in "Polish Flowers," see Hertz, *The Jews in Polish Culture*, 210–11.

130. Aaron, *Bearing the Unbearable*, 11–12.

131. Halina Birenbaum, *Wołanie o pamięć* (Oświęcim: Muzeum Oświęcim-Brzezinka, 1999), 119.

132. JHIA 301/5063 (Jakub Ewinson), 2.

133. Szymon Rogoziński, "Pieśń ujdzie cało. Pamięci Władysława Szlengela," *Opinia* 16 (1947), quoted in Engelking, Leociak, *The Warsaw Ghetto*, 599.

5. Assimilated Inhabitants of the Warsaw Ghetto after the *Gross Aktion*

1. Stanisław Gombiński (Jan Mawult), trans., *Words to Outlive Us*, 113.

2. Władysław Szlengel, "It's High Time," in Aaron, *Bearing the Unbearable*, 86.

3. Stefan Ernest, trans., *Words to Outlive Us*, 307.

4. Julian Hirshaut, *Jewish Martyrs of Pawiak* (New York: Holocaust Library, 1982), 40. For more on Jewish inmates of Pawiak see Katarzyna Person, "Pawiak w świadomości żydowskich mieszkańców okupowanej Warszawy," *Kwartalnik Historii Żydów*, no. 4 (2010): 411–23.

5. Vladka Meed, *On Both Sides of the Wall*, trans. S. Meed (Tel Aviv: Beit Lohamei Hagetaot, 1972), 182.

6. Stefan Ernest, trans., *Words to Outlive Us*, 307.

7. The most recent study of the subject is Agnieszka Haska, *"Jestem Żydem, chcę wejść."* In English see Abraham Shulman, *The Case of Hotel Polski* (New York: United States Holocaust Memorial Museum, 1982).

8. One of them was prominent activist Stefan Lubliner who worked in the Jewish Order Service and cooperated with the Polish Underground. On Lubliner not participating in deportations see JHIA S/366 (Kolekcja Jerzego Lewińskiego), "Protokół z posiedzenia Centralnego Sądu Partyjnego w dniu 12.06.1948." On his contacts with the Polish underground see "Protokół z posiedzenia Centralnego Sądu Partyjnego w dniu 22.05.1948" in the same collection. See also Joseph Lichten, "Notes on the Assimilation and Acculturation," 126.

9. JHIA AR I/730 (*Żagiew* 02.1942), 2. In the autumn of 1942, another group functioning under the same name appeared in the ghetto. It was described by Israel Gutman as "an organization of an obscure nature, suspected of being responsible for provocative acts designed to sow confusion and fear within the ghetto." According to Gutman, among its supporters may have been Gestapo agents. Israel Gutman, *The Jews of Warsaw, 1939–1943: Ghetto, Underground, Revolt*, trans. I. Friedman (Bloomington: Indiana University Press, 1982), 349. See also JHIA 301/5006 (Bronisław Mirski), 3. Members of this organization were executed in a large campaign conducted by the Revisionist *Żydowski Związek Wojskowy* fighters in the winter of 1942. However, there is reason to believe that the issues of the periodical in the Ringelblum Archive, dated to the first half of 1942, are not connected to this group, which did not constitute itself until after the summer of 1942.

10. Marian Fuks, "Adam Czerniaków i Jego dziennik," in *Adama Czerniakowa dziennik getta warszawskiego*, 17. On Ber Mayzels, the Orthodox rabbi of Warsaw, see Efraim F. Kupfer, *Ber Mayzels, zayn antayl in di kampen far der frayhayt fun Poylishn folk un der gelaykhbarekhtikung fun di Yidn* (Warsaw: Yidish Bokh, 1952).

11. JHIA AR I/740 (*Iton ha-Tnua* 12.1940/01.1941), 85.

12. Ibid., 98.

13. JHIA AR I/700 (*Za naszą i waszą wolność*, no. 3 [1941]), 8.

14. Teresa Prekerowa, "The Jewish Underground and the Polish Underground," *Polin* 9 (1996): 153.

15. Interview with Irena Tarłowska, in Engelking, *Na łące popiołów*, 152.

16. According to Laurence Weinbaum: "It is also clear and must have been to Jabotinsky as well, that at least in some measure the Polish authorities saw their relationship with the NZO (New Zionist Organization) as a way to legitimize their efforts to rid Poland of the Jews, silence critics of Polish policy on the Jewish question and bring about a further division of Zionist forces. This, then, would open the door to Poland's playing a greater role in the determination of the future of the Jewish people and the Zionist enterprise." Laurence Weinbaum, "Jabotinsky and the Poles," *Polin* 5 (1991), 165. On the subject see also Jerzy Tomaszewski, "Vladmir Jabotinsky's Talks with Representatives of the Polish Government," *Polin* 3 (1988), 276–93.

17. August Grabski, Maciej Wójcicki, *Żydowski Związek Wojskowy—historia przywrócona* (Warszawa: ŻIH, 2008), 40.

18. Joseph Trumpeldor (1880–1920) was a Zionist activist and organizer of the Jewish immigration to Palestine, who after his death in the battle of Tel Hai became a Zionist hero.

19. The Ringelblum Archives contain only two copies of Revisionists' publications: *Hamedinah* (1940) in Yiddish, a one-issue publication in memoriam of Vladimir Jabotinsky (AR I/737), and *Magen Dawid* in Polish and Yiddish (one issue, with no date) (AR I/744). As for the activities of *Mizarachi*, the only information available is that of a commune of its thirty members living together in a refugee point in the Warsaw Ghetto. AAN 202/II-28, quoted in Engelking, Leociak, *The Warsaw Ghetto*, 677.

20. Marianowicz, *Life Strictly Forbidden*, 4.

21. YIVO archives no. 245/584, dated 1939, quoted in Alina Cała, "The Social Consciousness of Young Jews in Interwar Poland," *Polin* 8 (1994), 52.

22. YVA E/438 (Pola Rotszyld).

23. Zivia Lubetkin, *In the Days of the Destruction and Revolt*, trans. I. Tubbin (Tel Aviv: Hakibbutz Hameuchad, 1981), 21.

24. Zuckerman, *A Surplus of Memory*, 70.

25. Blatman, Gutman, "Youth and Resistance Movements in Historical Perspectives," 20.

26. JHIA AR I/698 (*Neged Hazarem* 02/03 1941), 31.

27. Bernard Goldstein, *Five Years in the Warsaw Ghetto* (Edinburgh: AK, 2005), 72.

28. As Bernard Goldstein wrote: "Some of the secondary schools held final examinations, for which Polish inspectors were smuggled into the ghetto to 'legalize' the diplomas. These were then carefully hidden away against the day when the parents would present their children for admission into Polish institutions of higher learning." Goldstein, *Five Years in the Warsaw Ghetto*, 72.

29. Zuckerman, *A Surplus of Memory*, 70.

30. AR I/697 (Awangarda Młodzieży. Pismo Żydowskiej Młodzieży Marksistowskiej 4.10.1941, 2).

31. Blatman, Gutman, "Youth and Resistance Movements in Historical Perspectives," 7.

32. AR I/698 (*Neged Hazarem* 02.03.41 p. 28). See also Lubetkin, *In the Days of the Destruction and Revolt*, 43.

33. VHA 4687 (Interview with Irene Borton).

34. Rudi Assuntino and Wlodek Goldkorn, *Strażnik. Marek Edelman opowiada*, trans. I. Kania (Kraków: Znak, 1999), 74.

35. For example, Marek Edelman, who had the opportunity to rescue people out of the Umschlagplatz, claimed later in his memoirs that he gave preference to those who were in his organization, rather than to personal friends. Bereś, Burnetko, *Marek Edelman*, 112.

36. Simhah Rotem, *Memoirs of a Warsaw Ghetto Fighter: The Past Within Me*, trans. B. Harshav (New Haven: Yale University Press, 1994), 22.

37. See also Sakowska, "Dwie generacje, dwie formy oporu warszawskiego getta," 207.

38. VHA 28478 (Interview with Marysia Warman).

39. Rotem, *Memoirs of a Warsaw Ghetto Fighter*, 110. See also an interview with Inka Blady Szwajger in Anka Grupińska, *Ciągle po kole: Rozmowy z żołnierzami getta warszawskiego* (Warszawa: Wyd. Książkowe Twój Styl, 2000), 187.

40. Bereś, Burnetko, *Marek Edelman*, 163. For a very interesting analysis of relations between Zionists and PPR see Adolf Berman, "Blok Antyfaszystowski (ze wspomnień)," *Biuletyn Żydowskiego Instytutu Historycznego* 114–15, no. 2–3 (1980): 77–98.

41. On the discussion of the lack of reaction of the Polish underground and the government-in-exile to the summer 1942 deportations, see Adam Puławski, *W obliczu Zagłady. Rząd RP na Uchodźstwie, Delegatura Rządu RP na Kraj, ZWZ-AK wobec deportacji Żydów do obozów zagłady (1941–1942)* (Lublin: IPN, 2009), 535–48.

42. According to a ŻZW member, Adam Halperin, Betar youth was already armed and trained before leaving for Hrubieszów. See Adam Halperin, "Betar's Role in the Warsaw Ghetto Uprising," in *The Catastrophe of European Jewry: Antecedents, History, Reflections: Selected Papers*, ed. Y. Gutman, L. Rothkirchen (Jerusalem: Yad Vashem, 1976), 500. According to Dawid Wdowiński, the armed group was formed only after youth returned from Hrubieszów in June and September 1942. See David Wdowiński, *And We Are Not Saved* (New York: Philosophical Library, 1963), 56. On the other hand, according to the research of Dariusz Libionka, there is no reason to believe that the creation of the ŻZW was a direct consequence of the return of Betar members from the Hrubieszów farm. See Dariusz Libionka, Laurence Weinbaum, "A New Look at the Betar 'Idyll' in Hrubieszów," *Yad Vashem Studies* 37, no. 1 (2009): 85–108.

43. There are testimonies that just before the uprising ŻOB and ŻZW leaders met up to discuss their involvement in the fighting. See interview with Simhah Rotem in Grupińska, *Ciągle po kole*, 247.

44. Korus Bezpieczeństwa—from autumn of 1939 until 1941 under the name Organizacja Wojskowa (OW, Military Organization), from 1941 until November 1943 under the name Organizacja Wojskowa–Kadra Bezpieczeństwa, and finally from November 1943 under the name Korpus Bezpieczeństwa—was an organization associated with the AK, close to the political circles of Stronnictwo Demokratyczne.

Polska Ludowa Akacja Niepodległościowa, created in 1939, initially formed part of ZWZ-AK, and was later autonomous. In November 1943 PLAN formed *Komitet Ludowy*, the armed force of which became *Polska Armia Ludowa* (PAL). The organization had a strong left-wing program that included nationalization of production, planned economy, and formation of a federation of Central European countries.

45. See Dariusz Libionka, "ZWZ-AK i Delegatura Rzadu Polskiego wobec eksterminacji Żydów Polskich," in *Polacy i Żydzi pod okupacją niemiecką 1939–1945. Studia i Materiały*, ed. A. Żbikowski (Warszawa: IPN, 2006), 72.

46. Zuckerman, *A Surplus of Memory*, 131. Describing the help from AK expected by ŻOB in a report to Delegatura, Henryk Woliński asked for: "a/ greater number of arms as the received 10 parts are not enough for organizing armed resistance or other action of a group, rather than individual, character, b/ help with organizing purchase of arms; the funds for which would be provided by the Jewish side c/ instruction and instructors. There is a lack of instructors as individuals with appropriate qualifications have different functions in the police and do not have necessary trust of the armed organisation." AAN 202/XV – 2, 81.

47. See Władysław Bartoszewski, "Solidarity Actions at the Warsaw Ghetto Walls," in *Righteous among Nations: How Poles Helped the Jews 1939–1945*, ed. W. Bartoszewski, Z. Lewin, 555–70 (London: Earlscourt Publications Limited, 1969). It is not certain if the ghetto fighters were aware during the uprising of the solidarity actions at the ghetto walls.

48. Libionka, "ZWZ-AK i Delegatura Rządu Polskiego," 79. On this basis, Libionka doubts whether AK ever promised ŻOB their participation in armed fights in April.

49. See Yehuda Helman, "The Fate of the Last Fighters of the Jewish Military League in Warsaw," *Dapim: Studies on the Shoah* (1991), 21. Quoted in Grabski, Wójcicki, *Żydowski Związek Wojskowy*, 36.

50. Bereś, Burnetko, *Marek Edelman*, 128.

51. Ludwik Landau, *Kronika lat wojny i okupacji*, vol. 3 (Warszawa: PWN, 1962), 370. Those were obviously not the only rumors circulating in Warsaw during the uprising. According to one of the testimonies: "Warsaw was talking about treasures found in the ghetto: cellars full of furs, suitcases full of golden dollars, ten kilograms of gold" (JHIA 301/4651 [Frajnd]), 15.

52. *Wiadomości*, no. 40, Apr. 24, 1943 (Publication of the AK, published 1941–1945, targeted mainly at intelligentsia). Quoted in *Wojna żydowsko-niemiecka: polska prasa konspiracyjna 1943–1944 o powstaniu w getcie Warszawy*, ed. P. Szapiro (London: Aneks, 1992), 47.

53. *Biuletyn Informacyjny AK*, no. 17 (172), Apr. 29, 1943 (Main publication of the General Command of the AK, published 1939–1945). Quoted in *Wojna niemiecko-żydowska*, 69.

54. *Wiadomości*, no. 42, Apr. 29, 1943. Quoted in *Wojna niemiecko-żydowska*, 74.

55. Hirszfeld, *Historia*, 320.

56. Władysław Szlengel, "Kartka z dziennika akcji," www.zchor.org/szlengel/poems2.htm (accessed September 2012). The defense of the Polish garrison in Westerplatte between September 1–7, 1939, became a symbol of Polish heroism during the Second World War.

57. Kassow, *Who Will Write Our History?*, 330.

58. Ernest, *O wojnie wielkich Niemiec z Żydami Europy*, 14.

59. AAN Delegatura Rządu na Kraj (202/XV-1–2).

60. *Nurt Młodych*, no. 4, Apr. 30, 1943. Quoted in *Wojna niemiecko-żydowska*, 76.

61. On this point see *Wojna niemiecko-żydowska*, 11.

62. See, for example, JHIA 301/3073 (Jerzy Himelblau), 3.

63. Chaskielewicz, *Ukrywałem się w Warszawie*, 42.

64. AAN Dzienniki, kroniki, pamiętniki 231/I (Aurelia Wyleżańska).

65. Zylberberg, *A Warsaw Diary*, 161.

66. See Barbara Engelking, Dariusz Libionka, *Żydzi w powstańczej Warszawie* (Warszawa: Centrum Badań nad Zagładą Żydów, 2009), 97–100. The authors reject as unreliable information that ŻZW fighters also formed their own unit within AK. On this see Chaim Lazar, *Muranowska 7: The Warsaw Ghetto Rising* (Tel Aviv: Massada, 1966), 327.

67. JHIA 301/5719 (Danuta Dąbrowska). On the subject see Edward Kossoy, "The Gęsiówka Story: A Little Known Page of Jewish Fighting History," *Yad Vashem Studies* 32 (2004): 322–50. More in-depth research on KL Warschau and Gęsiowka can be found in Bogusław Kopka, *Konzentrationslager Warschau. Historia i następstwa* (Warszawa: IPN, 2007). According to Rotem, ŻOB attempted to get former Gęsiówka prisoners transferred from AK to the Jewish unit within the AL; this, however, proved impossible in the growing chaos of the uprising. See Rotem, *Memoirs of a Warsaw Ghetto Fighter*, 124.

68. One of the most illustrious cases was Krzysztof Kamil Baczyński, the most famous young poet of the Polish underground. See Joanna Rostropowicz-Clark, "Krzysztof Kamil Baczyński, a Poet Hero," *Polin* 13 (2000): 166–78.

69. BIP AK was treated with suspicion by many from the right wing of the AK. A few of its members of Jewish origin were murdered in June 1944 in unclear circumstances, most probably by the extreme-right AK members. See Janusz Marszalec, "Morderstwo

na Makowieckim i Widerszalu. Stara sprawa, nowe pytania, nowe wątpliwości," *Zagłada Żydów: Studia i Materiały* 3 (2007): 25–53. See also Michał Komar, Władysław Bartoszewski, *Skąd pan jest? Wywiad rzeka* (Warszawa: Świat Książki, 2006), 101–10.

70. Stanisław Aronson, "Walka o niepodległość Polski i Izraela-wspomnienia," in *Społeczność Żydowska w PRL przed kampanią antysemicką lat 1967–1968 i po niej* (Warszawa: IPN, 2009), 199.

71. Interview with Simhah Rotem in Grupińska, *Ciągle po kole*, 225.

72. MPW AHM Jan Karpiński (Klapper), interviewed by Małgorzta Brama, June 2007.

73. JHIA 301/1508 (Anonymous), 2; and Willenberg, *Bunt w Treblince*, 146.

74. AYV O.3/1617 (Alicja Grelewska), quoted in Engelking, Libionka, *Żydzi w powstańczej Warszawie*, 89.

75. JHIA 301/5063 (Jakub Ewison), 9.

76. JHIA 301/1508 (Anonymous), 4.

77. *Narodowe Siły Zbrojne* was a nationalistic, right-winged paramilitary organization created in September 1942. In March 1944 NSZ split; its more moderate part was subordinated to AK.

Socjalistyczna Organizacja Bojowa was a socialist military organization operating from March 1943, politically connected to PPS and subordinated to the AK.

Polska Armia Ludowa was a leftist organization operating from April 1943. On September 12, 1944, together with AL and KB it formed *Połączone Siły Zbrojne* (pol. Joint Armed Forces).

78. See A.K. Kunert ed., *Żydzi Polscy w Służbie Rzeczypospolitej* (Warszawa: Rada Ochrony Pamięci Walki i Męczeństwa, 2002), 40. The proclamation written on August 3 was not published by the Polish underground press until August 11. On August 23, a similar proclamation, calling "all workers and working intelligentsia to immediately join the uprising" was published by the Bund. Engelking, Libionka, *Żydzi w powstańczej Warszawie*, 49.

79. Zuckerman, *A Surplus of Memory*, 423. It is still not clear why exactly the unit joined the AL and not the AK. For the story of the creation of the unit see Engelking, Libionka, *Żydzi w powstańczej Warszawie*, 35–37 and 42–43.

80. MPW AHM Jan Karpiński (Klapper), interviewed by Małgorzata Brama, June 2007.

81. Zuckerman, *A Surplus of Memory*, 539.

82. See Edelman *Strażnik*, 102. Also JHIA 301/1539 (Efraim Krasucki), 5.

83. Chaim Goldstein, *The Bunker* (Philadelphia: Jewish Publication Society of America, 1970), 106. See also Willenberg, *Bunt w Treblince*, 146.

84. VHA 25555 (Interview with Helena Balicka).

85. See MPW AHM Wiktor Abrahamer "Grom," interviewed by Małgorzata Brama, June 2007.

86. JHIA 301/4443 (Wacław Myzia).

87. Temkin-Bermanowa, *Dziennik z Podziemia*, 59.

88. Zylberberg, *A Warsaw Diary*, 17. See also Temkin-Bermanowa, *Dziennik z Podziemia*, 148.

89. Paulsson, *Secret City*, 197. The exact number of Jews killed by Poles during the Warsaw Uprising is very difficult to establish. There are very few Polish sources on the subject and basically all Jewish testimonies available today are based on second-hand information and gossip circulating during the uprising.

90. Marek Szapiro, *Nim słońce wzejdzie. Dziennik pisany w ukryciu 1943–1944*, ed. Feliks Tych (Warszawa: ŻIH, 2007), 656.

91. Szapiro, *Nim słońce wzejdzie*, 670.

92. Artur Ney, "Pamiętnik," *Biuletyn Żydowskiego Instytutu Historycznego* 189, no. 1 (1999): 67.

93. JHIA 302/103 (Irena Grochem), 1.

94. Paulsson, *Secret City*, 167.

6. Holocaust Survivors in Post-War Poland: Conclusion

1. Samuel Puterman, trans., in *Words to Outlive Us*, 440.

2. Albert Stankowski, "Nowe spojrzenie na statystyki dotyczące emigracji Żydów z Polski po 1944 roku," in *Studia z historii Żydów w Polsce po 1945 r.*, ed. G. Berendt, A. Grabski, A. Stankowski (Warszawa: ŻIH, 2000), 109.

3. See Jan. T. Gross, *Fear: Anti-Semitism in Poland after Auschwitz: An Essay in Historical Interpretation* (Princeton: Princeton University Press, 2006).

4. Stankowski, "Nowe spojrzenie," 111.

5. Jerzy Tomaszewski, *Najnowsze dzieje Żydów w Polsce w zarysie (do 1950 roku)* (Warszawa: PWN, 1993), 424.

6. Tomaszewski, *Najnowsze dzieje Żydów*, 419.

7. Ibid., 404.

8. I use this term after Shulamit Volkov. See Shulamit Volkov, "The Dynamics of Dissimilation: Ostjuden and German Jews," in *The Jewish Response to German Culture: From the Enlightenment to the Second World War*, ed. J. Reinharz, W. Schatzberg, 192–211 (London: Brandeis Univerity Press, 1985).

9. Engelking, *Na łące popiołów*, 108.

10. On this see Andrzej Paczkowski, "Jews in the Polish Security Apparatus: An Attempt to Test the Stereotype," *Polin* 16 (2003): 451–64.

11. Joanna Michlic, *Poland's Threatening Other: The Image of the Jew from 1880 to the Present* (Lincoln: University of Nebraska Press, 2006), 206.

12. Alina Cała, August Grabski, "Provincial Jewish Committee of Warsaw (WKŻ) (1944–1949)," in *Żydzi Warszawy: Materiały konferencji*, 246.

13. Cała, Grabski, "Provincial Jewish Committee of Warsaw," 252.

14. Grzegorz Berendt, *Życie żydowskie w Polsce w latach 1950–1956. Z dziejów Towarzystwa Społeczno-Kulturalnego Żydów w Polsce* (Gdańsk: Wydawnictwo UG, 2006), 130.

15. Irena Hurwic-Nowakowska, *A Social Analysis of Postwar Polish Jewry*, trans. J. Michałowicz (Jerusalem: The Zalman Shazar Center for Jewish History, 1986), 27.

16. Karen Auerbach, "Rodziny żydowskie z domu w Alejach Ujazdowskich 16 w powojennej Warszawie. Dylematy etyczne w badaniach nad asymilacją w Polsce Ludowej," in *Społeczność żydowska w PRL przed kampanią antysemicką lat 1967–1968 i po niej*, ed. G. Berendt (Warszawa: IPN, 2009), 149–51.

17. For more, see Gabriel Finder, Alexander Prusin, "Jewish Collaborators on Trial in Poland, 1944–1956," *Polin* 20 (2007): 122–48.

18. Engel, "Who Is a Collaborator?," 367.

19. Raul Hilberg, *Perpetrators Victims Bystanders: Jewish Catastrophe 1939–1945* (New York: HarperCollins, 1992), 159.

Glossary

Aleynhilf. (yid. Self help) popular name for ŻTOS (pol. Jewish Society for Social Help), in November 1941 transformed into ŻOS (pol. Jewish Social Help), an organization coordinating welfare activities in the Warsaw Ghetto. Even though it was officially subordinated to the German established Jüdische Soziale Selbsthilfe, Aleynhilf remained largely independent and within its organizational framework there were numerous clandestine social and cultural organizations.

American Jewish Joint Distribution Committee. (AJDC) organization set up in 1914 to provide aid to Jews in Europe through organization of healthcare, vocational training, and provision of credit to workers. It functioned legally in the Warsaw Ghetto until December 1941, financing soup kitchens, providing help for children and refugees, and supporting clandestine activities.

Armia Krajowa. (AK, pol. Home Army) underground resistance organization sanctioned by the Polish government-in-exile, the military arm of the Polish Underground State, formed in February 1942. Its largest undertaking was the Warsaw Uprising, an attempt to liberate Warsaw, lasting from August 1 to October 2, 1944.

Armia Ludowa. (AL, pol. People's Army) a resistance group allied with Polska Partia Robotnicza (PPR, pol. Polish Workers Party), set up in January 1944 to support Soviet Union military actions. AL remained outside the framework of the Polish Underground State.

Aktion. deportation of the Warsaw ghetto's inhabitants to Treblinka which began on July 22, 1942, and lasted until September 21, 1942. The second Aktion, between January 18–21, 1943, was interrupted by the January revolt—armed resistance by the ghetto inhabitants.

Bund. (Algemeyner Yidisher Arbeter Bund in Poyln un Rusland, yid. General Jewish Workers' Alliance in Poland and Russia) Jewish socialist party founded in 1897, which propagated the program of national Jewish autonomy. In interwar Poland the Bund cooperated closely with the PPS (Polska Partia Socjalistyczna, pol. Polish Socialist Party).

Centos. (Centralne Towarzystwo Opieki nad Sierotami, pol. the Central Association for the Care of Orphans) an organization set up in 1924 and devoted solely to helping children. In interwar Warsaw, and later in the Warsaw Ghetto, it operated as the main children's relief agency, financing and running children's kitchens, orphanages, day-care centers, and libraries.

Hasid. (heb. pious) follower of the religious renewal movement which began in the mid-eighteenth century in Podolia and spread through most of eastern Europe.

Delegatura Rządu Rzeczypospolitej na Kraj. a provisional government for Poland. An agency of the Polish government-in-exile and the highest authority in the Underground Polish State framework during the Second World War.

Einsatz Reinhardt. (ger. Operation Reinhardt) code-name for the action of murdering Jews in the Generalgouvernement.

Endecja. popular name for Polish National Democratic Party (Narodowa Demokracja), a nationalist political movement, calling for the exclusion of Jews from Polish economic life. The principal ideologue of Endecja was Roman Dmowski.

Gazeta Żydowska. (pol. Jewish Newspaper) German-controlled newspaper, published three times a week between 1940 and 1942 in Kraków. It was the only newspaper distributed legally in the ghettos of Generalgouvernement.

Generalgouvernement. an administrative-territorial unit comprising part of Nazi-occupied Poland, established on October 26, 1939. It was divided into Warsaw, Kraków, and Lublin districts, with a capital in Kraków. After the Nazi invasion of the Soviet Union, the fifth province—Galicja—was added to its territory.

Government of the Republic of Poland in Exile. (pol. Rząd Rzeczypospolitej Polskiej na Uchodźctwie) the successor of the Polish government, formed in France in September 1939. After the fall of France it operated from London.

Hashomer Hatzair. (heb. Young Guard) pioneering socialist-Zionist youth movement, set up in 1913 in Galicia. During the war, its members played an important part in organizing civil and armed resistance against the Germans.

Haskalah. (heb. Enlightenment) ideological and social movement among European Jews which resulted from the European Enlightenment, advocating secular education and use of national languages. Its adherents were known as *maskilim.*

House Committees. organizations of Jewish self-administration, composed of inhabitants of one or a few apartment buildings. They were initially established in 1939 to fulfill air-raid duties.

Jewish Order Service. organization set up in October 1940 to take over the duties of the "Navy Blue" police in the newly established ghetto. It was headed by a pre-war colonel of the Polish State Police, Józef Szeryński, and soon became synonymous with the abuses of power.

Judenrat. administrative bodies established by the Germans in occupied countries. They had varying structures, areas of responsibility, and relations with both the Jewish communities whom they administered and the local Nazi authorities.

Jewish Self-Help Agency. (JSS, ger. Jüdishe Soziale Selbsthilfe) Jewish welfare organization, which functioned legally in the Generalgouvernement.

Kahal. Jewish communal body in a particular locality, carrying out religious and social functions. In Polish often referred to as *gmina* (pol. community).

Kehilah. community of Jews in a particular locality.

Komunistyczna Partia Polski. (KPP, Pol. Communist Party of Poland) political party founded in 1916, which operated illegally in Poland from March 1919. It was dissolved in 1938, after almost all of its leaders were murdered during the Great Purge in the Soviet Union.

Mekhes. (heb. levy) term used in Poland to refer to converts from Judaism into Christianity.

Mikvah. a pool of water used in Judaism for ritual bathing.

Mitzvah. one of 613 commandments to be adhered to by religious Jews.

Oyneg Shabes. (heb. Joy of Sabbath) A group organized by historian Emanuel Ringelblum to work on the Underground Archive of the Warsaw Ghetto. Its aim was to document the fate of the Jews of Poland by collecting documentation of their everyday life, conducting surveys and research. Documents from the Archive are now housed in the Jewish Historical Institute in Warsaw.

ORT. (rus. The Society for Handicrafts and Agricultural Work) organization for the development of vocational training among Jews set up in 1880 in Tsarist Russia. In the Warsaw Ghetto, in cooperation with the Judenrat, it trained students in twenty-four different trades.

Parówki. (pol. steam baths) a largely ineffective method of combating Typhus epidemics in the ghetto through forced bathing of the inhabitants of affected buildings and disinfections of their apartments and belongings.

Pawiak. popular name for the largest Gestapo prison in Poland, located in the Warsaw Ghetto. Among those incarcerated in Pawiak were mainly Poles, but also those who were caught on the "Aryan" side of Warsaw and were suspected of having a Jewish identity. Jews from the ghetto were imprisoned in the ghetto central prison, Gęsiówka, from mid-1941.

Placówki. (pol. placements) places of Jewish forced labor within the borders of Warsaw, which functioned until 1943.

Poalei Tzion. (heb. Workers of Zion) a Zionist labor organization which began in the Russian Empire in the early twentieth century and later split into left and right wings.

Points. places housing deportees and refuges arriving into the ghetto.

Polnische Polizei. (pol. Polish Police) an organization set up by the German administration, largely based on the pre-war Polish State Police. To distinguish between the two bodies, inhabitants of Warsaw usually referred to it as the "Navy Blue" police.

Polska Partia Socjalistyczna. (PPS, Polish Socialist Party) Polish socialist, pro-independence party, founded in 1892. In the early twentieth century it was led by Józef Piłsudski, but later moved into opposition. During the Second World War, it formed part of the Polish Underground State.

Polska Partia Robotnicza. (PPR, pol. Polish Workers Party) communist party set up in Warsaw in January 1942 and subordinated to the political decisions of the Soviet Union.

Shabbes Goy. (yid. Sabbath gentile) a non-Jew undertaking tasks which are prohibited to religious Jews on Sabbath.

Shop. German enterprise in the ghetto.

Szmalcownictwo. jargon term for the blackmailing of Jews who were illegally staying on the "Aryan" side in Nazi-occupied Poland.

Tarbut. (heb. culture) a network of Zionist schools set up in 1922, with Hebrew as the language of instruction.

Thirteen. popular name for the Office to Fight Usury and Speculation, a Gestapo collaboration unit, operational in the ghetto between autumn 1940 and July 1941. It was headed by Abraham Gancwajch.

Towarzystwo Popierania Rozwoju Rolnictwa wśród Żydów. (TOPOROL, pol. Jewish Agricultural Development Organization) organization set up by Joint in 1933 in order to prepare Jewish youth for agricultural work.

Towarzystwo Ochrony Zdrowia. (TOZ, pol. The Society for the Preservation of Health) welfare organization set up in 1922 to deal with the organization of health care for the Jewish Community in Poland. In the ghetto it conducted healthcare activities in parallel to those of the Judenrat, and was financed primarily by the JOINT.

Transferstelle. (ger. Transport Authority) an office controlling the legal transport of goods in and out of the ghetto.

Tsisho. (yid. Central Yiddish School Organization) a network of secular, socialist schools in interwar Poland, supported by, among others, the Bund and Poalei Tzion Left.

Umschlagplatz. (ger. reloading point) railroad siding first used for goods entering and leaving the ghetto, then from the summer of 1942 as a collection point during deportations from the ghetto.

Werkshutz. (ger. factory guard service) German, Ukrainian, and Jewish units employed to guard German workshops in the ghetto.

Wiadomości Literackie. (pol. Literary News) weekly literary magazine published in Warsaw between 1924 and 1939 by Mieczysław Grydzewski.

Yikor. (yid. Jewish Cultural Organization) illegal cultural organization and a branch of the Jewish Social Self-Help, set up in the Warsaw Ghetto in 1941. It was aimed at promoting Yiddish language and culture.

Yishuv. (heb. settlement) the Jewish settlement in Palestine before the founding of the State of Israel.

Żydowska Organizacja Bojowa. (ŻOB, pol. Jewish Fighting Organization) armed resistance group organized in its final form on October 15, 1942. Its political leadership was formed by ***Żydowski Komitet Narodowy.*** (pol. Jewish National Committee) In January 1943 ŻOB organized the first armed resistance against deportations from the Warsaw Ghetto and in April 1943 participated in the Warsaw Ghetto Uprising.

Żydowski Związek Wojskowy. (ŻZW, pol. Jewish Military Alliance) an armed organization set up in October 1939, composed mainly of members of pre-war right-wing Zionist parties. Its units participated in the Warsaw Ghetto Uprising.

Żydokomuna. (pol. Judo-communism) an anti-Semitic motif linking Jews with communism.

Bibliography

Archival Sources

Jewish Historical Institute Archive (JHIA):

- Testimonies (collection 301)
- Diaries (collection 302)
- Social Courts Proceedings (collection 313)
- Underground Archive of the Warsaw Ghetto (Ringelblum Archive part I and II)
- Kolekcja Bernarda Marka

Yad Vashem Archive (YVA):

- Yad Vashem Collection of Testimonies (O.3)
- Documentation about the Polish Government in Exile in London (O.25)
- Various Testimonies, Diaries, and Memoirs Collection (O.33)
- Nazi Documentation (O.51)

Archiwum Akt Nowych (AAN):

- Rada Główna Opiekuńcza (Zespół 52)
- Delegatura Rządu RP na Kraj (Zespół 1325)
- Armia Krajowa (Zespół 1326)

The Shoah Foundation Visual History Archive (VHA)

Muzeum Powstania Warszawskiego, Archiwum Historii Mówionej (MPW AHM)

Published Primary Sources

Adler, Stanisław. *In the Warsaw Ghetto: 1940–1943: An Account of an Eyewitness*. Translated by Sara Chmielewska-Philip. Jerusalem: Yad Vashem, 1982.

Arad, Yitzhak, ed. *Documents on the Holocaust: Selected Sources on the Destruction of the Jews of Germany and Austria, Poland and the Soviet Union*. Jerusalem: Yad Vashem, 1981.

Aronson, Stanisław. "Walka o niepodległość Polski i Izraela-wspomnienia." In *Społeczność żydowska w PRL przed kampanią antysemicką lat 1967–1968 i po niej*, edited by Grzegorz Berendt, 148–55. Warszawa: IPN, 2009.

Assuntino, Rudi, and Wlodek Goldkorn. *Strażnik. Marek Edelman opowiada.* Translated by Ireneusz Kania. Kraków: Znak, 1999.

Auerbach, Rachela. "Lament Rzeczy Martwych." *Przełom*, no. 2 (1946): 7.

Auerbach, Rachela. "Z ludem pospołu. O losie pisarzy i artystów żydowskich w getcie warszawskim," *Nasze Słowo*, no. 19 (1947): 10, 1; (1948): 9 and 11; (1948): 11.

Bartoszewski, Władysław. *The Warsaw Ghetto: A Christian's Testimony.* Translated by Stephen G. Cappellari. London: Lamp Press, 1989.

Bauman, Janina. *Winter in the Morning: A Young Girl's Life in the Warsaw Ghetto and Beyond, 1939–1945.* London: Virago, 1986.

Bereś, Witold, and Marek Burnetko. *Marek Edelman. Życie Po prostu.* Warszawa: Świat Książki, 2008.

Berg, Mary. *The Diary of Mary Berg: Growing Up in the Warsaw Ghetto.* Edited by Susan Lee Pentlin. Oxford: Oneworld, 2006.

Berland, Marian. *Dni długie jak wieki.* Warszawa: Niezależna Oficyna Wydawnicza, 1992.

Berman, Adolf. "The Fate of Children in the Warsaw Ghetto." In *The Catastrophe of European Jewry: Antecedents, History, Reflections: Selected Papers.* Edited by Israel Gutman. Jerusalem: Yad Vashem, 1976.

Berman, Adolf. *Vos der goyrl hoṭ mir basherṭ: miṭ Yidn in Ṿarshe, 1939–1942.* Tel Aviv: Beit Lohamei Hagettaot, 1980.

Berman, Adolf. "Blok Antyfaszystowski (ze wspomnień)." *Biuletyn Żydowskiego Instytutu Historycznego* 114–15, no. 2–3 (1980), 77–98.

Birenbaum Halina, *Wołanie o pamięć.* Oświęcim: Wyd. Państ. Muzeum Oświęcim-Brzezinka, 1999.

Borwicz, Michał, ed. *Pieśń ginących: z dziejów twórczości Żydów pod okupacją niemiecką.* Warszawa: Wyd. Centralnej Żydowskiej Komisji Historycznej, 1947.

Borwicz, Michał, ed. *Pieśń ujdzie cało. Antologia wierszy o Żydach pod okupacją niemiecką.* Warszawa: Wyd. Centralnej Żydowskiej Komisji Historycznej, 1947.

Browning, Christopher R., and Israel Gutman, eds. "The Reports of the Jewish 'Informer' in the Warsaw Ghetto—Selected Documents." *Yad Vashem Studies* 17 (1986): 248–94.

Chaskielewicz, Stefan. *Ukrywałem się w Warszawie: styczeń 1943–styczeń 1945*. Kraków: Społeczny Instytut Wydawniczy Znak, 1988.

Czerniaków, Adam. *The Warsaw Diary of Adam Czerniakow: Prelude to Doom*. Edited by Raul Hilberg, Stanislaw Staron, Josef Kermisz. Chicago: Ivan R. Dee, 1999.

David, Janina. *A Square of Sky: Memoirs of Wartime Childhood*. London: Eland, 1992.

Donat, Aleksander. *The Holocaust Kingdom: A Memoir*. New York: Holocaust Library, 1978.

Edelman, Marek. *I była miłość w getcie*. Warszawa: Świat Książki, 2009.

Engelking, Barbara. "O tym jak z wewnątrz getta patrzono na stronę aryjską z profesorem Israelem Gutmanem rozmawia Barbara Engelking." *Zagłada Żydow. Studia i Materiały* 1 (2005): 230–33.

Ernest, Stefan. *O wojnie wielkich Niemiec z Żydami Europy 1939–1943*. Edited by Marta Młodkowska. Warszawa: Czytelnik, ŻIH, 2003.

Fischer, Ludwig. *Raporty Ludwiga Fischera, gubernatora Dystryktu Warszawskiego 1939–1944*. Edited by Krzysztof Dunin-Wąsowicz et al. Warszawa: Książka i Wiedza, 1987.

Friedman, Philip, ed. *Martyrs and Fighters: The Epic of the Warsaw Ghetto*. London: Routledge and Kegan, 1952.

Goldstein, Bernard. *Five Years in the Warsaw Ghetto (The Stars Bear Witness)*. Translated and edited by Leonard Shatzkin. Edinburgh: A.K., 2005.

Goldstein, Chaim. *The Bunker*. Translated by Esther Malkin. Philadelphia: Jewish Publication Society of America, 1970.

Gran, Wiera. *Sztafeta Oszczerców. Autobiografia śpiewaczki*. Paris: self-published, 1980.

Grodzieńska, Stefania. *Urodził go "Niebieski Ptak."* Łódź: Akapit Press, 1990.

Grupińska, Anka. *Ciągle po kole: Rozmowy z żołnierzami getta warszawskiego*. Warszawa: Wyd. Książkowe Twój Styl, 2000.

Gryberg, Michał, ed. *Words to Outlive Us: Voices from the Warsaw Ghetto*. Translated by Philip Boehm. New York: Henry Holt and Company, 2002.

Hartglas, Apolinary. *Na pograniczu dwóch światów*. Edited by Jolanta Żyndul. Warszawa: Rytm, 1996.

Hirshaut, Julian. *Jewish Martyrs of Pawiak*. New York: Holocaust Library, 1982.

Hirszfeld, Ludwik. *Historia jednego życia*. Warszawa: Czytelnik, 2000.

Huberband, Shimon. *Kiddush Hashem: Jewish Religious and Cultural Life in Poland during the Holocaust*. Edited by Jeffrey S. Gurock and Robert S. Hirt. New York: Yeshiva University Press, 1987.

Kaplan, Chaim A. *Scroll of Agony: The Warsaw Diary of Chaim A. Kaplan*. Translated and edited by Abraham I. Katsh. Bloomington: Indiana University Press, 1999.

Katzenelson, Yitzhak. *Vittel Diary (22.5.43–16.9.43)*. Translated by Myer Coben. Tel Aviv: The Ghetto Fighters House, 1964.

Katzenelson, Yitzhak. *Song of the Murdered Jewish People*. Translated by Noah H. Rosenbloom. Ghetto Fighters House, 1983.

Kermish, Joseph, ed. *To Live With Honor and Die with Honor: Selected Documents from the Warsaw Ghetto Underground Archives "O.S." ["Oneg Shabbath"]*. Jerusalem: Yad Vashem, 1986.

Komar, Michał, and Władysław Bartoszewski. *Skąd pan jest? Wywiad rzeka*. Warszawa: Świat Książki, 2006.

Korczak, Janusz. *The Ghetto Years 1939–1942*. Translated by Jerzy Bachrach. Tel Aviv: The Ghetto Fighters House, 1980.

Koźmińska-Frejlak, Ewa. "Świadectwo milczenia . . . Rozmowa z Jerzym Lewińskim, byłym funkcjonariuszem Służby Porządkowej getta warszawskiego." *Zagłada Żydów. Źródła i materiały* 2 (2006): 245–79.

Kula, Witold. *Dziennik czasu okupacji*, edited by Marcin Kula. Warszawa: PIW, 1994.

Landau, Ludwik. *Kronika lat wojny i okupacji*, vol. 1, edited by Zbigniew Landau and Jerzy Tomaszewski. Warszawa: PWN, 1962.

———. *Kronika lat wojny i okupacji*, vol. 3, edited by Zbigniew Landau and Jerzy Tomaszewski. Warszawa: PWN, 1963.

Lewin, Abraham. *A Cup of Tears: A Diary of the Warsaw Ghetto*. Edited by Antony Polonsky, translated by Christopher Hutton. London: Fontana, 1990.

———. "Twilight Days: Missing Pages from Avraham Lewin's Warsaw Ghetto Diary, May–July 1942." Edited by Havi Ben-Sasson and Lea Preiss. *Yad Vashem Studies* 33 (2005): 7–60.

Lewin, Aleksander, ed. *Janusz Korczak w getcie: nowe źródła*. Warszawa: Latona, 1992.

Likiernik, Stansław. Interviewed by Patrycja Bukalska. www.fzp.net.pl/media.html (accessed September 2009)

Lubelska, Wanda. *Listy z getta*. Warszawa: Biblioteka Narodowa, 2000.

Lubetkin, Zivia. *In the Days of the Destruction and Revolt.* Translated by Ishai Tubbin. Tel Aviv: Hakibbutz Hameuchad, 1981.

Makower, Henryk. *Pamiętnik z getta warszawskiego. Październik 1940– Styczeń 1943.* Edited by Noemi Makower. Wrocław: Zakład Narodowy im. Ossolińskich, 1987.

Marianowicz, Antoni. *Life Strictly Forbidden.* Translated by Alicia Nitecki. London: Vallentine Mitchell, 2004.

Mazor, Michael. *The Vanished City: Everyday Life in the Warsaw Ghetto.* Translated by David Jacobsòn. New York: Marsilio, 1993.

Meed, Vladka. *On Both Sides of the Wall.* Translated by Steven Meed. Tel Aviv: Beit Lohamei Hagettaot, 1972.

Ney, Artur. "Pamiętnik." *Biuletyn Żydowskiego Instytutu Historycznego* 189, no. 1 (1999): 49–70.

Reich-Ranicki, Marcel. *The Author of Himself: The Life of Marcel Reich-Ranicki.* Translated by Ewald Osers. London: Weidenfeld and Nicolson, 2001.

Ringelblum, Emanuel. *Ksovim fun geto,* vol. 1. Varshe: Yidish Bukh, 1961.

———. *Ksovim fun geto,* vol. 2. Varshe: Yidish Bukh, 1963.

———. *Polish-Jewish Relations during the Second World War.* Edited by Joseph Kermish and Shmuel Krakowski. Jerusalem: Yad Vashem, 1974.

———. *Notes from the Warsaw Ghetto: The Journal of Emmanuel Ringelblum.* Translated by Jacob Sloan. New York: Schocken Books, 1988.

Rogoziński, Szymon. *My Fortunate Life.* Melbourne: Bookaburra, 2000.

Rotem, Simhah. *Memoirs of a Warsaw Ghetto Fighter: The Past Within Me.* Translated by Barbara Harshav. New Haven: Yale University Press, 1994.

Rufeisen-Schupper, Hela. *Pożegnanie Miłej 18.* Kraków: Beseder, 1996.

Seidman, Hillel. *Togbukh fun varshaver geto.* Buenos Ayres: Tsentral-farband fun Poylishe Yidn in Argentine, 1947.

Seksztajn, Gela. "Fragment Dziennika." *Nasze Słowo* no. 6–7 (1948), 37.

Shandler, Jeffrey, ed. *Awakening Lives: Autobiographies of Jewish Youth in Poland before the Holocaust.* London: Yale University Press, 2002.

Shaskes, Chaim. *Bleter fun a Geto Togbukh.* New York: C.H. Glants, 1943.

Starkopf, Adam. *There Is Always Time To Die.* Edited by Gertrude Hirschler. New York: Holocaust Library, 1981.

Stawski, Mieczysław. *Deszcz pada wszędzie.* Stockholm: Jedność, 1981.

Szapiro, Marek. *Nim słonce wzejdzie. Dziennik pisany w ukryciu 1943–1944.* Edited by Feliks Tych. Warszawa: ŻIH, 2007.

Szapiro, Paweł, ed. *Wojna żydowsko-niemiecka: polska prasa konspiracyjna 1943–1944 o powstaniu w getcie Warszawy*. London: Aneks, 1992.

Szczęsna, Joanna. "I już nic nie było jak przedtem. Rozmowa z Markiem Edelmanem." *Gazeta Wyborcza*. Apr. 22, 1999. http://wyborcza.pl/1,89798,5119367.html (accessed September 2012).

Szelestowska, Maria. *Lubię żyć*. Warszawa: Czytelnik, 2000.

Szereszewska, Helena. *Memoirs From Occupied Warsaw 1940–1945*. Translated by Anna Mariańska. London: Vallentine Mitchell, 1997.

Szlengel, Władysław. "Paszport." Translated by Robert Gliniak. www.zchor.org/szlengel/poems2.htm (accessed September 2012)

Szpilman, Władysław. *The Pianist: The Extraordinary Story of One Man's Survival in Warsaw, 1939–45*. Translated by Anthea Bell. London: Gollancz, 1999.

Szwajger Blady, Adina. *I Remember Nothing More: The Warsaw Children's Hospital and the Jewish Resistance*. Translated by Tasja Darowska and Danusia Stok. London: Collins-Harvill, 1990.

Szyfman, Arnold. *Moja tułaczka wojenna*. Warszawa: MON, 1960.

Śmigielska, Irena. *Skradzione lata*. Warszawa: ŻIH, 2001.

Temkin-Bermanowa, Barbara. *Dziennik z Podziemia*. Edited by Anka Grupińska, Paweł Szapiro. Warszawa: Twój Styl, 2000.

Tomkiewicz, Mina. *Of Bombs and Mice: A Novel of War-time Warsaw*. Translated by Stefan Gazel. London: George Allen and Unwin, 1970.

Turkow, Jonas. *Azoy iz es geven: Khurbn Varshe*. Buenos Aires: Tsentral-farband fun Poylishe Yidn in Argentine, 1948.

Wasser, Hersh. "Daily Entries of Hersh Wasser." Edited by Josef Kermish. *Yad Vashem Studies* 15 (1983): 201–82.

Wdowiński, David. *And We Are Not Saved*. New York: Philosophical Library, 1963.

Weiss, Pnina. "The Memoirs of Pnina Weiss—Wife of a Member of the First Judenrat in Warsaw." Edited by Esther Farbstein. *Yad Vashem Studies* 33 (2005): 61–100.

Willenberg, Samuel. *Bunt w Treblince*. Edited by Andrzej Żbikowski. Warszawa: Biblioteka "Więzi," 2004.

Wiszniewicz, Joanna. *A jednak czasem miewam sny: historia pewnej samotności*. Warszawa: Agencja Wydawnicza "Tu," 1996.

Wiszniewicz, Joanna. *Z Polski do Izraela. Rozmowy z pokoleniem '68*. Warszawa: Karta, 1992.

Zuckerman, Yitzhak. *A Surplus of Memory: Chronicle of the Warsaw Ghetto Uprising*. Translated and edited by Barbara Harshav. Berkeley: University of California Press, 1993.

Zylberberg, Michael. *A Warsaw Diary: 1939–1945*. London: Vallentine Mitchell, 1969.

Żywulska, Krystyna. *Pusta Woda*. Michałów-Grabina: Instytut Wydawniczy Latarnik, 2008.

Secondary Sources

Aaron, Frieda. *Bearing the Unbearable: Yiddish and Polish Poetry in the Ghettos and Concentration Camps*. Albany: SUNY Press, 1990.

Adamczyk-Garbowska, Monika. "Literatura jidysz w polskich przekładach dawnej i dziś." In *Jidyszland—polskie przestrzenie*. Edited by Ewa Geller and Monika Polit, 158–69. Warszawa: Wydawnictwo UW, 2008.

Auerbach, Karen. "Rodziny żydowskie z domu w Alejach Ujazdowskich 16 w powojennej Warszawie. Dylematy etyczne w badaniach nad asymilacją w Polsce Ludowej." In *Społeczność żydowska w PRL przed kampanią antysemicką lat 1967–1968 i po niej*, edited by Grzegorz Berendt, 148–55. Warszawa: IPN, 2009.

Bacon, Gershon. "National Revival, Ongoing Acculturation—Jewish Education in Interwar Poland." *Simon Dubnow Institut* 1 (2002): 71–92.

Bartal, Israel, and Magdalena Opalski. *Poles and Jews: A Failed Brotherhood*. Hanover: Brandeis University Press, 1992.

Bartoszewski, Władysław. "Solidarity Actions at the Warsaw Ghetto Walls." In Bartoszewski and Lewin, eds., 555–70.

Bartoszewski, Władysław, and Zofia Lewin. *Righteous Among Nations: How Poles Helped the Jews, 1939–1945*. London: Earlscourts Publications, 1969.

Ben-Sasson, Havi. "Christians in the Ghetto: All Saint's Church, Birth of the Holy Virgin Mary Church and the Jews of the Warsaw Ghetto." *Yad Vashem Studies* 31 (2003): 153–73.

Ben-Sasson, Havi. "'Chcemy wierzyć w inną Polskę' Stosunki żydowsko-polskie w podziemnej prasie żydowskiej Getta Warszawskiego." *Zagłada Żydów: Studia i materiały* 1 (2005): 96–113.

Berendt, Grzegorz. *Życie żydowskie w Polsce w latach 1950–1956. Z dziejów Towarzystwa Społeczno-Kulturalnego Żydów w Polsce*. Gdańsk: Wydawnictwo UG, 2006.

Berenstein, Tatiana. "Żydzi warszawscy w hitlerowskich obozach pracy przymusowej." *Biuletyn Żydowskiego Instytutu Historycznego* 67, no. 3 (1968): 39–65.

Blatman, Daniel, and Israel Gutman. "Youth and Resistance Movements in Historical Perspectives." *Yad Vashem Studies* 23 (1993): 1–71.

Blobaum, Robert. *Antisemitism and Its Opponents in Modern Poland*, Ithaca: Cornell University Press 2005.

Browning, Christopher R. *The Origins of the Final Solution: The Evolution of Nazi Jewish Policy, September 1939–March 1942*. London: William Heinemann, 2004.

Bułat, Mirosława M. "Cwiszn cwej teaters-na pograniczu dwóch teatrów. Źródła jidysz w badaniach nad kontaktami międzykulturowymi w polskim teatrze-kilka przypomnień, szereg uzupełnień." In *Jidyszland—polskie przestrzenie*, edited by Ewa Geller and Monika Polit, 121–41. Warszawa: Wydawnictwo UW, 2008.

Burgess, Ernest W., Robert E Park. *Introduction to the Science of Sociology*. Chicago: University of Chicago Press, 1921.

Cała, Alina. *Asymilacja Żydów w Królestwie Polskim (1864–1897)*. Warszawa: PIW, 1989.

———. "The Social Consciousness of Young Jews in Interwar Poland." *Polin* 8 (1994).

Cała, Alina, and August Grabski. "Provincial Jewish Committee of Warsaw (WKŻ) (1944–1949)." In *Żydzi Warszawy: Materiały konferencji w 100. rocznicę urodzin Emanuela Ringelbluma*, edited by Eleonora Bergman, 241–58. Warszawa: ŻIH, 2000.

Czarnecki, Antoni. "Parafia Wszystkich Świętych." In *Za co groziła śmierć. Polacy z pomocą Żydom w czasie okupacji*. Edited by Władysław Smólski. Warszawa: PAX, 1981.

Datner, Helena. *Ta i tamta strona: żydowska inteligencja Warszawy drugiej połowy XIX wieku*. Warszawa: ŻIH, 2007.

Dawidowicz, Lucy. *The Jewish Presence: Essays on Identity and History*. New York: Holt, Rinehart and Winston, 1977.

Dembowski, Peter F. *Christians in the Warsaw Ghetto: An Epitaph for the Unremembered*. Notre Dame: University of Notre Dame Press, 2005.

Dobroszycki, Lucjan. *Reptile Journalism: The Official Polish-language Press under the Nazis, 1939–1945*. Translated by Barbara Harshav. London: Yale University Press, 1994.

Eisenbach, Artur. *Emancypacja Żydów na ziemiach polskich 1785–1870 na tle europejskim*. Warszawa: PIW, 1988.

Endelman, Todd. "Assimilation." In *The YIVO Encyclopedia of Jews in Eastern Europe*, vol. 1, edited by Gershon D. Hundert, 81–87. New Haven: Yale University Press, 2008.

———. "Jewish Converts in Nineteenth-Century Warsaw. A Quantitative Analysis." *Jewish Social Studies* 4, no. 1 (1997): 28–59.

Engel, David. "Who Is a Collaborator? The Trials of Michal Weichert." In *Jews in Poland*, vol. 2, edited by Sławomir Kapralski, 339–70. Krakow: Judaica Foundation, 1999.

Engelking, Barbara. *Holocaust and Memory: The Experience of Holocaust and Its Consequences: An Investigation Based on Personal Narratives*. Edited by Gunnar S. Paulsson, translated by Emma Harris. London: Leicester University Press, 2001.

———. *Na łące popiołów, Ocaleni z Holocaustu*. Warszawa: Cyklady, 1997.

Engelking, Barbara, and Jacek Leociak. *The Warsaw Ghetto: A Guide to the Perished City*. Translated by Emma Harris. New Haven: Yale University Press, 2009.

Engelking, Barbara, and Dariusz Libionka. *Żydzi w powstańczej Warszawie*. Warszawa: Centrum Badań nad Zagładą Żydów, 2009.

Finder, Gabriel, and Alexander Prusin. "Jewish Collaborators on Trial in Poland, 1944–1956." *Polin* 20 (2007): 122–48.

Frankel, Jonathan. "Assimilation and the Jews in Nineteenth-Century Europe." In *Assimilation and Community: The Jews in Nineteenth-century Europe*, edited by Jonathan Frankel, Steven J. Zipperstein, 1–38. Cambridge: Cambridge University Press, 1992.

Friedman, Philip. "For Your Freedom as Well as Ours." In *Their Brothers' Keepers*, 111–29. New York: Crown Publishers, 1957.

Friedman, Philip. *Roads to Extinction: Essays on the Holocaust*. New York: Jewish Publication Society of America, 1980.

Frost, Shimon. *Schooling as a Socio-political Expression: Jewish Education in Interwar Poland*. Jerusalem: The Magnes Press, The Hebrew University, 1998.

Geller, Ewa. "The Jews of Warsaw as a Speech Community. Homage to Warsaw Yiddish." In *Żydzi Warszawy: Materiały konferencji w 100. rocznicę urodzin Emanuela Ringelbluma*, edited by Eleonora Bergman, 109–26. Warszawa: ŻIH, 2000.

Grabowski, Jan. *Ja tego Żyda znam!' Szantażowanie Żydów w Warszawie 1939–1943*. (Warszawa: IFiS PAN, 2004).

Grabowski, Jan. "Jewish Defendants in German and Polish Courts in the Warsaw District." *Yad Vashem Studies* 35 (2007): 49–81.

Grabowski, Jan. *Rescue for Money: Paid Helpers in Poland, 1939–1945*. Jerusalem: Yad Vashem, 2008.

Grabski, August; Wójcicki, Maciej. *Żydowski Związek Wojskowy-historia przywrócona*. Warszawa: ŻIH, 2008.

Groński, Marek. *Proca Dawida: kabaret w przedsionku piekieł*. Warszawa: Muza, 2007.

Gross, Jan. T. *Fear: Anti-Semitism in Poland after Auschwitz: An Essay in Historical Interpretation*. Princeton: Princeton University Press, 2006.

Grupińska, Anka. *Odczytanie listy. Opowieści o powstańcach żydowskich*. Kraków: Wydawnictwo Literackie, 2002.

Guesnet, François. *Polnische Juden im 19. Jahrhundert: Lebensbedingungen, Rechtsnormen und Organisation im Wandel*. Köln: Böhlau, 1998.

Gutman, Israel. "Adam Czerniakow—The Man and his Diary." In Gutman and Rothkirchen, eds., 451–90.

———. *The Jews of Warsaw, 1939–1943: Ghetto, Underground, Revolt*. Translated by Ina Friedman. Bloomington: Indiana University Press, 1982.

———. *Resistance: The Warsaw Ghetto Uprising*. Boston: Houghton Mifflin, 1994.

Gutman, Israel, and Livia Rothkirchen, eds. *The Catastrophe of European Jewry: Antecedents, History, Reflections: Selected Papers*. Jerusalem: Yad Vashem, 1976.

Gutman, Israel, and Shmuel Krakowski. *Unequal Victims: Poles and Jews During World War Two*. New York: Holocaust Library, 1986.

Halperin, Adam. "Betar's Role in the Warsaw Ghetto Uprising." In Gutman and Rothkirchen, eds., 549–58.

Haska, Agnieszka. *"Jestem Żydem, chcę wejść!" Hotel Polski w Warszawie, 1943*. Warszawa: IFiS PAN, 2006.

Heller, Celia. *On the Edge of Destruction: Jews of Poland between the Two World Wars*. New York: Columbia University Press, 1977.

Hempel, Adam. *Pogrobowcy klęski: rzecz o policji "granatowej" w Generalnym Gubernatorstwie 1939–1945*. Warszawa: PWN, 1990.

Hertz, Aleksander. *The Jews in Polish Culture*. Translated by Richard Lourie. Evanston, IL: Northwestern University Press, 1988.

Hilberg, Raul. *Perpetrators Victims Bystanders: Jewish Catastrophe 1939–1945*. New York: HarperCollins, 1992.

———. *Sources of Holocaust Research: An Analysis*. Chicago: Ivan R. Dee, 2001.

Holzer, Jerzy. "Relations between Polish and Jewish Left Wing Groups in Interwar Poland." In *The Jews in Poland*, edited by Ch. Abramsky, M. Jachimczyk, A. Polonsky, 140–46. Oxford: Basil Blackwell, 1986.

Hurwic-Nowakowska, Irena. *A Social Analysis of Postwar Polish Jewry*. Translated by Jerzy Michalowicz. Jerusalem: The Zalman Shazar Center for Jewish History, 1986.

Jabłonowski, Marek. "Związek Żydów Uczestników Walk o Niepodległość Polski." In *Żydzi w Obronie Rzeczypospolitej*, edited by Jerzy Tomaszewski, 113–24. Warszawa: Cyklady, 1996.

Jagodzińska, Agnieszka. *Pomiędzy: Akulturacja Żydów Warszawy w drugiej połowie XIX wieku*. Wrocław: Wydawnictwo Uniwersytetu Wrocławskiego, 2008.

———, ed. *W poszukiwaniu religii doskonałej? Konwersja a Żydzi*. Wrocław: Wydawnictwo Uniwersytetu Wrocławskiego, 2011.

Janczewska, Marta. "Obozy pracy przymusowej dla Żydow na terenie dystryktu warszawskiego." In *Prowincja noc: Życie i zagłada Żydów w dystrykcie warszawskim*, edited by Barbara Engelking, Jacek Leociak, and Dariusz Libionka, 271–320. Warszawa: IFiS PAN, 2007.

Janion, Maria. *Pułkownik żydowski: życiorys romantycznyf i nieromantyczny*. Kraków: Judaica, 2008.

Janion, Maria. *Bohater, spisek, śmierć. Wykłady żydowskie*. Warszawa: WAB, 2009.

Jockheck, Lars. "Vom Agenten zum Kollaborateur? Die Zusammenarbeit des jüdischen Publizisten Fritz Seifter aus Bielitz mit deutschen Behörden in den 1930er und 1940er Jahren." In *"Kollaboration" in Nordosteuropa. Erscheinungsformen und Deutungen im 20. Jahrhundert*, edited by Joachim Tauber, 192–205 (Wiesbaden: Harrassowitz, 2006).

Kassow, Samuel D. "Polish Jewish Relations in the Writings of Emanuel Ringelblum." In *Contested Memories: Poles and Jews during the Holocaust and its Aftermath*, edited by Joshua Zimmerman, 142–57 (London: Rutgers University Press, 2003).

———. *Who Will Write Our History? Emanuel Ringelblum, the Warsaw Ghetto, and the Oyneg Shabes Archive*. Bloomington: Indiana University Press, 2007.

Kavanaugh, Sarah. *ORT, the Second World War and the Rehabilitation of Holocaust Survivors*. London: Vallentine Mitchell, 2008.

Kopka, Bogusław. *Konzentrationslager Warschau. Historia i następstwa*. Warszawa: IPN, 2007.

Kossoy, Edward. "The Gęsiówka Story: A Little Known Page of Jewish Fighting History." *Yad Vashem Studies* 32 (2004): 322–50.

Kunert, Andrzej K., ed. *Żydzi Polscy w Służbie Rzeczypospolitej 1939–1945. Wybór źródeł*. Warszawa: Rada Ochrony Pamięci Walki i Męczeństwa, 2002.

Kupfer, F. *Ber Mayzels, zayn antayl in di kampen far der frayhayt fun Poylishn folk under gelaykhbarekhtikung fun di Yidn*. Warsaw: Yidish Bokh, 1952.

Landau-Czajka, Anna. *Syn będzie Lech . . . Asymilacja Żydów w Polsce międzywojennej*. Warszawa: Neriton, 2006.

Langer, Lawrence E. *Holocaust Testimonies—The Ruins of Memory*. New Heaven: Yale University Press, 1991.

Libionka, Dariusz. "Antisemitism, Anti-Judaism, and the Polish Catholic Clergy during the Second World War, 1939–1945." In Blobaum, ed., 233–64.

———. "ZWZ-AK i Delegatura Rządu Polskiego wobec eksterminacji Żydów Polskich." In *Polacy i Żydzi pod okupacja niemiecka 1939–1945. Studia i Materiały*, edited by Andrzej Żbikowski, 15–207. Warszawa: IPN, 2006.

Libionka, Dariusz, and Laurence Weinbaum. "A New Look at the Betar 'Idyll' in Hrubieszow." *Yad Vashem Studies* 37, no. 1 (2009): 85–108.

Lichten, Joseph. "Notes on the Assimilation and Acculturation of Jews in Poland." In *The Jews in Poland*, edited by Ch. Abramsky, M. Jachimczyk, A. Polonsky, 106–29. Oxford: Basil Blackwell, 1986.

Madaj, Karol, and Małgorzata Żuławik. *Proboszcz getta*. Warszawa: IPN, 2010.

Marczak-Oborski, Stanisław. *Teatr czasu wojny. Polskie życie teatralne w latach II wojny światowej, 1939–1945*. Warszawa: PIW, 1967.

Markowska, Marta, ed. *The Ringelblum Archive: Annihilation—Day by Day*. Warszawa: KARTA, 2008.

Marszalec, Janusz. "Morderstwo na Makowieckim i Widerszalu. Stara sprawa, nowe pytania, nowe wątpliwości." Zagłada Żydów. *Studia i Materiały* 2 (2007): 25–53.

Martin, Sean. "Jewish Youth Between Tradition and Assimilation: Exploring Jewish Identity in Interwar Kraków." *The Polish Review* 16, no. 4 (2001): 461–77.

Mendelsohn, Ezra. "Jewish Assimilation in the Polish Lands." In *Jewish Assimilation in Modern Times*, edited by Bela Vago, 141–50. Boulder, CO: Westview Press, 1981.

———. *Zionism in Poland: The Formative Years, 1915–1926*. New Haven: Yale University Press, 1981.

Meritchak, Benjamin. *Jews-Officers in the Polish Armed Forces 1939–1945*. Tel Aviv: Association of Jewish War Veterans of Polish Armies in Israel, 2001.

Michlic, Joanna. *Poland's Threatening Other: The Image of the Jew from 1880 to the Present*. Lincoln: University of Nebraska Press, 2006.

Michman, Dan. *The Emergence of Jewish Ghettos during the Holocaust*. Translated by Lenn J. Schramm. Cambridge: Cambridge University Press, 2011.

Molisak, Alina, and Zuzanna Kołodziejska, ed. *Żydowski Polak, polski Żyd. Problem tożsamości w literaturze polsko-żydowskiej*. Warszawa: Elipsa, 2011.

Nalewajko-Kulikov, Joanna. *Strategie Przetrwania. Żydzi po Aryjskiej stronie Warszawy*. Warszawa: Neriton 2004.

Opalski, Magdalena. "Polish-Jewish Relations and the January Uprising: the Polish Perspective." *Polin* 1 (1988): 68–80.

Paczkowski, Andrzej. "Jews in the Polish Security Apparatus: An Attempt to Test the Stereotype." *Polin* 16 (2003): 451–64.

Paulsson, Gunnar S. "Ringelblum Revisited Polish-Jewish Relations in Occupied Warsaw, 1940–1945." In *Contested Memories: Poles and Jews during the Holocaust and Its Aftermath*, edited by Joshua Zimmerman, 173–92. London: Rutgers University Press, 2003.

———. *Secret City: The Hidden Jews of Warsaw, 1940–1945*. London: Yale University Press, 2002.

Pentlin, Susan L. "Holocaust Victims of Privilege." In *Problems Unique to the Holocaust*, edited by H. J. Cargas, 25–42. Lexington: The University Press of Kentucky, 1999.

Person, Katarzyna. "The Initial Reception and First Publications from the Ringelblum Archive in Poland, 1946–1952." *Gal-Ed* 23 (2012), 59–76.

———. "Pawiak w świadomości żydowskich mieszkańców okupowanej Warszawy." *Kwartalnik Historii Żydów*, no. 4 (2010): 411–23.

Piątkowska, Renata. *Roman Kramsztyk. Między "Ziemiańską" a Montparnassem*. Warszawa: Neriton, 2004.

Pickhan, Gertrud. "Yiddishkayt and Class Consciousness: The Bund and Its Minority Concept." *East European Jewish Affairs* 39, no. 2 (2009): 249–64.

Podolska, Aldona. *Służba Porządkowa w getcie warszawskim w latach 1940–1943*. Warszawa: Wydawn. Fundacji "Historia pro Futuro," 1996.

Polen, Nehemia. *The Holy Fire: The Teachings of Rabbi Kalonymos Kalman Shapira, the Rebbe of the Warsaw Ghetto*. Northvale, NJ: Jason Aronson, 1994.

Polonsky, Antony. "Warszawska Szkoła Rabinów: Orędowniczka narodowej integracji w Królestwie Polskim." In *Duchowość żydowska w Polsce. materiały z międzynarodowej konferencji dedykowanej pamięci Profesora Chone Shmeruka, Kraków, 26–28 kwietnia, 1999*, edited by Michał Galas, 287–307. Kraków: UJ, 2000.

———. "'Why Did They Hate Tuwim and Boy So Much': Jews and 'Artificial Jews' in the Literary Polemics of the Second Polish Republic." In Blobaum, ed., 189–209.

Prekerowa, Teresa. "The Jewish Underground and the Polish Underground." *Polin* 9 (1996): 148–57.

Prokop-Janiec, Eugenia. *Polish-Jewish Literature in the Interwar Years*. Translated by Abe Shenitzer. Syracuse: Syracuse University Press, 2003.

Puławski, Adam. *W obliczu zagłady. Rząd RP na Uchodźctwie, Delegatura Rządu RP na Kraj, ZWZ-AK wobec deportacji Żydów do obozów zagłady (1941–1942)*. Lublin: IPN, 2009.

Quercioli Mincer, Laura. "The Controversy over Mickiewicz's Jewish Origin." *Polin* 19 (2007): 447–57.

Roland, Charles G. *Courage under Siege: Starvation, Disease, and Death in the Warsaw Ghetto*. New York: Oxford University Press, 1992.

Rosman, Moshe. *How Jewish Is Jewish History?* Oxford: The Littman Library of Jewish Civilization, 2007.

Roskies, David. "Landkentenish: Yiddish Belles Lettres in the Warsaw Ghetto." In *Holocaust Chronicles: Individualizing the Holocaust through Diaries and Other Contemporaneous Personal Accounts*, edited by Robert M. Shapiro, 11–30. Hoboken, NJ: KTAV, 1999.

Rostropowicz-Clark, Joanna. "Adam Mickiewicz's 'Forty and Four' or the Dangers of Playing with Kabbalah." *Polin* 7 (1992): 57–62.

———. "Krzysztof Kamil Baczyński, a Poet Hero." *Polin* 13 (2000): 166–78.

Rotkirchen, Livia. "The Zionist Character of 'Self-Government' of Terezin." In *The Nazi Holocaust*, vol. 6, edited by M. Marrus, 986–1020. Jerusalem: Yad Vashem, 1979.

Rudnicki, Adolf. *Lato*. Łódź: Książka, 1946.

Sakowska, Ruta. *Dwa etapy: hitlerowska polityka eksterminacji Żydów w oczach ofiar: szkic historyczny i dokumenty*. Wrocław: Zakład Narodowy im. Ossolinskich, 1986.

———. "Komitety Domowe w getcie warszawskim." *Biuletyn Żydowskiego Instytutu Historycznego* 61, no. 1 (1967): 59–86.

———. *Ludzie z dzielnicy zamkniętej. Z dziejów Żydów w Warszawie w latach okupacji hitlerowskiej październik 1939–marzec 1943*. Warszawa: PWN, 1993.

Sakowska-Pups, Ruta. "O działalności teatralnej w getcie warszawskim." *Biuletyn Żydowskiego Instytutu Historycznego* 69, no. 1 (1969): 47–70.

Sandrow, Nahma. *Vagabond Stars: A World History of Yiddish Theater*. New York: Harper and Row, 1977.

Schatz, Jaff. *The Generation: The Rise and Fall of the Jewish Communists of Poland*. Berkeley: University of California Press, 1991.

Schmeruk, Chone. "Hebrew-Yiddish-Polish: A Trilingual Jewish Culture." In *The Jews of Poland Between Two World Wars*, edited by Israel Gutman, 285–311. London: University Press of New England, 1989.

Shore, Marci. *Caviar and Ashes: A Warsaw's Generation's Life and Death in Marxism, 1918–1968*. New Haven: Yale University Press, 2006.

Shulman, Abraham. *The Case of Hotel Polski*. New York: United States Holocaust Memorial Museum, 1982.

Skibińska, Alina. *Źródła do badań nad zagładą Żydów na okupowanych ziemiach polskich. Przewodnik archiwalno-bibliograficzny*. Warszawa: Cyklady, 2007.

Stankowski, Albert. "Nowe spojrzenie na statystyki dotyczące emigracji Żydów z Polski po 1944 roku." In *Studia z historii Żydów w Polsce po 1945 r.*, edited by Grzegorz Berendt, August Grabski, Albert Stankowski. Warszawa: ŻIH, 2000.

Steffen, Katrin. *Jüdische Polonität. Ethnizität und Nation im Spiegel der polnischsprachigen jüdischen Presse 1918–1939*. Gottingen: Vandenhoeck & Ruprecht, 2004.

Steinlauf, Michael. "Jewish Theater in Poland." Polin 16 (2003): 71–92.

———. "Mark Arnshteyn and Polish-Jewish Theatre." In *The Jews of Poland Between Two World Wars*, edited by Israel Gutman, 399–411. London: University Press of New England, 1989.

Szarota, Tomasz. *Okupowanej Warszawy dzień powszedni. Studium historyczne.* Warszawa: Czytelnik, 1982.

———. *U progu zagłady. Zajścia antyżydowskie i pogromy w okupowanej Europie: Warszawa, Paryż, Amsterdam, Antwerpia, Kowno.* Warszawa: Sic!, 2000.

Teter, Magdalena. "Jewish Conversions to Catholicism in the Polish-Lithuanian Commonwealth of the Seventeenth and Eighteenth Centuries." *Jewish History* 17, no. 3 (2003): 257–83.

Tomaszewski, Jerzy. *Najnowsze dzieje Żydów w Polsce w zarysie (do 1950 roku).* Warszawa: PWN, 1993.

———. "Vladmir Jabotinsky's Talks with Representatives of the Polish Government." *Polin* 3 (1988): 276–93.

———, ed. Żydzi w obronie Rzeczypospolitej: materiały konferencji w Warszawie 17. i 18. października 1993 r. Warszawa: Cyklady, 1996.

Trunk, Isaiah. "Religious, Educational and Cultural Problems in the Eastern European Ghettos under German Occupation." *YIVO Annual of Jewish Social Studies* 14 (1965): 159–95.

———. *Judenrat: The Jewish Councils in Eastern Europe under Nazi Occupation.* New York: Macmillan, 1972.

Umińska, Bożena. "Recenzja: Jacek Leociak, Tekst wobec zagłady (O relacjach getta warszawskiego)." *BŻIH* 190, no. 2 (1999): 172.

Urbaniak, Violetta, and Bolesław Woszczyński, eds. *Źródła archiwalne do dziejów Żydów w Polsce.* Warszawa: Naczelna Dyrekcja Archiwów Państwowych, 2001.

Urynowicz, Marcin. "Adam Czerniaków a Muzeum im. Matthiasa Bersohna przy Gminie Żydowskiej w Warszawie 1908–1940." *Biuletyn Żydowskiego Instytutu Historycznego* 228, no. 4 (2008): 477–89.

———. *Adam Czerniaków. Prezes Getta Warszawskiego.* Warszawa: IPN, 2009.

Volkov, Shulamit. "The Dynamics of Dissimilation: Ostjuden and German Jews." In *The Jewish Response to German Culture: From the Enlightenment to the Second World War*, edited by Jehuda Reinharz and Walter Schatzberg, 192–211. Hannover: Brandeis University Press, 1985.

Waxman, Zoë. *Writing the Holocaust: Identity, Testimony, Representation.* Oxford: Oxford University Press, 2006.

Webber, Jonathan. "Jewish Identities in the Holocaust Martyrdom as a Representative Category." *Polin* 13 (2000): 128–46.

Weeks, Theodore R. *From Assimilation to Antisemitism: The 'Jewish Question' in Poland, 1850–1914.* DeKalb: Northern Illinois University Press, 2006.

———. "Poles, Jews and Russians, 1863–1914: The Death of the Ideal of Assimilation in the Kingdom of Poland." *Polin* 12 (1993): 242–56.

Weinbaum, Laurence. "Jabotinsky and the Poles." *Polin* 5 (1991): 156–72.

Weiss, Aharon. *Hamishtara hayehudit baGeneral-Gouvernement uvi-Shlezia Ha'ilit bitkufat ha-Shoa.* Jerusalem: The Hebrew University, 1973.

Wodziński, Marcin. *Haskalah and Hasidism in the Kingdom of Poland: A History of Conflict.* Translated by Sarah Cozens. Oxford: The Littman Library of Jewish Civilization, 2005.

Young, James E. *Writing and Re-writing the Holocaust.* Bloomington: Indiana University Press, 1988.

Żbikowski, Andrzej. "Żydowscy przesiedleńcy z dystryktu warszawskiego w getcie warszawskim, 1939–1942 (z pogranicza opisu i interpretacji)." In *Prowincja noc. Życie i zagłada Żydów w dystrykcie warszawskim.* Edited by Barbara Engelking, Jacek Leociak, and Dariusz Libionka. Warszawa: IFiS Pan, 2007.

Index